Philanthropy in Children's Periodicals, 1840–1930

Nineteenth-Century and Neo-Victorian Cultures
Series editors: Ruth Heholt and Joanne Ella Parsons

Recent books in the series
Domestic Architecture, Literature and the Sexual Imaginary in Europe, 1850–1930
Aina Martí-Balcells

Assessing Intelligence: The Bildungsroman and the Politics of Human Potential in England, 1860–1910
Sara Lyons

The Idler's Club: Humour and Mass Readership from Jerome K. Jerome to P. G. Wodehouse
Laura Fiss

Michael Field's Revisionary Poetics
Jill Ehnenn

Narrative, Affect and Victorian Sensation: Wilful Bodies
Tara MacDonald

The Provincial Fiction of Mitford, Gaskell and Eliot
Kevin A. Morrison

Women's Activism in the Transatlantic Consumers' Leagues, 1885–1920
Flore Janssen

Queer Books of Late-Victorian Print Culture
Frederick D. King

British Writers, Popular Literature and New Media Innovation, 1820–45
Alexis Easley

Philanthropy in Children's Periodicals, 1840–1930: The Charitable Child
Kristine Moruzi

http://www.edinburghuniversitypress.com/
series-nineteenth-century-and-neo-victorian-cultures

Philanthropy in Children's Periodicals, 1840–1930
The Charitable Child

Kristine Moruzi

EDINBURGH
University Press

Edinburgh University Press is one of the leading university presses in the UK. We publish academic books and journals in our selected subject areas across the humanities and social sciences, combining cutting-edge scholarship with high editorial and production values to produce academic works of lasting importance. For more information visit our website: edinburghuniversitypress.com

© Kristine Moruzi 2024

Edinburgh University Press Ltd
13 Infirmary Street
Edinburgh EH1 1LT

Typeset in 11/13pt Sabon
by Cheshire Typesetting Ltd, Cuddington, Cheshire, and
printed and bound in Great Britain

A CIP record for this book is available from the British Library

ISBN 978 1 3995 2135 2 (hardback)
ISBN 978 1 3995 2137 6 (webready PDF)
ISBN 978 1 3995 2138 3 (epub)

The right of Kristine Moruzi to be identified as the author of this work has been asserted in accordance with the Copyright, Designs and Patents Act 1988, and the Copyright and Related Rights Regulations 2003 (SI No. 2498).

Contents

List of Illustrations	vi
Acknowledgements	viii
1. Introduction: Children, Charity, and the Periodical Press	1
2. Charitable Publics	22
3. Charitable Agency	59
4. Charitable Motivation	99
5. Charitable Subjectivity	132
6. Transnational Charity	166
7. Charitable Habits	201
8. Conclusion: Charitable Children, Real and Imagined	239
Bibliography	246
Index	267

Illustrations

Figures

2.1 Endpaper, *Young Helpers' League Magazine*, January 1892–December 1894, np.   32

2.2 C. J. Staniland, 'Little Annie's Christmas', *Aunt Judy's Magazine*, November 1871, 120.   39

2.3 'Habitations Formed', *Young Helpers' League Magazine*, January 1892–December 1894, 28.   45

2.4 First subscription list from *Aunt Judy's Magazine*, February 1868, 256.   50

3.1 First page of 'Contributions from Districts' in *Wesleyan Missionary Society Annual Report*, 1856, 27.   78

3.2 'Juvenile Christmas Offerings for 1855', *Wesleyan Juvenile Offering*, May 1856, 2.   81

3.3 'Head of the List, Fern Street, Bolton', *At Home and Abroad*, 1901, 11.   84

3.4 'Collectors at Bethesda, Cheltenham', *At Home and Abroad*, 1901, 45.   85

4.1 'Turned Out!', *Young Helpers' League Magazine*, 1901–2, 93.   114

4.2 'What Our Leaguers Work For', *Young Helpers' League Magazine*, 1901–2, 96.   116

4.3 'A Hint for Companions', *Young Helpers' League Magazine*, 1901–2, 101.   119

5.1 'Medal Winners', *Ups and Downs*, September 1895, 5.   143

5.2 'With Our Friends', *Ups and Downs*, December 1895, 5.   144

List of Illustrations   vii

5.3 'Faithful in that which is least', *Ups and Downs*,
     January 1896, 11.   149
5.4 'Our Old Friends Directory', *Ups and Downs*,
     October 1895, np.   152
7.1 Cover of *The Red Cross Junior*, September 1922.   211
7.2 Cover of *The Junior Red Cross Record for New
     South Wales*, March 1919.   219

Tables

3.1 Juvenile Contributions to the Wesleyan Missionary
     Society (1841–1919).   74
5.1 Numbers of boys and girls emigrated between 1867
     and 1897 ('Our Emigrants', *Ups and Downs*, January
     1898, 83).   146
5.2 Subscribers to the Old Friends Directory published in
     Ups and Downs (1895–1896) by sailing date.   153

Acknowledgements

The inspiration from this project came when I was doing archival work for my PhD a number of years ago. A subscription list in *Aunt Judy's Magazine* raised many questions that have finally culminated in this book. I wish to acknowledge the Australian Research Council, which supported this research through a Discovery Early Career Research Award. That funding made it possible to visit numerous archives and libraries in Canada, Australia, New Zealand, and the United Kingdom that were necessary to complete this work, and I am grateful to the archivists and librarians who facilitated my visits. The School of Communication and Creative Arts at Deakin University also supported this research with a well-timed period of research leave in which to complete the manuscript.

Many friends, family, and colleagues have inquired about the status of this book and supported me in its long development, including reading chapters and providing welcome advice. Thank you to Michelle J. Smith, Sue Chen, Paul Venzo, Emma Whatman, Liz Little, Karen Le Rossignol, Kate Moruzi, and Natalie Coulter. Charlotte and James Barry could always be relied upon to have a G&T on hand. Lara Hedberg and Sarah Moruzi provided excellent and timely research assistance at key points during the project. Sam Chu has reminded me that writing books is cool; his enthusiasm is appreciated! Thanks to Doug and Eden Sharp for their gracious hospitality whenever I was passing through London on yet another research trip.

Much of the work appearing in this book began as conference papers presented at the meetings of the Research Society for Victorian Periodicals, the Society for the History of Children

Acknowledgements   ix

and Youth, and the Australasian Victorian Studies Association. I thank the organisers of these events and the audience members for their insightful questions and remarks. Portions of Chapter 2 first appeared in *Victorian Periodicals Review* (50.1 [Spring 2017]). Portions of Chapters 4 and 7 were initially developed for chapters published in *Affect, Emotion and Children's Literature: Representation and Socialisation in Texts for Children and Young Adults* (Routledge, 2014) and *The Embodied Child: Readings in Children's Literature and Culture* (Routledge, 2014), respectively. I am grateful for the permission to publish these revised materials.

Over the years, I have appreciated having numerous conversations about the role of charity in contemporary society. Thanks especially to Jim and Gerry Sharp and George and Anne Marie Moruzi for sharing their insights. I was particularly delighted by a story my dad shared recently about regularly attending Sunday School in 1940s rural British Columbia with ten cents for the church collection. He diligently contributed one of the five-cent coins to the collection plate each week, but the other was spent on a piece of gum from the gumball machine at the corner store in the hopes that he would eventually get the prize from the machine, a miniature trophy. After we ended our call, he sent me a picture of his prize, saved after all these years. This story is wonderful reminder that children can be guided towards certain charitable habits and behaviours, but ultimately, they make decisions for themselves.

Over the course of this research, my daughters Kate and Sarah have moved from childhood to adulthood. It has been a pleasure and a privilege to share that journey with them, and I thank them for their support throughout this project. My husband Mike now knows more about charity than he ever wanted and will undoubtedly be pleased to see this book in print. His steadfast support makes everything possible.

Dedication

To Mom and Dad,
for instilling the spirit of adventure that led me down this path

1

Introduction
Children, Charity, and the Periodical Press

Drawing on a wealth of material from children's periodicals from the Victorian era to the 1920s, this book examines how the concept of the charitable child is defined through the press. Charitable ideals became increasingly prevalent at a time of burgeoning social inequities and cultural change, shaping expectations that children were capable of and responsible for charitable giving. While the child as the object of charity has received considerable attention, less focus has been paid to how and why children have been encouraged to help others.[1] Yet the ways in which children were positioned to see themselves as people who could and should help – in whatever forms that assistance might take – are crucial to understanding how children and childhood were conceptualised in the past. Children were undoubtedly important contributors to charitable causes; Frank Prochaska observes that '[t]he financial contributions of children can be found in virtually every type of nineteenth-century charity'.[2] Children accompanied their mothers as they performed charitable work, and children's charitable activity was 'enormous' in foreign and home missions, temperance societies, animal protection efforts, and Bible missions.[3] While some attention has been paid to specific charities and their efforts to raise children's awareness of their cause, no systemic approach has been taken to examine how print contributed to the broader cultural environment in which this charity work took place.[4]

Philanthropy in Children's Periodicals, 1840–1930: The Charitable Child aims to begin to fill this gap by exploring how children's magazines and children's columns in adult newspapers encouraged children to help other children, defining a philanthropic role for young people that is reinforced through the press. It uses children's print culture to examine the relationship between chil-

1

dren and charitable institutions in the nineteenth and early twentieth centuries and foreground children's active roles. Not only does this approach demonstrate children's agency and responsiveness to the needs of others during this period, but it also shows how ideas of charity were articulated in printed materials for children. Charitable ideals for children were mobilised in periodicals and traversed boundaries based on class, gender, and race. The ubiquity and frequency of children's periodicals and children's columns in adult newspapers meant that young people were regularly exposed to charitable ideas in both fictional and non-fictional materials in ways that reinforced the expectation that they should help others in need.

One such example appears in the 1889 volume of *Band of Hope Review* (1851–1937). In the story 'Cyril's Sacrifice', twelve-year-old Cyril laments that his father will not be able to make his annual Christmas contribution to the Orphan Asylum. Cyril has no money of his own, for he always spends it as soon as it arrives. The only item of value he owns is a beautiful model man-of-war ship, which he has spent the last two years building. He decides to sell the ship and, with the money from the sale, orders oranges and apples and toys to be shared with the orphan children. Cyril's willingness to part with his ship inspires the man who purchased it to return it to the boy in recognition of his 'self-denying kindness'.[5] The accompanying illustration depicts the ship laden with fruit and the headmistress distributing toys to the young orphans in the foreground. This story and illustration operate together to reflect the dynamic relationship between the child as charitable donor and the child as object of charity that is emblematic of charitable relations in the nineteenth century. Although the story highlights Cyril's sacrifice and the important work he performs to enable the orphans to receive their Christmas treat, the illustration is designed to encourage viewers to imagine the happiness of the young people receiving their gifts. *Band of Hope Review* is one of many children's periodicals published in the nineteenth and early twentieth centuries that aimed to instruct young readers about specific charitable causes and how they could help others in need. The illustration focuses readerly attention on the children in need of assistance, but the accompanying narrative instructs children on the sacrifices they should make to help others. While the narrator is sympathetic to Cyril's dilemma, readers are reminded that a sacrifice 'which costs nothing is generally worth nothing'.[6] The value of his charitable work comes from the sacrifice he willingly makes to give the children a happy holiday celebration.

This example is emblematic of the reciprocal giving that is defined and reinforced through children's periodicals in the nineteenth century. The period between 1840 and 1930 is central to this examination because it was characterised by the expansion of periodicals for young people and concomitant concerns about appropriate reading for a young audience. The reduction in paper prices around 1850 in England meant that the number of periodicals expanded rapidly in the second half of the century. Magazines became more affordable, and children were seen as an emerging market. At the same time, with the publication of cheap magazines containing stories of crime and intrigue, adults became increasingly concerned about what children of all classes were reading and whether it was appropriate for a young audience.

The nineteenth century is also a key period for understanding the rise of charity. Alan Kidd explains how the 'social fabric of Victorian England was permeated by charity and repercussions of the charitable relationship. Directly or indirectly, philanthropy affected the social and cultural life of the time.'[7] Although debates about the appropriate form of charity persisted throughout the century, with some arguing for a tax-supported system of relief while others felt that individual charity was more appropriate, rapid industrialisation and urbanisation meant cities were flooded with new inhabitants living in extremely marginal conditions. This 'new class of poor' was a concern because it signalled social instability, declining health, and inadequate social policy.[8] Childhood as a period of innocence and vulnerability was an important development of the nineteenth century and prompted legislation to protect child workers and provide mandatory education. At the same time, social welfare programmes were virtually non-existent, and poor and neglected children had little recourse except for the streets. Charitable organisations were left to fill the many welfare and health gaps in the nineteenth and early twentieth centuries, which they did by appealing for funds to help children. Then, as now, children were centrally positioned in fundraising campaigns designed to solicit financial support for organisations dedicated to improving children's lives and providing them with better opportunities.

This book foregrounds the role of print culture in the develop-

4   Philanthropy in Children's Periodicals, 1840–1930

ment of a charitable ethic for children by enabling a more sophisticated understanding of how young people engaged with printed materials. It also considers how these materials were mobilised by charitable institutions to educate children, encourage them to think charitably, and motivate them to act on behalf of the charity. It draws on a range of British, Canadian, Australian, New Zealand, and American children's periodicals and children's pages to demonstrate how ideologies of charity were promulgated at a time when the needs of poor and neglected children were becoming increasingly urgent. The periodical press was mobilised to raise child readers' awareness of and support for a variety of charitable campaigns including missionary activities, hospitals, temperance activities, impoverished and neglected children, returning soldiers, and the Red Cross. These charities publicised their activities in print and encouraged children to contribute in a variety of ways including fundraising, staging performances, hosting charity bazaars, and making items to be donated or sold.

Defining charity in the nineteenth century

The definitions for charity and philanthropy found in the *Oxford English Dictionary* are remarkably similar. The term 'charity' is described as '[b]enevolence to one's neighbours, especially to the poor', while 'philanthropy' has a wider scope as 'practical benevolence, now especially as expressed by the generous donation of money to good causes'.[9] The difference in these definitions lies primarily in charity's focus on the poor, while philanthropy is more broadly applied to good causes. According to Robert H. Bremner, charity and philanthropy 'have so much in common . . . that the words are often used interchangeably', but one area of difference is in their 'degree of interest in the poor' since charity, with its Judeo-Christian underpinnings, 'has an abiding commitment to relieve the poor, orphans, the friendless, and the homeless'.[10] In contrast, philanthropy is 'secular in origin' and 'has not been as closely as involved with the poor'.[11] By the end of the nineteenth century, Bremner argues, philanthropy had come to mean 'contributions of money to a variety of causes intended to benefit all classes of society'.[12]

In this book, I tend to use the term 'charity' to describe the actions by children to raise funds for various causes, inspired by David Owen's *English Philanthropy, 1660–1960* (1964) and

W. K. Jordan's *Philanthropy in England, 1480–1660: A Study of the Changing Pattern of English Social Aspirations* (2006). Both of these surveys of English philanthropy are focused on significant donations of money. Owen, for instance, is not interested in the 'good works, personal service, or labors in the public interest' unless they are accompanied by 'substantial contributions of money'.[13] Similarly, Jordan uses wills and living gifts to identify charitable benefactions since most sizeable donations would have been recorded.[14] They both position these donations as a form of philanthropy, as their book titles suggest, and as a reaction to 'changing social conditions, although this response might [have been] influenced by such factors as the religious imperative, humanitarianism or personal example of the elite'.[15] During the Victorian era, philanthropy played a vital role in the effort to ameliorate problems resulting from poverty and industrialism, which, as Owen points out, were understood to be a 'permanent element in the social structure'.[16] The outpouring of voluntary labour and money may have been prompted by a variety of complex motives such as 'humanitarian impulses, religion, social aspirations' or, as Jordan explains, simply by the desire to belong 'to a culture which regards such actions as worthy'.[17]

Most of the children's donations discussed in this book – and the work that accompanied those donations – seem to me to be rather more charitable than philanthropic in their orientation. Children's benevolent work throughout this period was typically oriented towards helping poor children, and the amounts of their contributions are small enough to be considered alms giving. Understanding children's benevolence through the lens of gift theory informs my analysis of children's charitable behaviours. Marcel Mauss's theory of the gift describes a social obligation to give and the obligation to repay.[18] Alan Kidd, drawing on Mauss, explains that giving behaviour can be understood in relation to collectivist and individualist traditions. The collectivist tradition of giving is based on the 'reciprocity of the gift relationship' between the donor and the recipient, in which each is 'obliged to perform both functions of giving and receiving', thus establishing the 'social adhesive of mutual ties'.[19] The individualist tradition is based on self-interest to achieve the best outcome for the donor, yet this utilitarian concept is limited in helping to understand children's charitable behaviour in the nineteenth and early twentieth centuries. While benefits undoubtedly accrued through public rec-

6   Philanthropy in Children's Periodicals, 1840–1930

ognition and social standing to young people who contributed to various charitable causes, they are seemingly insufficient to account for the ubiquity of this benevolence. As Kidd explains,

> Choices are made in a social, political, cultural and ethical context. Even judged by the individual calculus of exchange theory, voluntary co-operative behaviour, including charity, cannot be rationalized as a mechanism of self-interest without the intervention of an internalized social ethic to impel voluntary action.[20]

The social norms that are operating on young people include reciprocity but also 'the norm of beneficence and the norm of social responsibility'.[21] These norms are both defined by and reinforced through the charitable publics that are created in the pages of children's magazines and enable both collectivist and individualist gift giving. They were designed to induct children into patterns of charitable giving that would continue into adulthood.

Children's periodicals and children's columns

In the nineteenth century, children of all classes were routinely introduced to charitable causes through magazines, fiction, and other printed ephemera. Children's print culture thus forms the basis for this study, of which the periodical is an essential component. The range of these periodicals and the strategies employed to maintain both readership and commitment to the charitable cause reflect the highly competitive fundraising environment, especially in the last decades of the nineteenth century and during the First World War. Nonetheless, these magazines and the charitable causes found in their pages reflect a consistent attitude towards children as people who could and should help others. The periodical is an important medium for these charitable campaigns because it helped to reflect, but also to produce, the understanding of children as charitable. Lyn Pykett explains that Victorian periodicals cannot be seen as simply 'evidence' of the culture in which they are published. They are instead 'a central component of that culture ... and can only be read and understood as part of that culture and society, and in the context of other knowledges about them'.[22] Children's magazines reflect the negotiation and redefinition of charity and childhood that was ongoing between 1840 and 1930. The children reading – and appearing in – these magazines at the beginning of this period had different expectations of their periodicals than those at the end of this period. As we shall see, children increasingly expected to be able to participate in their magazines through competitions and correspondence, and they eagerly sought visual materials. The shift in ideas and attitudes about child, childhood, and charity over the century were both produced by, and reflected in, children's print culture.

The rapid increase in the number of children's periodicals occurs alongside widespread concerns about the quality of materials being published for young readers. In Edward Salmon's 1888 critique, he describes how children's magazines, 'with certain notable exceptions, are in every sense of the word dreadfuls', with 'no limit on their number or their pernicious influence'.[23] He is referring to the rise of penny dreadfuls containing stories of crime and intrigue that were both cheap and readily available to young readers. He was concerned about the form and content of children's magazines, praising the Religious Tract Society's *Boy's Own Paper* (1879–1967) because it was read by boys 'in the slums' as well as in 'the best homes'.[24] A magazine with a wide audience that crossed classes was more likely to contain material appropriate for all young readers. Moreover, magazines extolling moral values such as charity and responsibility were unlikely to be criticised for their tone, explaining why Salmon makes no mention of missionary magazines, focusing instead on commercial publications.

The sheer volume of charitable campaigns appearing in children's periodicals and in children's columns made it challenging to select the examples to be discussed in this book. Chronologically, it begins with the *Wesleyan Juvenile Offering* (1844–1878) because it is one of the earliest magazines to actively incorporate fundraising into its pages. It was launched in the same year as the *Juvenile Missionary Magazine* (1844–1885), and these two magazines reflect the Christian orientation that was embedded in most nineteenth-century charitable giving in the English-speaking world. The book concludes with the Junior Red Cross magazines that emerged out of the First World War in which the religious orientation of much of the previous century has given way to a secular framework of international service. In between these two bookends, a range of magazines are explored to see how charitable ideologies are embedded and how children are encouraged to support the charitable causes in their pages.

How charitable causes are presented in these magazines prompts

8   Philanthropy in Children's Periodicals, 1840–1930

a consideration of their material form and their objectives. Many children's magazines can be understood as charity magazines. Most charitable organisations in the nineteenth century created publications aimed at adult supporters as a vehicle for defining their charitable cause, organising its (mostly volunteer) workforce, and acknowledging contributions. As children were increasingly seen as a legitimate source of charitable support, these adult publications began to include content aimed at younger readers. Then, as the amount of children's content increased and as readerships were differentiated, a children's magazine was often established to separate the contents and clearly delineate its objectives for young members.[25] The Wesleyans, accordingly, began publishing the *Wesleyan Juvenile Offering* rather than including content in their adult missionary magazine, the *Wesleyan Methodist Magazine* (1744–1960?). Similarly, Barnardo's *Young Helpers' League Magazine* (1892–1929?) emerged from his *Night and Day* (1877–), the Waifs and Strays Society published *Brothers and Sisters* (1890–1920?) out of *Our Waifs and Strays* (1882–1920?), and the Red Cross began publishing Junior Red Cross magazines.[26]

Children's charity magazines are a specific subset of the adult charity magazine. They are typically less interested in the corporate structures that underpin the organisation, although the children's magazine presented an opportunity for the charity to define its children's structure in relation to the adult organisation. Like the adult charity magazines, the children's magazines were designed both to entertain and to inform readers about the charitable cause. Each magazine included content that satisfied its charitable goals and was presumably designed to attract readers. For the *Wesleyan Juvenile Offering*, this initially meant letters from missionaries, reports on missionary activities, and some short fiction and poetry depicting children engaged in religious activities. However, this content shifted over time to include more material written by children and more evidence of their participation in charitable efforts.

Each children's charity magazine was undoubtedly aware of its multiple readerships. First and foremost was its readership of children. Producing content that was age appropriate in terms of language and messaging was essential. At the same time, some of these magazines contained content that was designed to be read aloud by adults and then discussed with young members. In fact, varying levels of literacy were an important factor, especially for magazines that were wide-ranging in the audiences they sought

Children, Charity, and the Periodical Press 9

to attract. Nonetheless, the educational element of the charity magazine in constructing and reinforcing a charitable identity for its members was crucial. The gradual development of charitable branding through badges and certificates contributed to children's identification with and support for a particular cause. This identification was an important aspect of the charity's long term, strategic objectives insofar as attracting children to the charity was important not only for its short-term goals of raising awareness and fundraising, but also for its longer-term objective of building its adult community of supporters.

The perennially ageing readership of charitable children's magazines was an ongoing challenge to both charitable support and periodical readership. To define a readership based on age meant that the magazine was always concerned about attracting new readers to replace the ones who were becoming too old for the magazine. At the same time, having spent time and energy attracting young people to the cause, the charity ideally wanted to retain these young adults as part of their adult membership. This required a deft strategy in which the initial rationale for supporting the charity was transformed as the charitable supporter's subjectivity shifted. Most of the campaigns discussed in this book are aimed at helping children since children were naturally assumed to want to help others like themselves. This assumption was embedded in Romantic ideologies of childhood as a time of innocence and vulnerability. Children would, it was assumed, readily sympathise with other children whose circumstances were less fortunate than their own, whether it was because they were separated from God, or poor and sick, or orphans. Moreover, child readers of the charity magazines were instructed about their responsibility to help those less fortunate. As they became adults, the shared identity as children was no longer relevant, but ideally the responsibility they felt would continue.

The ubiquity of charity in the nineteenth century means that charitable work was also encouraged in non-charity children's magazines. Samuel Beeton's *Boy's Own Magazine* (1855–74) raised funds in support of a drinking fountain.[27] Edwin Brett's *Boys of England* (1867–99) encouraged boys to contribute funds to the magazine's lifeboat fund, raising £350 for Southend's first lifeboat.[28] Readers of *Good Words for the Young* (1868–87) were encouraged to support children affected by the 1877 famine in India.[29] As will be explored in more detail in Chapter 2, *Aunt*

10 Philanthropy in Children's Periodicals, 1840–1930

Judy's Magazine (1866–85) provided significant support for the Great Ormond Street Hospital for Children. The girls' magazine *Atalanta* (1887–98) raised money for an 'Atalanta Cot' at the Royal Alexandra Hospital in Rhyl and printed letters soliciting support for organisations like the Girl's Friendly Society.[30] The *Girl's Own Paper* (1880–1914) supported the Princess Louise Home, established in 1835 and run by the National Society for the Protection of Young Girls, through fundraising and bazaars. Readers responded enthusiastically to the Countess of Aberdeen's appeal that they support working girls in London through the establishment and maintenance of a girls' home.[31] The variety of magazines and charitable interests reflect the dynamic nature of charity and children's print during this period. Any magazine intended for young readers might include some requests for children's charitable work. The difference from charity magazines is that the charitable focus is just one of many interests embedded in the magazine content.

The discussion of children's print culture thus far has focused exclusively on magazines. Yet children's columns in adult newspapers were another important venue through which children were inducted into charitable habits and behaviours. These columns offered materials to young readers who otherwise might not have had access to content developed specifically for them. The newspaper was presumably already being read by other household members such as parents or perhaps older siblings, and the inclusion of a children's column enabled access to age-appropriate materials. Because they were included in newspapers, these materials were often more local than national, and, with their emergence later in the nineteenth century, provided participatory opportunities for young people. Thus, these columns operate differently from children's charity magazines since they tend not to be focused on a single charitable cause – if they have any at all – and instead include a wider range of content designed to appeal to a broad range of young readers who would hopefully continue to read the newspaper as they aged.

While many children's columns appeared in the British regional press from the 1880s, Australian and New Zealand newspapers also began to include material for children. The differences in the colonial publishing industries meant that neither country had the population nor the demand to justify the publication of dedicated children's magazines.[32] Instead, they sought to attract children to their papers by including children's columns, which contained appropriate materials for young readers, often focused more on local events and activities, and provided regular weekly opportunities for participation and engagement.[33] As a microcosm of a children's periodical, these columns often include fiction, poetry, jokes and puzzles, and robust correspondence sections as well as a strong editorial persona. This editor is an important figure in the development of a charitable ethos in the children's column.

By bringing together a range of children's print culture between 1840 and 1930 from English-speaking countries, the clear similarities in ideals of childhood are evident. Yet this ninety-year period is also marked by significant change as various local and federal governments came to understand the need to develop social welfare programmes around the turn of the twentieth century and took on more fiscal responsibility for those in need. At the same time, many charitable organisations were able to use their children's periodicals to continue to position children as valuable contributors to their efforts.

Children as charitable actors

Understanding the real impact of these charitable campaigns on children is difficult to ascertain. Undoubtedly, a portion of children's financial contributions came directly from parents or other adults. Despite many charities strongly urging children to make sacrifices, as Cyril did in the story from *Band of Hope Review* with which this chapter began, children's actual motivations and behaviours are not always, or even often, visible. Nonetheless, drawing on the sociology of childhood, this book understands the child as a social actor who can participate in the world. Evidence of children's charitable participation is promoted and displayed in the pages of children's magazines and elsewhere. Children were actively engaged in supporting these causes, which is important because participation, in these and other democratic events, 'was not clear cut or naturally occurring; it was something that had to be solicited, encouraged, guided, and directed'.[34] The magazine was an essential component of children's charitable engagement but was not, of course, the only one. As Viviana A. Zelizer explains, 'the meaning and consequences of children's work depend on the social setting in which the work occurs', and our understanding is informed by an examination of 'the web of social relations in

12   Philanthropy in Children's Periodicals, 1840–1930

which these children's efforts take place'.[35] A child's interest and ability to support a charitable cause was enabled by a range of social, educational, and economic factors.

Childhood is a social construction that varies over time, in different locations, and across race, class, and gender. That certain children are encouraged to participate in different kinds of charity, while others are positioned as the objects of charity, reflects the extent to which childhood was constructed in certain ways for some children and in different ways for others. The Indigenous child, for example, is typically subject to missionary definitions of childhood as heathen, yet also capable of redemption and salvation. The poor, female child is frequently portrayed as being at risk of temptation and ruin. These children are commonly understood to require charitable intervention. Indeed, the concept and construction of childhood dependency 'has frequently been used to naturalize a lack of autonomy, not only for the young, but for all sorts of subservient people'.[36] In contrast, the white, middle-class child is assumed to have enough autonomy to be able to actively participate in charity work. However, children in need of charity sometimes also saw themselves as people who could help others as well, thus resisting the social construction of their childhood.

Childhood is a constituent part of the social order.[37] The induction of children into patterns of philanthropy was undoubtedly guided, at least in part, by a desire to encourage habits of charitable giving that would continue into adulthood, when children would presumably have more money available to them. Childhood thus offers a rich site to 'delineate relations of power' in which children are instructed about how to be in the world.[38] Every periodical campaign to raise young people's awareness of a charitable cause can be seen as an attempt to develop a collaboration between young readers and adult organisers. As Marah Gubar describes, collaboration can be 'employed to evoke a range of relationships of coproduction', which 'need not (and rarely [do]) refer to a perfectly reciprocal bond between equals'.[39] Gubar is referring to Golden Age children's stories where children are 'capable of reshaping stories' and can be conceived of as 'artful collaborators' in constructing their identities.[40] These identities are developed 'not in a vacuum but in reaction to the directives of the society they inhabit and the texts they read'.[41]

Not all the magazines featuring charitable campaigns include

Children, Charity, and the Periodical Press   13

children's correspondence, but numerous examples of children's written support for these charitable causes appear in their pages. Editorial influence is important since children who wished to see their letters or reports of their activities in print presumably understood the kinds of content that would be acceptable for publication. This meant that letters resisting the charitable construction of childhood are unlikely to appear. Nonetheless, the sheer volume of children's contributions across the period indicates tacit acceptance of the charitable ideal, at least to a certain extent. As William Corsaro writes, 'the notion that children are active agents in their own development and socialization is now generally accepted'.[42] He explains that children develop individually while the collective processes of which they are a part continue to change. Importantly, he suggests, he must consider 'the nature of children's *membership*' in local cultures and '*the changes in their degree or intensity* of membership and participation over time'.[43] A child's charity work, often evident through financial contribution or other kinds of activity, represents a commitment to support a particular cause at a particular moment in time. Extrapolating based on a few limited examples of one child's participation is challenging since the child may not have participated over a long period of time, their contribution may be a one-off, and their interest may be related to the social benefits accrued through their participation.

Book structure

This book is organised both thematically and chronologically as it answers a series of questions about how children's magazines situate charity, the degree of charitable agency that can be attributed to young people, how they were motivated to act, and how habits of charity were created and reinforced. It also considers the extent to which charitable practices circulated throughout the English-speaking world and how someone who had been a charitable recipient could be transformed into a charitable donor. A series of case studies bring together a thematic framework designed to elucidate a question with one or more examples for analysis. The examples have been selected because they are indicative of how children's periodicals and children's columns were facilitating charitable work through their pages. While there are many other magazines that could have been chosen, these are typical of the

14   Philanthropy in Children's Periodicals, 1840–1930

charitable activities and the shifts in children's print culture during the period.

Chapter 2, 'Charitable Publics', the most wide ranging in terms of chronology and examples, considers the shifts in charitable practices through children's print. It examines the strategies deployed in children's magazines to create what I call a 'charitable public', inspired by Lauren Berlant's idea of 'intimate publics'. These strategies, which were deployed in many different magazines and used to support different causes, were designed to introduce young readers to the specific cause and incorporate content that both extolled the cause and rewarded children's engagement with it. This included descriptions of children performing charity work, information about the charity, reports on monetary contributions, and other forms of engagement with young readers. Yet, despite these similarities, these materials also show how magazines responded to the changing expectations of their readers alongside some of the subtleties of the specific charitable causes. Nonetheless, this chapter focuses on the centrality of print to the development of a charitable ethos for children.

Aunt Judy's Magazine is used in this chapter to identify some typical strategies employed by magazine publishers to encourage children's charitable giving. This example is set alongside other examples in Britain, Canada, Australia, and New Zealand, including missionary periodicals like the *Wesleyan Juvenile Offering*, charity magazines like Barnardo's *Young Helpers' League Magazine*, the temperance *Band of Hope Review* and the Red Cross Junior magazines, and children's pages. By foregrounding a specific magazine such as *Aunt Judy's Magazine*, which was a commercial magazine that sponsored cots at the Great Ormond Street Children's Hospital, this chapter identifies and explores specific magazine strategies designed to create a charitable public and promote a cause. It considers the role of informational articles, fiction, illustrations and photos, subscription lists, fundraising activities, reports on charity recipients, and other paratextual materials in developing an ideal charitable child who understands his or her responsibility to help those in need. It uses a variety of different examples of charitable publics produced through children's magazines during the nineteenth and early twentieth centuries across different charitable activities supporting missionary work, children's hospitals, temperance, and children's health. Even as they drew upon evolving ideas about children and child-

Children, Charity, and the Periodical Press   15

hood as well as new technologies, they demonstrate the centrality of print in the production of charitable publics that promoted a charitable ideal for children between 1840 and 1930.

Having identified how a space for charitable ideas and activity was created in children's periodicals, Chapter 3 on 'Charitable Agency' questions the extent to which young readers of the magazine can be considered charitable agents and how the magazine went about encouraging that agency. The charitable ethos that is evidenced in children's behaviours through the periodical press is part of a pattern of behaviours designed and implemented by adults. That children were often following adult directions in supporting a charitable cause does not negate their charitable agency. Children willingly following adult directions about charitable work can still be considered agents, as Susan Miller explains. Children's active participation in the charitable infrastructures described in Chapter 2 can be positioned alongside the material contributions they made to the cause as evidence of their charitable activity. This chapter draws on examples from the *Wesleyan Juvenile Offering*, which became *At Home and Abroad* (1879–1974), to explore how children were trained about religion, missionary works, and charity in the Wesleyan Missionary Society and how the magazine depicts children's charitable activities and encourages them to be charitable agents.

This chapter focuses specifically on the monetary contributions made by children as an indicator of their charitable agency. While children's motivations for fundraising and performing other types of charitable support can be opaque, the longevity of a magazine like the *Wesleyan Juvenile Offering* and the ongoing financial contributions from children indicate a commitment that is part of the cultural framework. While this sentiment may have been temporary for some children, for others it may have been an important part of their individual subjectivity as charitable beings. Regardless, it suggests that children of the nineteenth and early twentieth centuries were interested in helping others through their charitable work.

Moreover, given that the runs of *Wesleyan Juvenile Offering* and *At Home and Abroad* extend beyond the time period covered in this book, this example offers a new perspective of how one religious periodical used print aimed at young people to raise awareness of its charitable cause, while also responding to cultural and social shifts in ideas about children and childhood to attract and

16   Philanthropy in Children's Periodicals, 1840–1930

retain readers' interest in the magazine and its charity work. In particular, this chapter explores the language of charitable giving, the charitable agency enacted by children through their contributions, and how the magazine encouraged children's regular participation in fundraising campaigns.

Chapter 4, on 'Charitable Motivation', considers how the magazine motivated readers to participate in charitable work. The question of motivation is a complex one that draws upon the role of reading in the nineteenth century. Critics were concerned about the impact of low-quality reading materials on young readers, and those concerns were persuasive because of the widespread belief of reading's impact on moral development. This chapter lays out how charitable motivation has been theorised before considering how it manifests in Barnardo's *Young Helpers' League Magazine* and its impact on readers. Narrative and visual strategies appearing in the magazine encouraged an emotional and affective response that was intended to be transformed into action by either directly assisting those in need or raising funds to support the charitable cause. These strategies were so common in the magazines that young writers adopted similar techniques in their own contributions. These examples show how children were motivated to be charitable through an editorial strategy juxtaposing negative emotions associated with 'pitiful' children against the positive potential of the cause to produce change through material support.

While many of the magazines discussed in this book are aimed at middle-class children, not all of them are. The missionary and temperance magazines, in particular, were targeted at least as much at working-class and poor children given their literacy and teetotalism objectives. Working-class children were unquestionably part of the charitable public defined in certain magazines. While some of their giving is elided by the practice of aggregating collections, in other cases working-class children are explicitly identified as ideal charitable donors. Chapter 5, on 'Charitable Subjectivity', turns to another aspect of the Barnardo's charity – the emigration of young people to Canada – to show how these emigrated children, the recipients of charity themselves, were encouraged to make financial contributions to assist others to emigrate. Barnardo's *Ups and Downs* (1895–1914) is a Canadian magazine aimed in part at the British children who had been sent to Canada. It demonstrates how children, no matter their circumstances, were expected to help others. Letters and updates from these children appear

Children, Charity, and the Periodical Press   17

regularly in the magazine, and they demonstrate what Kendall R. Phillips describes as 'rhetorical maneuvers' as the young writers adopted multiple subject positions as grateful charity recipients and beneficent charitable donors who understood their responsibilities to assist others. Martin Gorsky describes this 'charitable co-operation' as visible in a range of activities and institutions 'in which working-class members were present, as small subscribers, as enthusiastic recipients and as workers' in order to improve their social standing.[44] The young people's participation in charitable giving in *Ups and Downs* reflects a sophisticated negotiation of their charitable subjectivities as both recipients and agents of charity.

Chapter 6, on 'Transnational Charity', argues that children's charitable work is transnational insofar as philanthropic discourses were circulating throughout the Anglo-American world and the ideologies of both childhood and children's charity were also circulating through children's print culture. It examines two children's columns, one in the New Zealand *Otago Witness* and the other in the South Australian *Adelaide Observer*. They offer a different mode of engagement with young readers because of their presence in adult newspapers. The publication of extensive correspondence sections in both columns offers a window into New Zealand and South Australian childhood and how young readers understood their charitable obligations. The charity work evident in these columns reflects a transnational mode of charity that foregrounds the local but also extends beyond it.

The chapter discusses the 'Our Little Folks' column in the *Otago Witness* (1876–1932), in which the child readers initiate the idea of collecting money for Barnardo's. This outward-looking focus is sometimes in tension with local need, as is evident in other charitable campaigns conducted through its pages. The 'Children's Column' of the *Adelaide Observer* (1843–1904) mobilises a more focused strategy through the development of the Sunbeam Society. These child readers enact transnational charity through their participation in other British charity organisations and through their active engagement with other international charitable causes around the world. Once again, however, local need is at times in tension with international charities, as competing demands were placed on limited funds. These examples reflect not only the extent to which ideas about children's charity were circulating in British colonies like New Zealand and Australia, but also the degree to

18   Philanthropy in Children's Periodicals, 1840–1930

which these children were interested in and willing to raise funds for international causes.

The final chapter on 'Charitable Habits' explores the Junior Red Cross, an organisation that explicitly established transnational practices after the First World War by the sharing of ideas, materials, and child-authored content. Yet the focus here is on how charitable habits could be established and promoted through the Junior Red Cross magazines published in Canada, New South Wales, and the United States. The Junior Red Cross was explicit in its goals to embody its charitable aims of service, health, and citizenship. Pierre Bourdieu's idea of *habitus* provides a framework for understanding how charitable habits are created among young people through the pages of their magazines. I examine the three earliest Junior Red Cross organisations in Canada, Australia, and the United States to explore how they produced a *habitus* of charity incorporating elements of service, health, and international friendliness through their magazines. Each organisation published its own Junior Red Cross magazine, with the Australian *Junior Red Cross Record* and the American *Junior Red Cross News* both launching in 1919 and the *Canadian Red Cross Junior* in 1922. These publications emerged out of a shared understanding of how children had already been assisting with the war effort and how, in peace time, they could turn their attention to other worthwhile objectives. While all three reflect the same broad objectives of the Junior Red Cross, each magazine also demonstrates its own unique implementation. More was expected of Junior Red Cross members than simply raising awareness and funds for a particular charitable cause. Instead, young people were also expected to transform themselves physically and ideologically. These charitable habits were practised through individual and collective action that was repeated over time to enable this transformation.

Through this comparison of charitable campaigns appearing in children's print culture between 1840 and 1930, I develop a new history of children's charity that shows how children's magazines and children's columns in newspapers reflect a dynamic charitable environment in which children were encouraged to make significant contributions. Print culture was central to the definition of children's charity during this period, and the comparison of campaigns and periodicals across time and place enables a better understanding of how childhood was understood. Examining

Children, Charity, and the Periodical Press   19

these periodicals alongside one another highlights not only the prevalence of children's charitable work but also the similar strategies deployed in their pages to encourage specific behaviours from child readers.

Notes

1. See, for example, Shurlee Swain and Margot Hillel, *Child, Nation, Race and Empire: Child Rescue Discourse, England, Canada and Australia, 1850–1915* (Manchester: Manchester University Press, 2010); Lydia Murdoch, *Imagined Orphans: Poor Families, Child Welfare, and Contested Citizenship in London* (New Brunswick: Rutgers University Press, 2006); Ellen Boucher, *Empire's Children: Emigration, Welfare, and the Decline of the British World, 1869–1967* (Cambridge: Cambridge University Press, 2014).
2. Frank Prochaska, *Women and Philanthropy in the Nineteenth Century* (Oxford: Clarendon, 1980), 75.
3. Prochaska, *Women and Philanthropy*, 74.
4. See, for example, Susan Ash, *Funding Philanthropy: Dr. Barnardo's Metaphors, Narratives and Spectacles* (Liverpool: Liverpool University Press, 2016); Michelle Elleray, *Victorian Coral Islands of Empire, Mission, and the Boys' Adventure Novel* (Abingdon: Milton, Taylor & Francis Group, 2020); Hugh Morrison, '"Little vessels" or "little soldiers": New Zealand Protestant Children, Foreign Missions, Religious Pedagogy and Empire, *c.*1880s–1930s', *Paedagogica Historica* 47, no. 3 (2001): 303–21 and Hugh Morrison, '"Impressions Which Will Never Be Lost": Missionary Periodicals for Protestant Children in Late Nineteenth-Century Canada and New Zealand', *Church History* 82, no. 2 (2013): 388–93.
5. Jennie Chappell, 'Cyril's Sacrifice', *Band of Hope Review* (1889): 46.
6. Chappell, 'Cyril's Sacrifice', 46.
7. Alan J. Kidd, 'Philanthropy and the 'Social History Paradigm',' *Social History* 21, no. 2 (May 1996), 180.
8. David Owen, *English Philanthropy, 1660–1960* (Cambridge: Belknap Press, 1964), 134. Regarding the history of philanthropy in England, see also W. K. Jordan, *Philanthropy in England, 1480–1660: A Study of the Changing Pattern of English Social Aspirations* (London and New York: Routledge, 2006); Robert H. Bremner, *Giving: Charity and Philanthropy in History* (New Brunswick: Transaction Publishers, 2000), and Martin Gorsky,

20 Philanthropy in Children's Periodicals, 1840–1930

Patterns of Philanthropy: Charity and Society in Nineteenth-Century Bristol (Woodbridge: The Royal Historical Society and The Boydell Press, 1999).

9. *Oxford English Dictionary*, s.v. 'charity, n', September 2023. https://doi.org/10.1093/OED/3068262751. *Oxford English Dictionary*, s.v. 'philanthropy, n', July 2023 https://doi.org/10.1093/OED/4790171312.

10. Bremner, *Giving*, xi, xii.

11. Bremner, *Giving*, xii.

12. Bremner, *Giving*, xii. See also Gorsky, *Patterns*, 12–14.

13. Owen, *English Philanthropy*, 1.

14. Jordan, *Philanthropy in England*, 22–4.

15. Gorsky, *Patterns*, 3.

16. Owen, *English Philanthropy*, 4.

17. Owen, *English Philanthropy*, 6. Jordan, *Philanthropy in England*, 144.

18. Marcel Mauss, *The Gift: The Form and Reason for Exchange in Archaic Societies* (Abingdon: Routledge, 2002).

19. Kidd, 'Philanthropy and the "social history paradigm",' 183.

20. Kidd, 'Philanthropy and the "social history paradigm",' 184.

21. Kidd, 'Philanthropy and the "social history paradigm",' 184.

22. Lyn Pykett, 'Reading the Periodical Press: Text and Context', *Victorian Periodicals Review* 22, no. 3 (1989): 102.

23. Edward Salmon, *Juvenile Literature As It Is* (London: Henry J. Drane, 1888), 184.

24. Salmon, *Juvenile Literature*, 186.

25. Swain and Hillel point out that magazines 'became the primary means by which each of the emerging [child rescue] organisations publicised its work' (21).

26. The emergence of *New South Wales Junior Red Cross Record* in 1919, its reincorporation into the adult publication in 1924, and then its re-emergence as a separate magazine for Junior members by 1930 indicates the at times porous nature of boundaries of both the charity magazine and its readers.

27. 'Drinking Fountain Fund', *Boy's Own Magazine* (July 1868): np.

28. Christopher Mark Banham, 'Boys of England', in *Dictionary of Nineteenth-Century Journalism in Great Britain and Ireland*, ed. Laurel Brake and Marysa Demoor (London: Academia Press and The British Library, 2009), 69.

29. 'The Famine-Stricken Children in India', *Good Words for the Young* (December 1877): 362–5.

30. 'The Atalanta Letter-Bag', *Atalanta* (December 1891): 187.

31. Ishbel Aberdeen, 'The Girl's Own Home', *Girl's Own Paper* (October 1882): 6–7.
32. See Chapter 2 on 'Colonial Girls' Print Culture' in Michelle J. Smith, Kristine Moruzi, and Clare Bradford, *From Colonial to Modern: Transnational Girlhood in Canadian, Australian, and New Zealand Children's Literature, 1840–1940* (Toronto: University of Toronto Press, 2018).
33. See Frederick Milton, 'Uncle Toby's Legacy: Children's Columns in the Provincial Newspaper Press, 1873–1914', *International Journal of Regional and Local Studies* 5, no. 1 (2009: 104–20) and Siân Pooley, 'Children's Writing and the Popular Press in England 1876–1914', *History Workshop Journal* 80, no. 1 (Autumn 2015): 75–98.
34. Cruikshank, Barbara. *The Will to Empower: Democratic Citizens and Other Subjects* (Ithaca: Cornell University Press, 1999), 97.
35. Viviana A. Zelizer, 'The Priceless Child Revisited', in *Studies in Modern Childhood: Society, Agency, Culture*, ed. Jens Qvortrup (Houndmills: Palgrave Macmillan, 2005), 185.
36. Karen Sánchez-Eppler, 'Childhood', in *Keywords for Children's Literature*, ed. Philip Nel and Lissa Paul (New York: New York University Press, 2011), 36.
37. Berry Mayall and Virginia Morrow, *You Can Help Your Country: English Children's Work During the Second World War* (London: Institute of Education, 2011), 20.
38. Lesley Ginsberg, 'Minority/Majority: Childhood Studies and Antebellum American Literature', in *The Children's Table: Childhood Studies and the Humanities*, ed. Anne Mae Duane (Athens: University of Georgia Press, 2013), 106.
39. Marah Gubar, *Artful Dodgers: Reconceiving the Golden Age of Children's Literature* (Oxford: Oxford University Press, 2009), 8.
40. Gubar, *Artful Dodgers*, 6.
41. Gubar, *Artful Dodgers*, 7.
42. William A. Corsaro, 'Collective Action and Agency in Young Children's Peer Cultures', in *Studies in Modern Childhood: Society, Agency, Culture*, ed. Jens Qvortrup (Houndmills: Palgrave Macmillan, 2005), 231.
43. Corsaro, 'Collective Action', 231. Emphasis in original.
44. Gorsky, *Patterns of Philanthropy*, 9.

2

Charitable Publics

In an early number of the first volume of *Young Helpers' League Magazine*, editor Thomas Barnardo describes a letter received by the League Secretary in which a lady writes that

> My little boy, who has joined the Young Helpers' League, is much perturbed as to whether he is obliged to give what he has collected (only a few shillings) to Dr. Barnardo's Homes, or whether he may, as a member of the League, give his money to the 'Church of England Society for Waifs and Strays'.[1]

The letter is rare textual evidence of the multiplicity of charitable organisations and how children's participation in them was a source of tension. The letter continues with how 'Our Vicar is very anxious to get small donations for the Church of England Waifs and Strays, and we wait your directions in the matter'.[2] With multiple organisations aiming to attract similar groups of potential fundraisers, capacity to attract new members was limited. That the boy's mother wrote to the magazine for clarification demonstrates the impact of these periodicals in guiding charitable giving.[3]

Periodicals were of vital importance to the development of children's charitable impulses in the nineteenth century and into the twentieth century. This chapter brings together the range of strategies that were mobilised in children's magazines to encourage children to see themselves as charitable donors and to do the work requested by the charities. Drawing on multiple examples, this chapter demonstrates how many magazines implemented similar strategies to attract child readers through a discussion of the charitable cause supported in the magazine, fiction that

22

depicted children performing charitable duties, information about the charity, reports on financial donations, and various forms of child engagement. These periodicals, spanning geographical distances and chronological timespans, also responded to the changing expectations of child readers and the different requirements of the charitable causes.

Children were active contributors to charitable causes in the nineteenth century, and children's periodicals were often the vehicle through which they were encouraged to make sustained contributions. The juvenile missionary magazines founded in the 1840s that encouraged child readers to donate to foreign missions reinforced these charitable aims by encouraging children to regularly attend Sunday schools where they would learn about the value of missions and receive regular updates on missionary activities and fundraising objectives. *Band of Hope Review and Sunday Scholar Friend* was similarly distributed through Sunday schools beginning in the 1850s to inform and instruct children about the importance of temperance, but it defined charity in ways that were more explicitly activist and less focused on financial donations. When *Aunt Judy's Magazine* first appealed to its child readers in 1868 to raise money for a cot at the Great Ormond Street Hospital for Sick Children, it took advantage of the charitable impulses initially fostered by missionary magazines. Yet it could not rely on the same organisational structures, such as Sunday schools and the community projects of the missionary society, to help promote children's commitment to its charitable cause. Instead, the magazine defined new strategies to engage readers and promote charitable giving.

The role of print is central to the development of children's charitable ethos during this period. The examples that are discussed in this chapter and elsewhere in this book have all mobilised the affordances of serial print publication to develop child readerships in support of their charitable causes. I argue in this chapter that the success of these periodicals in shaping children's attitudes towards their charitable cause is enabled through the charitable publics created through print. Drawing on Lauren Berlant's idea of 'intimate publics', I consider how 'charitable publics' were defined and reinforced in children's periodicals to produce charitable children who understood their responsibilities to help others. This chapter uses a variety of examples of charitable publics produced through children's magazines during the nineteenth and early twentieth centuries supporting missionary work, children's hospitals, temperance, and children's health. Even as they drew upon evolving ideas about children and childhood as well as new technologies, they demonstrate the centrality of print in the production of charitable publics that promoted a charitable ideal for children between 1840 and 1930 and the reality that those publics were strikingly similar.

Numerous strategies enabled the creation of these charitable publics, but they are underlaid by the fundamental assumption that children could and should provide assistance to others, especially those who are vulnerable because of their lack of religion, poverty, behaviour, or health. As I discussed in the previous chapter, children were encouraged to contribute to a variety of different charitable causes throughout the century and indeed charity was a fundamental concept to Victorians. Through print, charitable publics were created first by defining the charitable cause, encouraging young readers to join in, and then demonstrating the success of the charity and of the young people's efforts to support the cause.

Defining charitable publics

In *The Female Complaint: The Unfinished Business of Sentimentality in American Culture* (2008), Lauren Berlant uses women's culture to form the basis of her exploration of what she calls 'intimate publics'. As she explains in the preface, 'What makes a public sphere intimate is an expectation that the consumers of its particular stuff *already* share a worldview and emotional knowledge that they have derived from a broadly common historical experience.'[4] In children's periodicals, given the young age of the implied readership, the magazine is constituting the world view and emotional knowledge that produces charitable giving while also sharing contemporary social and cultural expectations about such giving, informed by religious beliefs that encourage care for others. The charitable public being created through the experience of reading the magazine alongside many other young readers generates the shared expectation that this public will create 'a better experience of social belonging' through the experiences of reading the magazine and contributing towards its charitable aims.[5] Like Benedict Anderson's argument that the press created an 'imagined community' enabling the development and spread of nationalism, this charitable public flourishes as an 'affective scene of identification among strangers that promises a certain experience of belonging and provides a complex of consolation, confirmation, discipline and discussion' about enacting charitable behaviours.[6] The magazines discussed in this chapter demonstrate the capacity of print to simultaneously create and make visible a charitable public comprised of young readers invested in the success of its charitable cause.

An intimate public operates as a space in which its participants share interests and desires. Berlant, referring to twentieth-century women's intimate publics, describes them as 'a market' that is open 'to a bloc of consumers' and claims 'to circulate texts and things that express those people's core interests and desires'.[7] This language is understandably informed by consumer culture, but children's capitalist participation has long been a site of contestation. Christopher Parkes details how 'the romantic view of childhood was responsible for initiating the gradual removal of the child from the workplace' in nineteenth-century Britain through a series of legislative changes that removed children's ability to work and eventually required them to attend school.[8] The idealised view of childhood innocence was felt to be incompatible with 'economically productive activity'.[9] This ideal sits in contrast to earlier evangelical views in which the child was seen 'as a competent collaborator, capable of working and playing alongside adults'.[10] These competing ideas of the child, Parkes argues, inform nineteenth-century capitalist society, which 'required the child to be a figure that could participate in commercial activity and yet remain innocent and uncorrupted'.[11]

The charitable public produced by children's magazines is defined by a shared set of beliefs about children that intersect with both definitions of childhood as contributors to commercial activity and as innocent. The editors expected child readers to participate in charitable activity while also remaining innocent and uncorrupted. This expectation was reasonable given how charitable causes were positioned in children's magazines. An idealised view of those in need is presented in the magazine, with minimal graphic material to disturb young readers. Moreover, when children are asked to raise funds, paid employment is never suggested as a source. Instead, they are encouraged to perform activities within a certain permissible range, such as asking family members to donate, encouraging friends and family to subscribe

26   Philanthropy in Children's Periodicals, 1840–1930

to the magazine, and performing ad hoc activities to generate funds. Thus, the charitable public defined for children is based on a set of 'core interests and desires' that enables its participants to '*feel* as though it expresses what is common among them, a subjective likeness that seems to emanate from their history and their ongoing attachments and actions'.[12] These commonalities are based on a set of understandings about what can be asked of children within contemporary definitions of childhood and charity. Children can be encouraged to participate and made to feel guilty if they are not doing enough; they can be expected to raise awareness of the cause and solicit donations or raise funds directly. In return, the magazine creating its charitable public will provide details about the cause, include regular updates about its successes and challenges, and continue to promote the cause as central to the magazine's ideological position.

The emotional aspect of the intimate public is essential to its development. Berlant defines publics as 'affective insofar as they don't just respond to material interests but magnetize optimism about living and being connected to strangers in a kind of nebulous *communitas*'.[13] Nowhere is this degree of optimism more apparent than in the charitable publics defined in children's periodicals. The persistent, repeated calls for charitable action appearing in their pages are testament to the beliefs that adult writers, editors, and publishers had in the ability – and the willingness – of children to make significant efforts to support charitable work. Children's manifest contributions to the cause also signal their optimism about the charity's ability to do good. The charitable public created through the magazine is based on this shared understanding among young readers of how they can be contributing members in which they mutually agree to work towards a charitable objective. Of course, not all children who felt that they were part of the charitable public necessarily understood their participation and engagement in the same way. As Berlant explains, being part of a public is 'a way of experiencing one's own story as part of something social, even if one's singular relation to that belonging is extremely limited, episodic, ambivalent, rejecting, or mediated by random encounters with relevantly marked texts'.[14] Although children's voices are not always a significant feature of children's magazines, some of their correspondence demonstrates the extent to which their interest in ensuring that they are correctly identified supersedes their interest in the cause itself. While children's engagement with the charitable public through the pages of a magazine is thus multifaceted and uneven, each individual experience contributes to the overarching public as a whole.

The social and cultural charitable contexts needed to enable a charitable public are produced through the charity magazine and commercial magazines with strong charitable links. The charity magazine is a distinct form of the company magazine, which Michael Heller identifies as emerging in the 1880s. One of its main functions is 'operational' insofar as it enables the organisation to function by 'informing, educating and entertaining employees and key stakeholders'.[15] The company magazine 'assisted in building the spirit or soul of the company' through its articulation of an *esprit de corps* and how it 'played a role in articulating, negotiating and representing commonly held values, beliefs and practices'.[16] These features of a company magazine can also be applied to the nineteenth- and early twentieth-century charity magazines, and to children's charity magazines in particular. They were embedded in the processes of cultural formation that understood readers are charitable donors. Heller's description of the function of company magazines in producing a corporate identity in which readers share values and beliefs echo Berlant's comments about 'intimate publics' in which such shared understandings enable belonging. The children's charity magazine is thus a valuable site through which to explore how a charitable public is created through its pages.

Defining the charitable cause

A charitable public in a children's magazine could only be created through a carefully defined charitable cause. Periodicals adopted different approaches to defining their charitable causes, often based on the cause itself, how the magazine was distributed, and the institutional support it received. Some periodicals depended on the regular weekly or monthly purchase of the next instalment, especially commercial magazines like *Aunt Judy's Magazine* as well as newspapers featuring children's columns. For these magazines, the charitable cause promoted in its pages was just one of many features that were intended to provide continuity across its issues alongside fiction, poetry, informational articles, correspondence, and illustrations. Nonetheless, when these commercial publications chose to support a charitable cause, they included a range

28   Philanthropy in Children's Periodicals, 1840–1930

of charitable content designed to define their charitable publics. Charity magazines, as discussed in Chapter 1, generally had more institutional support in the form of a subscription model and were often distributed through the structures of organisational membership. Moreover, a charity magazine could potentially take advantage of presumed knowledge about its cause.

A charitable public was created in children's periodicals by featuring children who were already helping others. One of the objectives in the first number of the monthly, twenty-four-page *Juvenile Missionary Magazine* (1844–87), published by the London Missionary Society, is explained as follows:

> As nothing but the blessing of God can make our attempts useful and successful we must pray for that. This Magazine will tell you by and by of children who have loved to pray, and grown up to be useful and happy, and lived to serve and honour the Saviour all their days.[17]

Prayer is essential for young people, and the young readers are presented with stories and letters featuring children who have also enjoyed prayer and then grown up to do God's work. In another example, James Sherman writes of how an eight-year-old girl approached him to offer to distribute tracts to tradesmen who keep their shops open on Sundays for she thinks they will not 'refuse to take them [from] a little girl'.[18] Sherman adopted her plan and, 'acting as a Missionary in the district, she has been the instrument of shutting up six shops which were formerly kept open'.[19] By including stories that feature young people doing the charity work, magazines were able to produce an implied – and actual – readership of young people who were defined by a shared interest in the welfare of others. Across a range of causes, these magazines consistently depicted children doing the important work of and for the charity.

In *Band of Hope Review and Sunday Scholar Friend* (1851–1937), a monthly, four-page, halfpenny children's magazine launched in 1851, its religious focus is mobilised specifically for its temperance cause.[20] The editor outlines the purposes of the magazine in the September 1852 issue:

> To counteract the fearful influence of the low-priced immoral prints upon the young; to stem the torrent of intemperance; to promote the better observance of the Lord's day; to inculcate kindness to animals;

to foster a love for peace, brotherly love, and obedience to parents; and to incite to a daily and diligent searching of the Holy Scriptures.[21]

The magazine aims to produce higher-quality literature for young people that contains temperance and religious messages designed to encourage a charitable public motivated by kindness, love, obedience, and regular Bible reading. Unlike some of the other magazines discussed in this chapter, in which the charitable public is defined primarily by its financial support of the cause, *Band of Hope Review* hopes that children will take the temperance pledge and spread its messages to other young people, but also, perhaps even more importantly, to adults who would benefit from its content. The editor reports that '[t]wo cases of reformation amongst drunkards, by the distribution of the paper amongst their *children*, have been communicated to us.'[22] By distributing the magazine to children through Sunday Schools and Ragged Schools, it hoped to obtain readers among both its readerships: the intended young people who were the target of the magazine and also the adults who cared for these young people and were more likely to have problems with drink. At the same time, the magazine was also distributed directly to those 'on board emigrant ships and canal boats; amongst railway men, &c., &c'. in the hopes of directly appealing to older, predominantly adult, readers.[23] The magazine thus aimed to attract a dual readership of both adults and children. While this was common with children's periodicals since young readers typically depended on adults to purchase the magazine on their behalf, in this case adults were explicitly part of the target readership.

This dual readership was in line with broader concerns about the problem of drink in the nineteenth century. Brian Harrison describes a concern in the 1850s that temperance work had become more focused 'on rearing the children in sobriety instead of reclaiming their parents'.[24] This corresponded to the rapid establishment of Bands of Hope beginning in 1847 and their continuing expansion throughout the century. Victoria Berridge explains how the 'reality of the temperance culture' encouraged working men (and later women) to join temperance movements in which membership was based on a shared appreciation of thrift and an interest in religious matters.[25] This reality also attracted child teetotallers, with over 3.5 million British school children registered as members in 1901.[26] These high membership numbers

30   Philanthropy in Children's Periodicals, 1840–1930

were enabled through a range of temperance campaign strategies based on 'both moral and economic arguments against drink', in which abstinence became a 'badge of 'respectability'.[27] Producing 'newspapers and tracts in their hundreds of thousands', temperance societies contributed to what Annemarie McAllister describes as a 'national cultural habitus' that critiqued the role of drink in contemporary society and in which periodicals were a vital contribution to temperance culture.[28] She notes the extraordinary circulation figures of the children's temperance press: in 1860–1, *Band of Hope Review* had over 250,000 readers.[29] The periodical was instrumental in creating change among its readers and had a pervasive influence throughout the second half of the century as its charitable public expanded.

The focus on children helping other children is explicit in magazines supporting home missions aiming at poor, disadvantaged children located in Britain. Organisations like the evangelical Barnardo's and the Anglican Waifs and Strays Society defined charitable publics on this basis. After Barnardo launched his charity in 1870, he became a prolific publisher of printed materials encouraging adults to support his charitable causes. Only with the 1892 launch of his quarterly children's charity publication *Young Helpers' League Magazine* did he create a venue and infrastructure to support children's charitable giving. His hope was that this 'vast army of child-helpers [can] wonderfully strengthen our hands and theirs, and give us aggressive power of no mean kind in carrying on our warfare against the powers of evil'.[30] Similarly, in describing the activities conducted by young members of the Children's Union of the Waifs and Strays Society, Helen Milman explains how '[t]he great charm about these entertainments is that everything has been done by the children themselves'.[31] Both of these organisations were keen to develop charitable publics defined by the young age of the charity workers, religious sentiment, and a desire to help other children.

Moreover, the charitable public developed for young people differed from the ones aimed at adults. Barnardo's children's magazine differed from his adult publication, *Night and Day*, since he was aware of the need to publish material suitable for a younger audience. In line with concerns identified in *Band of Hope Review*, Barnardo did not want children accessing materials that were seen to be inappropriate for them. He explains how '[m]any of the

Charitable Publics 31

narratives of child rescue' published for adults 'exhibit the seamy side of human nature'.[32] He explains that, since there are

> many aspects of our rescue work which it is not desirable that young children, whether boys or girls, should be familiar with ... we have but followed in the beaten and honoured track of the veteran Societies in launching ... our new quarterly magazine, intended for the perusal of the young.[33]

The tension between innocence and experience in this context differs from the economic productivity discussed previously. Here, the tension appears in relation to children's knowledge of the world and reflects a desire to protect young readers from some harsh realities of nineteenth-century life.

The endpaper for the first volume of *Young Helpers' League Magazine* (see Fig. 2.1) defines its charitable public including its target audience, who it aims to help, and its mission. This 'Union of Boys and Girls, Chiefly of the Upper and Middle Classes' encourages young people to consider how they can contribute to Barnardo's.[34] This magazine is not intended for poor children but is instead geared towards children who have the desire and the ability to help others. It also clearly identifies who is to be assisted by the charity, the 'crippled, blind, deaf and dumb, and sick children of the waif class'.[35] The motto of the organisation, 'Bear ye one another's burdens, and so fulfil the law of Christ' is a verse from the Bible (Galatians 6:2), which connects it to the evangelical Christian doctrine that people should help one another. The 'Daily Prayer' blesses 'all poor children throughout the world', but it is also a prayer to encourage 'our hearts' to be filled with 'loving desires' to help those poor children.[36] These upper- and middle-class children will form the charitable public of the magazine, reflecting their subject positions as children who will help others. This help is expected to come in a material form by becoming 'Companions of the "Young Helpers' League"' after completing the application form and enclosing one shilling, for which each Companion will receive 'a beautiful Card of Membership' as well as the 'admirably illustrated' quarterly *Young Helpers' League Magazine*.[37]

Boys and girls living 'in happy homes the wide world over' are invited to become Companions, which continues to position the child Companions as distinct from the children who will be helped.[38] This reflects broader cultural shifts in the last decades

Fig. 2.1 Endpaper, *Young Helpers' League Magazine*, January 1892–December 1894, np.

of the nineteenth century that Hugh Cunningham describes, in which 'the ideals and actuality of middle-class childhood became more powerfully interwoven with the remedies offered for the condition of the children of the poor'.[39] Middle-class children were understood to be inhabiting an idealised space characterised by 'the security of a good home and family, and contact with nature'.[40] The charitable public created through the magazine, then, was formulated to assist other less fortunate children to achieve some degree of access to similar formulations of childhood. It is developed through the magazine by reinforcing its community. As Barnardo explains in the preface to the first volume of *Young Helpers' League Magazine*, 'So it is to a wide, wide circle of warm-hearted co-workers that I dedicate this volume. It is *your* volume, for you have helped to make it, and it is *your* work that it records.'[41] He appeals to the readers of the magazine by directly addressing them and encourages them to see themselves as part of a 'wide, wide circle' of people who are working together to achieve common goals. Milman similarly explains that, although the plan to create the Children's Union is hers, '*you* have all got to carry it out'.[42] In both cases, the editors are aware that the success of the charitable public is dependent on children participating in the charitable work.

In the latter decades of the nineteenth century, as an increasing number of non-religious publishers began producing materials for children, religion ceased to be the only rationale by which children were encouraged to help others. The campaign in *Aunt Judy's Magazine* to support the Great Ormond Street Hospital for Sick Children beginning in 1868 marks a significant shift in the language associated with children's charity in which child health, rather than religious conversion, becomes most important. While a child's health was also entwined with ideas of class, these campaigns nonetheless reflected a distinct move away from religious charity to a more humanist rationale and rhetoric. The six-penny monthly had no explicit religious affiliation, published as it was by George Bell, and was aimed at both boys and girls. Editor Margaret Gatty, in her role as 'Aunt Judy', introduces the hospital as a source of charitable contributions in the correspondence section of the January 1868 issue by including a letter from Samuel Whitford, the hospital's secretary. He explains the hospital's plans to open a country branch and wonders whether 'the readers of your highly interesting and instructive magazine

34 Philanthropy in Children's Periodicals, 1840–1930

might not be induced . . . to contribute for the support of a *Cot*, to be called the "Aunt Judy's Magazine Cot"'.[43] He explains that £30 will be sufficient to fund the cot for a year, and he will send regular reports about the children who are treated. Gatty promises to acknowledge every donation received to support the cot, no matter how 'trifling', and to announce when the required sum has been collected.[44] In this case, the charitable public in support of the Great Ormond Street Hospital is created through a specific call to action for child readers in which Gatty presumes that children will be interested in and able to support the cause.

Although the market is characterised by fewer new religious publications for children in the last decades of the century, this is not to suggest that religious charitable giving declined during this period. In fact, as I discuss in more detail in the next chapter, the lengthy runs of children's religious periodicals reflect the longstanding ethos of charity embedded within religious institutions. Yet the appearance of charitable campaigns in non-religious magazines – or at least in magazines without an explicitly religious focus – demonstrate how charity was mobilised in the nineteenth century to address a myriad of social problems for which the state was ill-prepared or unwilling to respond. This distinction between private philanthropy and social support emerges from 'the Victorian ethos' that 'ascribed such evils as poverty, destitute old age, and even much of the suffering from unemployment to individual inadequacies rather than to any more general failure of the social mechanism'.[45] Thus Gatty's support for the 'Aunt Judy's Magazine Cot' emerges from the social necessity that the hospital was dependent on charitable giving for its operating costs because it received no other public funding.

The ethos of children's charity that is developed through print during much of the nineteenth century is transformed during the First World War since paper shortages meant that the role of magazines declined. The charitable goals during wartime became much wider, but often still had associations with children, including the Belgian Relief Fund and the Returning Soldiers' Fund. The rise of the Junior Red Cross and the appearance of their first children's magazines from the 1920s saw those charitable impulses being mobilised in print once paper was again widely available and affordable. With the Junior Red Cross, the aim of assisting children returns to the forefront, along with a more international focus. Like the Band of Hope, which intended to direct children

Charitable Publics 35

toward specific goals through temperance pledges, the Junior Red Cross invited children to sign pledges to improve health outcomes. The Junior Red Cross could 'do better work than the grown-ups, because good health depends largely on the practice of right health habits, and these are more easily learned in childhood than in adult life'.[46] As will be discussed in more detail in Chapter 7, the Junior Red Cross created a charitable habitus that defined its charitable public based on common aims to improve the circumstances of children's lives through better health after the war.

Healthy numbers of readers and charitable subscribers was an essential and ongoing concern for organisations wishing to maintain their charitable publics. Children's periodicals were regularly challenged by their 'perennially ageing readership', which meant that 'editors and publishers had to attend carefully to changes in the marketplace and evolving ideas about children and childhood'.[47] Along with the initial description of the charitable cause and its aims, charitable children's magazines periodically reminded readers about their goals and encouraged them to participate or, if they were already members or contributors to the cause, to invite their friends to also join the cause.

In establishing the Young Helpers' League, Barnardo alludes to the need to induct children into the charitable public he has already created for adults. In the 1892 Annual Report, he observes that 'one of the difficulties of such work as ours arises from the loss of old established friends by death or removal ... The eye turns with hope and expectation to the children of to-day, who will be the workers of tomorrow.'[48] Barnardo knows he must look to the future to ensure the availability of a steady supply of adult supporters of this work. He explains that '[w]hile thus learning to help others, this band of Companions of the Y. H. L. are themselves being unconsciously educated into quickened sympathy with sad and suffering childhood, a sympathy which we trust will *bear its fruit* in after years'.[49] The magazine, as Barnardo explains, is intended to be a recruiting tool. By creating a charitable public among his younger readers, he anticipates their continuing support as they become adults.

Yet the young people Barnardo was hoping to attract are the same ones temperance workers were concerned about losing from Bands of Hope. Even with a clearly defined pathway that encouraged young people to participate in temperance activities from a young age by joining Bands of Hope, teens gradually stopped

36   Philanthropy in Children's Periodicals, 1840–1930

attending meetings. The activities offered by Bands of Hope typically included regular meetings featuring songs, recitations, dialogues, readings, and magic lantern shows, as well as peripheral materials such as *Band of Hope Review*, pledge certificates, medals for new members, recruitment, and anniversaries, and badges as special honours. They were designed to be entertaining and to encourage regular attendance and participation among younger attendees, but they were not as attractive to older children. In a paper delivered at the annual meeting of the Durham branch of the Church of England Temperance Society, H. F. Clarke explains that '[a]ll will admit the unquestionable difficulty of retaining members in our Bands of Hope after they reach a certain age' as they begin to earn their living and gradually drift away, 'in other words, at the very period when they are most exposed to temptation'.[50] Clarke proposes establishing activities aimed at older members such as clubs focused on useful activities such as 'woodcarving, book-binding, fretwork, carpentry, [and] gymnastics' alongside 'needlework, knitting, &c'.[51] This aligns with another paper by Herbert T. James, in which he proposes an 'Industrial Band of Hope' where members are instructed in various useful handicrafts to learn new skills. Not only will these activities keep young members from wandering the streets, the sale of the work will also support the organisation.[52] Across various organisations, the urgent need to retain members was apparent. Not only did they wish to continue sharing and reinforcing the charitable objectives, but they also needed people who would contribute to the charity in material and financial ways as they became adults.

The serial print form provides an opportunity to reinforce these charitable publics. The seriality of periodicals is a vital factor for understanding how ideas about children and charity were communicated, shared, and reinforced. Children's periodicals were reflecting and mobilising discourses appearing elsewhere – in the press, in fiction, in the church, and on street corners – that encouraged young people to consider how they could assist poor, sick, or otherwise unfortunate children. Their weekly, monthly, or quarterly distribution provided the iterability that enabled the development of charitable publics and thereby the development of the charitable child who believed that they should help others and who understood themselves as part of the community of charitable givers. These individual issues were self-contained, but they also consisted of 'building blocks' in which key ideals in the magazine were developed and repeated over time with the appearance of each new number.[53] James Mussell explains how '[s]eriality . . . allows readers to differentiate between form and content, regarding form as that which stays the same and allowing content, which varies, to flow'.[54] The form of most children's periodicals remained consistent over time, often with regular features including editorials, fiction, informational articles, illustrations, and correspondence. The content necessarily differed across issues to maintain freshness for the keen young reader. Yet, within this variable content, creating a charitable public required regular and consistent messaging about the work of the charity. By publishing specific components related to charity – including regular reports about the charitable cause, subscription lists or fundraising totals, correspondence, and other relevant informational or fictional articles, the magazine develops an 'aggregate of knowledge' about charity that child readers absorbed each week or month and over time.[55]

The seriality of the magazines enabled the introduction of the charitable cause and a call to action as well as reinforcing the value of this action in practical and financial terms. In each issue, the magazine raised the visibility of the charitable cause. Charity magazines typically identified the cause in an initial number, sometimes setting financial targets for child contributors depending on their level of enthusiasm. In the example from *Aunt Judy's Magazine*, for example, the goal of £30 is established. The eventual total of more than £3,000 raised between 1868 and 1885 demonstrates how small contributions could be aggregated into large sums over time. Similarly, the *Wesleyan Juvenile Offering* included annual Christmas donation periods in which they encouraged their young readers to actively solicit contributions from friends and family. The *Juvenile Missionary Magazine* initially asked child readers to contribute to a missionary ship, a tangible outcome that they invited children to visit before its departure from London. Over the years, the juvenile association of the London Missionary Society raised funds for four separate ships as they sunk or needed to be replaced.

These charitable successes were made possible by the seriality of the periodical. With established distribution systems in place to provide access to young readers, magazines could advertise the specific charitable goal regularly and remind readers to do their best to support it. Even readers who may have begun reading the paper midway through a charitable campaign would relatively easily be able to identify the cause and decide to support it. The

38   Philanthropy in Children's Periodicals, 1840–1930

magazines were designed to reduce the barriers to entry and to encourage child participation through content that promoted the charity and identified how children could contribute.

The charitable cause itself was generally supported through other content appearing elsewhere in the magazine. The initial request in the correspondence section that readers support the 'Aunt Judy's Magazine Cot', for instance, was accompanied by an article on 'The Hospital for Sick Children'. 'Gwynfryn', the pseudonym of Dorothea Jones, describes the hospital, which contains 'little people, in very small beds ranged along the walls'.[56] The article concludes with the story of a desperately ill child who sends gifts to the hospital so that 'some of the poor children' can play with her toys.[57] The article and the concluding anecdote about a child contributor to the hospital introduce child readers to the charitable cause and to the idea that they could help sick children through their contributions. When the idea is formally introduced in the correspondence section at the end of the issue, readers would have already been exposed to the hospital and predisposed to see it as a cause worth supporting.

Even after the charity was well understood within *Aunt Judy's Magazine*, the magazine continued to offer other material beyond the specific updates about the cot to encourage readers to contribute. In 'Little Annie's Christmas', an illustrated poem appearing in November 1871, the eponymous protagonist lies alone, ill, and in pain on a ragged bed. The poem begins by describing how the 'sweet chimes of Christmas Day' are heard by many, but not those 'In the dark town, where crowded dwell / The poor in narrow courts and streets' like those where Annie lives (see Fig. 2.2).[58] Her bed lies on the floor, with a broken chair and window in the background. Happily, the 'little sufferer' is visited by Margaret, who also used to be unwell until she was treated at a children's hospital. She describes the hospital as 'like Heaven' with 'clean white beds', 'wholesome food', and relief from pain where they taught her to read and pray.[59] The Great Ormond Street Hospital is named specifically, but the poem is not resolved with Annie also being swept into its care. Instead, Margaret only hopes that Annie might also be able to be treated there. The image of the two girls together reflects the before and after of charitable giving. Margaret is grateful for the treatment she has received, while Annie's circumstances are desperately forlorn even though she is hopeful that someone will eventually come and carry her away.

Charitable Publics 39

Fig. 2.2 C. J. Staniland, 'Little Annie's Christmas', *Aunt Judy's Magazine*, November 1871, 120.

40   Philanthropy in Children's Periodicals, 1840–1930

In the final stanza, the narrator makes an appeal to readers to support the establishment of a new cot at the hospital. Shifting to directly address the reader, the narrator invites them to think of themselves as part of the charitable public by envisioning the many unfortunate children like Annie and asking whether they will let the suffering continue:

> Dear children, many Annies lie
> Exhausted on their bed of pain;
> Oh, will you let their weary cry
> Be uttered every day in vain?
> By little savings, could you not
> Support a new 'Aunt Judy's Cot?'[60]

The concluding couplet, with its different rhyme scheme, calls on each child to save their money and support a new cot at the hospital. Supporting content like this poem and illustration reinforce the charitable cause discussed elsewhere in the magazine and helped to produce its charitable public.

The seriality of the publication reiterates the charitable cause as one worthy of time and, if possible, financial support. It also produces and reinforces a group of young people who are interested in the success of both the magazine and its charitable cause. Moreover, across the months and years of the magazine's publication, it encourages young readers to help others by assuming that this content will be attractive and sufficiently interesting to motivate young people to support the cause.

Joining the charitable public

The strategies of commercial magazines supporting a charitable cause are somewhat different from those of charity magazines. It may have been easier for commercial magazines to attract readers and obtain charitable donors since the range of content meant that they could appeal to a wide audience, not only those who were presumably already interested in the charitable cause. Appeals like those appearing in *Aunt Judy's Magazine* offered an opportunity to attract readers to the cause if they were not already participating. Charity magazines had to attract new readers based on content falling within a narrower range informed by their charitable objectives. On the other hand, magazines with clear charitable objectives and appropriate materials for young people may have been more desirable to adult purchasers. The number of papers distributed for free, such as those handed out by missionary and temperance organisations, may have also influenced consumption habits among young readers.

Growing the membership of the charitable public supporting the charitable cause was an essential aspect of many magazines, although the ways they acknowledged this membership were intertwined with other elements of the magazine. This section looks at how the magazines supported the growing community of young readers who were engaged in performing charitable work by considering how the organisational structure is embedded into the magazines' content. This structural support encouraged children to participate in the charitable cause and join groups of other young people to support the cause.

For both the Wesleyan Missionary Society and the London Missionary Society, Sunday Schools provided the infrastructure to support the charitable cause and the distribution of its magazine. For the Wesleyans, children became part of a local branch, which was part of a circuit, and multiple circuits joined together to form a district. In the London Missionary Society, contribution amounts are listed in the annual reports by the Sunday School name and then the region in which the school was located.[61] Although *Wesleyan Juvenile Offering* was happy to report on new branches being established, fundraising numbers were typically reported at the district or circuit level, rather than at an individual branch level. As a consequence, child readers were positioned to see their contributions as part of a much larger collective action, a point discussed in more detail in the next chapter. Similarly, the *Juvenile Missionary Magazine* incorporated strategies that leveraged the Sunday School structure that was already in place. Cunningham explains how Sunday Schools were established to give order to children's lives on Sundays when they were not working and to provide 'the rudiments of religion and education which would shape the rest of their lives'.[62] The inclusion of charity work within this educational infrastructure was a natural outcome. The *Wesleyan Juvenile Offering* thus supported the work of the Sunday School and its ability to encourage charity work by identifying members based on the Sunday School in which they were located and noting when new Sunday School branches were established. The Sunday School distributed the magazine and used

42   Philanthropy in Children's Periodicals, 1840–1930

it as a teaching tool as well as a vehicle encouraging children to raise funds through donations.

Importantly, the existing Sunday School system provided an infrastructure for collecting funds. These funds were typically noted separately in annual reports, making children's financial contributions to the organisation more evident. The London district of the Wesleyan Methodist Missionary Society, for example, contained seven circuits, and each circuit had a different number of Sunday Schools. The district also included schools not located within a circuit. The results of the annual Christmas fundraising campaign by the children are listed in the annual reports. In the 1842 report, for instance, the children in the London district raised £718 9s 4d, contributing to an overall total of £4,721 7s 4d.[63]

Although the Band of Hope and Temperance Union was not formally affiliated with any of the Sunday Schools, people interested in establishing a juvenile society for young temperance members were strongly encouraged to approach the local Sunday School. In a handbook on how to form a Band of Hope, readers are informed that, for larger communities, 'it is more desirable to form a society in connection with a Sunday School' since otherwise the group might become too large to manage successfully. In villages with a smaller number of children and teachers, one Band of Hope for the community was advisable. Bands of Hope that are connected with schools are 'best' because 'parents will be more willing to allow their children to attend meetings at their own school', which is also often closer to home.[64] Moreover, the children will be known to the teachers, which provides a strong inducement for their attendance. A similar logic applies to the creation of a day school Band of Hope as long as someone on the staff is an abstainer. Meetings could be held once a fortnight or once a month, where

> the master, or some friend, would give an address; some of the children might recite pieces, and a Band of Hope melody be sung. This could all be done in thirty or forty minutes and the time made to pass so pleasantly that the children would be glad to remain for the extra time after the usual School hour; once a quarter an evening entertainment, preceded by a tea, might be given, which all paying members would attend.[65]

Although young people could become Band of Hope members without making the weekly half-penny payment, they were encouraged to

Charitable Publics   43

become paying members, which meant they would be given a temperance magazine each month, permitted to attend three quarterly tea meetings and entertainments, given access to free books from the library, and – for a small additional fee – attend the annual Summer Excursion.[66] As McAllister notes, the organisation was able to attract young members by 'providing regular activities for them in relatively pleasant surroundings, encouraging them to identity with a group [of children with similar interests]; rewarding them with markers and symbols of success, such as the medals they could proudly wear; and systematically fostering their abilities and skills'.[67]

These practical logistics offer information that is otherwise missing from *Band of Hope Review*, which is distinct for the small amount of content related to its organisational structure and the extensive amount of work happening outside the pages of the magazine. This is typical of charitable work discussed in children's magazines, which often elided the complexities of the work being done off the page. Given that the Band of Hope juvenile societies were specifically intended to promote the 'total abstinence from all intoxicating drinks (and tobacco) amongst the young' by requiring them to sign a pledge to abstain, the magazine's content was more focused on its pedagogical mission.[68] Although the Band of Hope and Temperance Union had a similar structure to that outlined for the Wesleyan Missionary Society, in which groups of young people came together as part of local societies that rolled up to a larger regional union, the magazine allocated little space in which to discuss the functioning of the organisation. The minimal space is likely because of its length. At only four pages, *Band of Hope Review* was considerably shorter than most other monthly charity magazines.

Although *Band of Hope Review* did not often refer to its organisational structure, the regional annual reports shed some light on the complexities of its organisation. Within the Oxfordshire Band of Hope and Temperance Union, for instance, are adult and juvenile societies that are involved to varying extents in its range of activities, including the annual conference and demonstration, lectures, social meetings, mission work, writing and distributing literature such as the *Oxford Temperance Herald*, and raising funds for the Christmas and New Year collection.[69] A total of £11 11s 3s was raised in 1881, and the amount contributed by young people is not identified in the annual report.[70] I would suggest that this indicates the relatively lesser importance placed on children's contributions. Children were requested, and incentivised, to

44   Philanthropy in Children's Periodicals, 1840–1930

become paying members to help offset the costs of food, entertainment, and temperance publications, but otherwise their collecting efforts were relatively modest. This differs significantly from some of the other charitable causes discussed here, in which children's financial contributions were essential to their ongoing success. For Bands of Hope, however, the children's pledges to abstain from all intoxicating drinks were equally as important as their proselytising efforts and perhaps even more crucial than their financial contributions.

If the organisation had a pre-existing structure like the missionary societies and their Sunday Schools, the magazines were able to capitalise on this for fundraising. Other organisations that lacked the infrastructure had to abandon any idea of organisation or create their own. *Aunt Judy's Magazine*, for instance, did not have an institutional structure to help support its charitable aims and made no efforts to organise its subscribers. It depended entirely on the magazine to encourage charitable giving. It did so through the inclusion of subscription lists that identified individual subscribers and their contribution amounts. Since organisations like Barnardo's, and later the Junior Red Cross, did not have the advantages of a pre-existing organisational structure, they created their own. Barnardo's developed the Young Helpers' League, in which boys and girls enrolled to become a 'Companion' of the League accompanied by a one shilling annual subscription.[71] These individual subscribers were grouped into local 'lodges' of twelve Companions, and two lodges were sufficient to form a 'habitation'. Although lists of individual contributions remained part of *Young Helpers' League Magazine*, these were accompanied by lengthy lists of 'Habitations Formed', including its lodges, names of the president, treasurer, and secretary, and the names of all members (see Fig. 2.3). Given that these lists could run up to three or four pages, Barnardo's was prepared to dedicate significant magazine space to describing its infrastructure and reporting on its success.[72] In an early number, the editor remarks, 'Considering that we have only been started three months, and that the larger number of our Companions have really *only been enrolled within the last six weeks*, we think our subscription list for the first quarter is a very good one'.[73] Comments such as this reinforce the importance and values of the organisation structure that underpins the establishment of the charitable public.

Habitations Formed.

Bedford Habitation. — This includes five Lodges: (1) Arrowsmith Girls' Lodge; (2) Arrowsmith Boys' Lodge; (3) Clapham Lodge; (4) Old Bedford Lodge; (5) Corrington Lodge. President: Lady Mance, Manora. — Treasurer: Colonel Stenhouse. — Secretary: Miss E. Hutchinson, "St. Andrews," Kimbolton Road, Bedford. Number of Companions, 75. — Henry Bateman, Henry H. Bristow, Florence G. Evans, Lilian Edwards, Francis Finch, Henry K. Finch, Florence Fink, Bessie Fink, Marguerite Fuller, Algernon Gamman, Edith Maud Gamman, Hubert C. Maydon, Louisa E. Payne, Mabel Louisa Pearse, Guy Raymond, Edgar J. Richmond, J. F. Sampson, Roy Neville Suter, Henry Thompson, Flora Toomey, Cecil F. Urquhart, Florrie Wilson, Edith Wilson, Maud Wilson, Lindsay Bashford, Florence M. Blake, Robert C. Campbell, Walter A. Campbell, Alice Mary Deverell, Marion Edwards, Beatrice Edwards, Maggie K. Forbes, Dorothy Hipwell, Isabel Hipwell, Eveline L. Mounsey, Geraldine Nangle, A. M. M. Thornber, Roy A. Wellesley, Frances S. M. Walsh, May Griffiths, John M. Laing, Roderic Laing, May Scott, Annie R. S. Ashwell, A. Abrahams, Frances Birney, Norah Gray, Alice May Green, Herbert W. Fforde, Gertrude Jackman, Iyde W. Jacob, Nellie Ottewill, Edith Ottewill, Jessie Ottewill, Violet M. Ponting, Edith M. Southwell, Rosina B. Orr, Walton R. Scott, Margaret Thomas, John E. Spurling, Irene Frances Beddall, Constance Eddison, Edith Eddison, Margaret Eddison, Arthur Gray, Anna B. Richardson, George Thomas, James Webster Watts, Charles Hamilton Mance, William Harold Watts, Isabel Winkfield, Agnes E. M. Winkfield, Leontine Dooman, Bertie Sampson.

Bristol.—Here there are two Habitations. (1) *Bristol Habitation.*—Treasurer, Miss Aplin, Leyton House, Warwick Road, Redland. Secretary, Mrs. Stanley, Newington Villa, Sydenham Road. (2) *St. Andrew's Habitation.*—Secretary: Miss Nicolson, 2, Belgrave Villas, Cotham Grove.

Number of Companions in both the above Bristol Habitations, 144.—Constance E. Collins, Maggie Croll, Faith Dening, Theodore Victor Green, Leonard P. Hunt, Louis W. Munroe, Alice J. Paddon, Mary Pascoe, Ida Clements, Vincent Clements, Amy L. I. Bartel, Mildred Smith, Katie Prewett, Marguerite Mellowes, Ida Mabel Blandford, Violet Herbert, Laurence A. G. Lane, Mabel Gundry Lane, Edith Gundry Lane, Margaret Isabella Brightman, Eveline G. Reynolds, Herbert John Reynolds, Gertrude Rowe, Mary H. H. Nicholson, Howard Bicknell, Elizabeth Annie Cross, John Leonard Gardner, Robert John Green, Stanley James Habgood, Charles G. Habgood, Willie Hobbs,

Fig. 2.3 'Habitations Formed', *Young Helpers' League Magazine*, January 1892–December 1894, 28.

46   Philanthropy in Children's Periodicals, 1840–1930

The Junior Red Cross faced a similar challenge when they began operating after the First World War because they lacked a formal structure to attract and retain children. They created 'Circles' in New Zealand and encouraged children to form one for their school.[74] The British Red Cross explained in their 1924 annual report that 'Links' were to be formed 'by organised groups of children and young persons between the ages of five and eighteen'.[75] They also note that '[t]here is no question of "competition" with existing organizations. If the school or club, or whatever the group may be, approves of [the Junior Red Cross objectives], or desires to strengthen its own work for them, it allies itself to the Red Cross by enrolling as a Link.'[76] This comment alludes to the potential tension between competing children's organisations across religious and secular lines where children might feel torn between different groups. For the Red Cross, at least, it was possible – and even encouraged – to belong to multiple institutions. Given its non-religious objectives of 'Health; Help to Sick and Suffering Children; [and] A Chain of Service linking Children of all Lands', the Red Cross presumably felt it could attract children united by these goals regardless of their religious affiliation. Thus, the New Zealand Junior Red Cross had circles at a number of religious schools, including the Anglican St Hilda's Collegiate School in Dunedin and St Mary's Diocesan School in Taranaki.[77] Indeed, as Chapter 7 discusses, the alignment between schools and the Junior Red Cross was an important factor in its success.

Through a range of strategies, children were encouraged to actively participate in charitable work through the magazine. The associated charitable organisation used the pages of the magazine to define its infrastructure and inform children about how they could participate. By joining the organisation, children became part of the charitable public that declared its shared concern for a particular group or issue and offered their time and money to support that cause.

Evidence of charitable success

Charitable success was another important aspect of creating and maintaining a charitable public. The magazine was an important venue through which to evaluate and report on its success. In some publications, fiction was a tool used to creative an imaginative space to envisage charitable success. Fundraising totals

Charitable Publics   47

are commonly listed and, depending on the amount, are either a source of pride or provoke a call to raise more funds. Reports of children who have been assisted by the charity were another key strategy since it relied on evidence from the charity itself. Together they tell a story of charitable success that encourages readers to join, or remain part of, the charitable public.

The success of the temperance movement in *Band of Hope Review* is primarily articulated through fiction that emphasises the importance of temperance and the possibilities of young people to affect change for themselves and for the adults around them. One such story is 'The Two Pledges', appearing in October 1860. 'Little Dennie' is the only son of a clergyman, and he has developed 'a love for strong drinks' through the example of his father.[78] After getting '*dead drunk*' at a festive gathering, he fails to see any danger of becoming a drunkard since, as he explains to his father, 'I am not afraid of it. You drink rum, father, every day, and you are not a drunkard.'[79] Dennie refuses to accept the bribe of a gold watch from his father in exchange for giving up rum, instead insisting that '[i]f it wrong for me to drink, it is wrong for you, and if you stop drinking, *I will*.'[80] Although the clergyman quails at the idea, 'the welfare of his child' requires that they both pledge to give up drink, with the father giving the gold watch to his son for as long as he abstains. The story concludes many years later, when Dennie is now a 'distinguished clergyman' still in possession of his watch. He tells his four young sons of 'his danger and his escape from the whirlpool of INTEMPERANCE'.[81] This story reflects the temperance move to teetotalism beginning in the 1850s rather than simply moderation, while also asserting the importance of both children and adults taking pledges of temperance.[82] Across multiple generations, the temperance pledge has the power to positively impact lives.

Aunt Judy's Magazine includes regular updates about the current cot inhabitant to demonstrate the positive impact of the Great Ormond Street Hospital. In Robert Frank's discussion of the motivations behind charitable giving, he explains that 'despite the importance of self-interested motives for most donors, a charitable organisation's appeal for support must focus primarily on the worthiness of its cause'.[83] The first person to take up residence in the 'Aunt Judy's Magazine Cot' was a ten-year-old girl named Mary, who was admitted for a hip complaint that required her to use a crutch.[84] Reports on Mary and other cot inhabitants focus

48   Philanthropy in Children's Periodicals, 1840–1930

on how the child's circumstances have improved as a result of their time in hospital. Mary is 'now very bright and happy' as a consequence of her hospital treatment.[85] Readers are later informed that some charitable women are seeking funding for Mary's admittance to a longer-term 'House of Relief', which they eventually secure in part through dedicated donations from magazine readers.[86] Over a year after the initial cot report appears, *Aunt Judy's Magazine* reports that Mary is 'enjoying the comforts of a happy home at Miss Percival's Institution' and can now write as well as read.[87]

These cot reports have multiple functions in the pages of the magazine. Their regular appearance emphasises the seriality of the magazine where readers might turn to the correspondence pages to check for updates about the current cot inhabitant. Margaret Beetham explains that '[s]ince the periodical depends on ensuring that the readers continue to buy each number as it comes out, there is a tendency in the form not only to keep reproducing elements that have been successful, but also to link each number to the next'.[88] The cot reports provide a degree of continuity across the monthly issues to encourage readers to purchase the latest number, to situate the 'Aunt Judy's Magazine Cot' as the charitable cause supported by the magazine, and to promote an ideal of charity to its readers.

In the first volume of the *Juvenile Missionary Magazine*, children are encouraged to raise money for the charitable work of the organisation, and the children's ongoing contributions are already apparent. The frontispiece depicts an 'exact representation' of a new missionary ship, the 'John Williams', that children have helped to purchase.[89] The illustration offers child supporters a tangible symbol of the charity's efforts. The launch of the ship at Harwich is cause for delight, with local children able to attend: 'The children . . . were regaled with plum-cakes and oranges, and returned to their homes delighted and highly gratified; and . . . to the latest hour of their lives, they will never forget the launching of the "New Missionary Ship".'[90] The charity's success is documented in the magazine on multiple fronts. It includes an illustration of the physical ship for all young contributors but also describes the entertainment enjoyed by the children and then – on the facing page – describes what happened to the ship after it launched. Although not yet ready to travel overseas, it is brought to London for fitting out and then to the West India Export Dock to receive cargo.[91]

Charitable Publics   49

Although the ship had not yet started its missionary work, the magazine reinforces the specific charitable cause through other ship-related content. This included regular reports on its progress throughout its long journey: 'No news has yet arrived' by 16 October 1844, after the ship's departure on 5 June.[92] While they were waiting for news, young readers of the magazine are told that

> Doubtless you often follow [the ship] in imagination as she pursues her course across the ocean. You will also think of those whom she is carrying to far distant shores, and you long for the period when you will hear of her safe arrival among islands of the South.[93]

The imaginative potential is innate in young readers as is the desire to ensure that the missionary workers have arrived safely. While the readers wait, the author of the piece, S. T., encourages them to do yet one more duty: to pray. The duty can be undertaken by everyone and should be accompanied by a prayer for personal salvation. The success of the charitable cause embedded within the *Juvenile Missionary Magazine* is multifaceted, incorporating personal prayer, charitable giving, and missionary activity.

The success of the charitable public produced through the magazine is evident in the names of contributors printed in each issue. In *Aunt Judy's Magazine*, the subscription lists became an important feature in the magazine, providing evidence of the fundraising done by young readers. The magazine begins with a modest list the month following the introduction of 'Aunt Judy's Magazine Cot'. The February 1868 list (see Fig. 2.4) indicates the range of different kinds of contributions, from individual subscribers like Mrs Fossett, who commits to an annual subscription of £1 1s, to a collection of clothing from 'Some little children in Yorkshire'.[94] The smallest monetary contributions are still relatively large at one shilling, but subsequent lists include smaller amounts of just three pennies. These lists of contributions appeared each month and are one of the main forms of content to reassert the importance of the charitable cause. Not only do they reward contributors, who were able to see their names in print, but they also potentially attract new contributors to become supporters of the cause.

The public nature of these lists meant that readers looked to them as a record of their charitable work and expected them to be

AUNT JUDY'S ANSWERS TO CORRESPONDENTS.

less fit it is, perhaps, to be classed with writings which, generally, only offer themselves for amusement. Still, it is not easy to draw an exact line of separation. There are juveniles of many ages, and there are tales of an intermediate character in the same way. As, for instance, some in which a young lady begins a child and ends as a wife and mother; after the fashion of those juggler's trees which you see grow up, bud, blossom and bear fruit before your eyes; but then, in most such cases, good teaching forms the really leading feature of the writing. This will be seen in several of the stories in the list forwarded by our correspondent; so that none, perhaps, are strictly novels (in our interpretation of the word). Nay, even in the Melchior volume—the least grown up of all—there is actually the Viscount who begins as a lad and ends as a married man.

How well good Miss Edgeworth knew all this! She had her children's books, and her intermediate juvenile tales, and her novels, all kept as distinct as possible!

The etymological origin of the word Novel, as applied to tales of real life, is an interesting subject of discussion, but far beyond investigation here. Of course the word means, literally, *something new;* and France, Italy, and Spain give it the same conventional application as ourselves. Some think that when the wild romances of knights and magicians were succeeded by tales of a more realistic character, these latter were called novels from their being a new style of literature. Further back still, certain additions to the law code of Justinian were called "Nouelles," so that Johnson gives, as the second meaning of Novel, "A law annexed to the code:" his first meaning being "A small tale, generally of love." However, our correspondent has asked only the present conventional use of the word, and we have satisfied her as well as we could.

Aunt Judy acknowledges with grateful pleasure the following subscriptions to the "Aunt Judy's Magazine Cot" at the Hospital for Sick Children:—

Mrs. Fossett, Surbiton (annual)	1	1	0
Miss M. A. Butler, Wantage (annual)	0	2	6
The Misses Dixon, Page Hall	1	0	0
Rosie, Chester	0	5	0
Waltham Abbey Sunday School, 1st class. Girls	0	3	6
E. B. M. L.	0	2	6
"Trot," Limerick	0	1	0
Jessie, Daisy, and Tiny Scott	0	2	0
Ada Morgan	0	1	0
Three English Children at Portobello.	0	2	6
Ellen and Emily, Brixton	0	2	6
Miss Emily A. Buttanshaw, Chinnor Tetsworth	1	0	0
C. J. & M. T.	0	1	3
Mrs. C. M. Griffiths	0	10	0
John and Arthur Shaw	0	1	6
Miss C. A. Martineau (annual)	0	10	0
Victoria and Charles Robert	1	0	0
"Some little Children in Yorkshire" . . . . A parcel of Clothing			
The Misses Brear, Bradford . A Box of Toys and Scraps.			

The children at a Country Parsonage write thus:—

"We cannot afford a great deal at a time, so we are going to set up a box, with a hole in the lid, and put in what we can ourselves, and get what we can from other people, so as to be able, *at the end of the year,* to send something towards 'Aunt Judy's Cot.' We do like your magazine so much! It is just what we wanted."

The Secretary also informs Aunt Judy that one clergyman is thinking of putting up a Contribution Box in the porch of his church for the benefit of the Hospital; and that several letters have reached him inquiring further particulars, and mentions the notice in the magazine. He also gratifies us much by announcing that he has of late received several fresh contributions to the Hospital generally, which he attributes in part to the "touching account of the charity" given in our pages.

Fig. 2.4 First subscription list from *Aunt Judy's Magazine*, February 1868, 256.

accurate. As Prochaska explains about women's charitable work in the nineteenth century, 'The long lists of subscribers, which commonly took up the bulk of the annual charitable reports, were in themselves a sign of status seeking.'[95] The subscribers to the 'Aunt Judy's Magazine Cot' were clearly interested in the performative aspects of the list, contacting Gatty when their names, locations, or contribution amounts were incorrectly identified. For instance, Gatty reports that the 'poor women at the mother's meeting' sent 1s 9d instead of the 9d listed in February 1869.[96] Similarly, 'Lucy, Ethel, May, and their Mamma' are from Wellingborough, rather than Sittingbourne.[97] Both errors were corrected in the following month. Their significance lies in the attention subscribers paid to the printed lists. Gatty evidently agreed, promising to print the names of every contributor regardless of the size of the contribution.

The seriality of the subscription lists also promoted the charitable cause. Although some contributors were anonymous, each time a reader made a named contribution, they presumably wished to see their name and contribution in print and would turn to the latest issue of the magazine to see their own donation and the gradually increasing balance. For commercial magazines like *Aunt Judy's Magazine*, then, the subscription lists and the charitable cause more broadly served to retain readers and potentially attract new ones. The subscription lists were a vital feature of many nineteenth-century magazines, helping to reinforce the charitable cause and ensure its success. Every issue of *Aunt Judy's Magazine* after February 1868 included a list of subscribers, which sometimes extended across multiple pages. The 'Aunt Judy's Magazine Cot' also inspired others and, by 1877, eighteen other cots had been funded. By 1885, eight cots had been funded in perpetuity (indicating that £2,000 had been raised for each cot), a further twenty-six cots through life donations, and thirteen through annual subscriptions.[98] The *Monthly Packet* was invited to support a Great Ormond Street Hospital cot as well, but subsequently decided to fund the 'Daisy Chain Cot' (after Yonge's domestic novel, *The Daisy Chain*) at the Cumberland Children's Hospital.[99] Although *Aunt Judy's Magazine* might have been the first to fund a named cot in a hospital, other magazines evidently felt this was an opportunity to attract new readers and signal their charitable ethos.

Advertising and reviews of *Aunt Judy's Magazine* highlight the vibrancy of the subscription lists appearing in the magazine.

52   Philanthropy in Children's Periodicals, 1840–1930

The prospectus for 1871 explains that a 'feature which has been found to have an unlooked-for interest is the subscription list for "Aunt Judy's Magazine Cot" [. . . which] is kept up entirely by the subscribers to the Magazine'.[100] In one of its regular reviews, *The Spectator* reports in 1879 how the magazine 'does one great practical work – it supports two cots at the Children's Hospital . . . and collects for it, both in money and goods; keeping its young donors fully informed of all it accomplished, and carefully acknowledging all their kind presents'.[101] The funding of the charitable cause, plus the magazine's support through content like the cot reports, indicate the importance of this material in attracting and retaining readers and charitable contributors.

The financial contributions of young people formed an important part of the annual fundraising of many organisations, although this could often be understood as a collective activity rather than an individual one. As will be discussed in more detail in Chapter 3, the Wesleyan Missionary Society encouraged regular contributions through its Christmas Juvenile Offerings and reported each year on the success of this fundraising campaign, listing amounts raised at circuit and district levels. In addition to providing regular reports on its juvenile associations after 1877, from 1901 it also identified the young people who had raised amounts over a certain threshold. Even when individual or local contributions are not listed in the magazine, those specifics were sometimes identified in annual reports that may have been shared with young people. Children's collective fundraising achievements were often listed separately in these annual reports, which highlighted the importance of these activities for the organisation as a whole. Prochaska emphasises that 'there is no means of determining how much of the money came from the children themselves and how much of it they collected from adults', but children were nonetheless important agents of this fundraising.[102]

Magazines were therefore vitally important to the development of children's charitable publics across the entirety of the period between 1840 and 1930. Ideas of charity were embedded in the magazine's content and a particular cause was defined in its pages. At the same time, the implied child reader was clearly and carefully positioned as someone who could help others, from regular prayer and doing God's work to more tangible actions like fundraising and indirect work that would enable children to donate their money to the cause. By emphasising the importance of the charitable cause, focusing on the shared values that underpinned charitable work, and reporting regularly on the successful activities undertaken by the charity, each magazine could simultaneously establish and reinforce its charitable public. This public was typically distinct within a given magazine, although children could and did participate in multiple charitable publics. This suggests that these publics could be malleable and fluid to a certain extent, and their ever-ageing populations meant that editors were always seeking to attract new members to retain its vibrant support for a given charitable cause.

Notes

1. 'Editor's Chat', *Young Helpers' League Magazine*, January 1892–December 1894, 25.
2. 'Editor's Chat', *Young Helpers' League Magazine*, 25.
3. Portions of this chapter were first published by Kristine Moruzi in '"Donations need not be large to be acceptable": Children, Charity and the Great Ormond Street Hospital in *Aunt Judy's Magazine*'. Copyright © 2017 The Research Society for Victorian Periodicals, *Victorian Periodicals Review*, volume 50, issue 1, Spring 2017, 190–213.
4. Lauren Berlant, *The Female Complaint: The Unfinished Business of Sentimentality in American Culture* (Durham: Duke University Press, 2008), viii. Emphasis in original.
5. Berlant, *The Female Complaint*, viii.
6. Benedict Anderson, *Imagined Communities: Reflections on the Origin and Spread of Nationalism* (London: Verso, 1991), 46. Berlant, *The Female Complaint*, viii.
7. Berlant, *The Female Complaint*, 5.
8. Christopher Parkes, *Children's Literature and Capitalism: Fictions of Social Mobility in Britain, 1850–1914* (Houndmills: Palgrave Macmillan, 2012), 2.
9. Hugh Cunningham, *Children of the Poor: Representations of Childhood since the Seventeenth Century* (Oxford: Blackwell, 1991), 230.
10. Gubar, *Artful Dodgers*, 9.
11. Parkes, *Children's Literature and Capitalism*, 3.
12. Berlant, *The Female Complaint*, 5.
13. Berlant, *The Female Complaint*, xi. Emphasis in original.
14. Berlant, *The Female Complaint*, x.

54   Philanthropy in Children's Periodicals, 1840–1930

15. Michael Heller, 'Company Magazines 1880–1940: An Overview', *Management & Organizational History* 3, no. 3–4 (2008): 187.

16. Heller, 'Company Magazines', 187, 188.

17. 'The Editor's Salam, Or Introductory Address', *Juvenile Missionary Magazine*, June 1844, 6.

18. James Sherman, 'Every One Can Do Something for Jesus Christ', *Juvenile Missionary Magazine*, July 1844, 34.

19. Sherman, 'Every One', 34.

20. In 1861, with the launch of a new series, the title changed to *Band of Hope Review*. The publication is referred to by the shorter title throughout.

21. 'To Our Readers', *Band of Hope Review and Children's Friend*, September 1852, 89.

22. 'To Our Readers', *Band of Hope Review*, 89. Emphasis in original.

23. 'To Our Readers', *Band of Hope Review*, 89.

24. Brian Harrison, *Drink and the Victorians: The Temperance Question in England, 1815–1872*, 2nd edition (Staffordshire: Keele University Press, 1994), 178.

25. Victoria Berridge, *Demons: Our Changing Attitudes to Alcohol, Tobacco, and Drugs* (Oxford: Oxford University Press, 2014), 43.

26. Gwylmor Prys Williams and George Thompson Brake, *Drink in Great Britain, 1900–1979* (London: Edsall & Co., 1980), 181.

27. Berridge, *Demons*, 37.

28. Berridge, *Demons*, 40. Annemarie McAllister, *Writing for Social Change in Temperance Periodicals: Conviction and Career* (New York: Routledge, 2023), 2.

29. Annemarie McAllister, '*Onward*: How a Regional Temperance Magazine for Children Survived and Flourished in the Victorian Marketplace', *Victorian Periodicals Review*, 48, no. 1 (Spring 2015): 46.

30. Eva Travers Evered Poole, 'Four Questions Fully Answered', *Night and Day* 16 (February 1892), 1.

31. Helen Milman, 'To the Children', *Our Waifs and Strays*, February 1889, 7.

32. 'The New Magazine for our Young Helpers', *Night and Day* 16 (February 1892), 15.

33. 'The New Magazine', 15.

34. Endpaper of *Young Helpers' League Magazine* 1 (January 1892–December 1894), np.

35. Endpaper, np.

36. Endpaper, np.

37. Endpaper, np.
38. Endpaper, np.
39. Cunningham, *Children of the Poor*, 230.
40. Cunningham, *Children of the Poor*, 230.
41. Thomas Barnardo, 'Preface', *Young Helpers' League Magazine* I (January 1892–December 1894), np. Emphasis in original.
42. Milman, 'To the Children', 7. Emphasis in original.
43. 'Aunt Judy's Correspondence', *Aunt Judy's Magazine*, January 1869, 192.
44. 'Aunt Judy's Correspondence', 192.
45. Owen, *English Philanthropy*, 211.
46. 'What Is the Junior Red Cross?' *Red Cross Junior*, June 1922, 3.
47. Kristine Moruzi, Beth Rodgers, and Michelle J. Smith. 'General Introduction: Reading, Writing, and Creating Communities in Children's Periodicals', in *The Edinburgh History of Children's Periodicals*, ed. Kristine Moruzi, Beth Rodgers, and Michelle J. Smith (Edinburgh: Edinburgh University Press, 2024), 10.
48. *Dr. Barnardo's Homes for Orphan and Destitute Children: Annual Report for 1891* (London: np, 1891), 11.
49. *Dr. Barnardo's Homes for Orphan and Destitute Children*, 11. Emphasis in original.
50. H. F. Clarke, *How to Avoid Leakage Between the Band of Hope and the Adult Society* (London: Church of England Temperance Society, [1894]), 3.
51. Clarke, *How to Avoid Leakage*, 4.
52. Herbert T. James, *Industrial Bands of Hope* (London: Church of England Temperature Publication Depot, 1891), 3.
53. Linda K. Hughes and Michael Lund, 'Textual/Sexual Pleasure and Serial Production', in *Literature in the Marketplace: Nineteenth-Century British Publishing and Reading Practices*, ed. John O. Jordan and Robert L. Patten (Cambridge: Cambridge University Press, 1995), 149.
54. James Mussell, 'Repetition: Or, "In Our Last",' *Victorian Periodicals Review*, 48, no. 3 (2015): 348.
55. Kristine Moruzi, 'Serializing Scholarship: (Re)Producing Girlhood in *Atalanta*', in *Seriality and Texts for Young People: The Compulsion to Repeat*, ed. Mavis Reimer, Nyala Ali, Deanna England, Melanie Dennis Unrau (Houndmills: Palgrave Macmillan, 2014), 169.
56. Gwynfryn, 'The Hospital for Sick Children', *Aunt Judy's Magazine*, January 1868, 173.

56   Philanthropy in Children's Periodicals, 1840–1930

57. Gwynfryn, 'The Hospital', 178.
58. E. M. L., 'Little Annie's Christmas', *Aunt Judy's Magazine*, November 1871, 122.
59. E. M. L., 122.
60. E. M. L., 122.
61. *The Report of the Directors to the Fifty-First General Meeting of the Missionary Society* (London: London Missionary Society, 1845), cxvi–cxvii. This list of Sunday Schools includes those from Wales, Scotland, and Ireland as well as Guernsey, Jersey, Brussels, Sydney, and South Africa.
62. Cunningham, *Children of the Poor*, 38.
63. *The Report of the Wesleyan Methodist Missionary Society* (London: Wesleyan Missionary Society, 1842), 96–7.
64. *The Band of Hope Manual: The Formation and Management of Bands of Hope (Junior and Senior)* (London: United Kingdom Band of Hope Union, nd), 4.
65. *The Band of Hope Manual*, 5.
66. *The Band of Hope Manual*, 10.
67. McAllister, '*Onward*', 43.
68. *The Band of Hope Manual*, 6.
69. *The Seventh Annual Report of the Oxfordshire Band of Hope and Temperance Union, 1881–82* (Oxford: Oxfordshire Band of Hope and Temperance Union, 1882), 3–6.
70. *The Seventh Annual Report*, 6.
71. 'Organization of the League, and Its Work', *Young Helpers' League Magazine*, January 1892–December 1894, 12.
72. 'Habitations Formed', *Young Helpers' League Magazine*, January 1892–December 1894, 28.
73. 'Editor's Chat', *Young Helpers' League Magazine*, January 1892–December 1894, 26. Emphasis in original.
74. 'The Junior Red Cross', *New Zealand Junior Red Cross Journal*, June 1927, 16.
75. *Report of the British Red Cross Society for the Year 1924* (London: np, 1924), 19.
76. *Report, 1924*, 19.
77. 'Activities of Circles', *New Zealand Junior Red Cross Journal*, February 1928, 7.
78. 'The Two Pledges', *Band of Hope Review and Sunday School's Friend*, October 1861, 231.
79. 'The Two Pledges', 231.
80. 'The Two Pledges', 231.

Charitable Publics   57

81. 'The Two Pledges', 231.
82. James Nicholls, *The Politics of Alcohol: A History of the Drink Question in England* (Manchester: Manchester University Press, 2009): 99–104. See also Harrison, *Drink and the Victorians*, 121–38 and Berridge, *Demons*, 36–47.
83. Robert Frank, 'Motivation, Cognition and Charitable Giving', in *Giving: Western Ideas of Philanthropy*, ed. J. B. Schneewind (Bloomington: Indiana University Press, 1996), 143.
84. 'Aunt Judy's Correspondence', April 1868, 379.
85. 'Aunt Judy's Correspondence', April 1868, 379.
86. 'Aunt Judy's Correspondence', June 1868, 165.
87. 'Aunt Judy's Correspondence', May 1869, 61–2.
88. Beetham, Margaret. 'Open and Closed: The Periodical as a Publishing Genre', *Victorian Periodicals Review* 22, no. 3 (1989): 97.
89. 'The New Ship "John Williams"', *Juvenile Missionary Magazine*, June 1844, 7.
90. William Hordle, 'Launching of the New Ship', *Juvenile Missionary Magazine*, June 1844, 10.
91. 'The "John Williams" in the West India Dock', *Juvenile Missionary Magazine*, June 1844, 11.
92. 'The "John Williams"', *Juvenile Missionary Magazine*, November 1844, 138.
93. S. T., 'Address to the Juvenile Contributors Towards the New Missionary Ship', *Juvenile Missionary Magazine*, October 1844, 109.
94. 'Aunt Judy's Correspondence', *Aunt Judy's Magazine*, February 1868, 256.
95. Prochaska, *Women and Philanthropy*, 40.
96. 'Aunt Judy's Correspondence', March 1869, 317.
97. 'Aunt Judy's Correspondence', 317.
98. The Quiver cot was one of these latter examples and was funded for twelve years through annual contributions to *Quiver: An Illustrated Magazine for Sunday and General Reading* (1861–1926). See Graham Law, 'Quiver', in *Dictionary of Nineteenth-Century Journalism in Great Britain and Ireland*, ed. Laurel Brake and Marysa Demoor (Ghent: Academia Press and The British Library, 2009), 525. The subtitle dates from 1865.
99. 'The Cumberland Street Children's Hospital', *The Monthly Packet of Evening Readings for Younger Members of the English Church*, January 1871, 92–5.

58   Philanthropy in Children's Periodicals, 1840–1930

100. *Address* (London: Bell & Daldy, 1871), 2.
101. 'Current Literature', *The Spectator*, 1 February 1879, 155.
102. Frank Prochaska, 'Little Vessels: Children in the Nineteenth-Century English Missionary Movement', *Journal of Imperial and Commonwealth History* 6, no. 2 (1978): 106.

3

Charitable Agency

In February 1844, a 'letter from an Old Missionary' celebrating 'the establishment of a Missionary Periodical for our children' was published in the second issue of the *Wesleyan Juvenile Offering: A Miscellany of Missionary Information for Young Persons* (1844–78).[1] He writes, 'I am persuaded that we have never yet sufficiently interested [children] in the cause of Foreign Missions'.[2] While this perceived lack of interest ignores the money children associated with the Wesleyan Missionary Society had already raised for the missionary cause – at this point more than £10,000 in the previous three years – the letter reinforces the connection between the children's periodical and missionary efforts. The periodical, he believes, is one important method by which children will be 'trained' in 'the exercise of charity'.[3]

This chapter draws on examples from the British *Wesleyan Juvenile Offering*, which became *At Home and Abroad* (1879–1974), to explore how children were trained about religion, missionary works, and charity in the Wesleyan Missionary Society and how the magazine depicts children's charitable activities and encourages them to be charitable agents.[4] One of the complexities of research on children's periodicals is attempting to tease out the extent to which children were agential in their charitable efforts and interrogating how much of their labour was voluntary. Children's agency is often understood in adversarial terms insofar as it only becomes visible when they resist dominant adult ideas and expectations. David F. Lancy has criticised this understanding of agency as a 'dogma' that 'denies the reality of culture', which accumulates through adaptations that 'are preserved from one generation to the next'.[5] Kristine Alexander calls for the term 'to

59

60   Philanthropy in Children's Periodicals, 1840–1930

be rethought and used far more critically', while Mona Gleason argues that 'the search for children's agency as *a priori* goal ... runs the risk of limiting, rather than expanding, our ability to show they contributed in significant ways to change over time'.[6] Lynn Thomas makes a similar argument in relation to gender studies that agency 'should not be the endpoint of our analyses'.[7] She notes a desire among scholars on Africa to combat 'negative and reductionist stereotypes of the continent' defined by 'helplessness, simplicity and victimization ... especially as applied to women'.[8] Asserting agency can become an impulse to resist stereotypes, yet limited sources can result in simplistic, overdetermined understandings of children's culture.

The charitable ethos that is evidenced in children's behaviours through the nineteenth- and early twentieth-century periodical press is part of a pattern of behaviours designed and implemented by adults. That children were often following adult directions in supporting a charitable cause does not negate their charitable agency. In this sense, I am following Susan Miller's evaluation of children's agency 'that rests on a continuum from opposition to assent'.[9] She writes that we should 'be attentive to the ways in which children willingly conform to adult agenda, not necessarily because youth acquiesce to power, but because their interests often align with those promoted by adults'.[10] Children's active participation in the charitable infrastructures described in the previous chapter can be positioned alongside the material contributions they made to the cause as evidence of their charitable activity.

This chapter examines examples of children's actions that can be interpreted as evidence of their charitable activity and explore the extent to which we can draw conclusions about their charitable beliefs. Here I am particularly interested in their financial contributions as evidence of this support. While we cannot necessarily know children's motivations in raising funds for an organisation and whether this work is evidence of charitable sentiment, the longevity of many charitable causes over months, years, and even decades suggests a commitment that is part of the cultural framework and not some transitory feeling. Of course, this sentiment may well have been temporary for some children, while for others it may have been an important part of their individual subjectivity as charitable beings. Nonetheless, it suggests that children of the nineteenth and early twentieth centuries were interested in helping others through their charitable work. This work, in my view, is evidence of how 'young people ... discovered that cooperation with adults provided them the best way to exercise their own agency' and demonstrates their 'socially significant place' in the charitable field.[11]

The Wesleyan Missionary Society was part of the evangelical revival that resulted in the establishment of Protestant missionary societies around the turn of the nineteenth century, including the Baptist Missionary Society (1792), the London Missionary Society (1790), and the Church Missionary Society (1799). As Anna Johnston explains, 'These societies were established to intervene directly in the lives of native "heathens" of the world – particularly those in the British colonies'.[12] The launch of *Wesleyan Juvenile Offering* in 1844 was one of the earliest children's periodicals that attempted to simultaneously provide religious instruction alongside developing a religious ethos aimed at charitable giving. Moreover, it provides a useful overview of how one religious periodical used print to raise awareness among young people of its charitable cause, while also responding to cultural and social shifts in ideas about children and childhood to attract and retain readers' interest in the magazine and its charity work. In particular, this chapter begins by exploring how the charitable agent is created through the language of charitable giving and how this language is used to reinforce the charitable ethos articulated elsewhere in the magazine. Then it demonstrates the charitable agency enacted by children through their substantial contributions for the Wesleyan Missionary Society each year. Finally, it analyses the methods employed in the magazine to inform children about the need for financial contributions and to encourage their regular and active participation in fundraising efforts and in its charitable public. Together these elements define and mobilise children's agency as charitable contributors in a specifically religious register, one that is repeated and transformed in other children's periodicals during this period.

The focus of the charitable agency defined and reinforced in the *Wesleyan Juvenile Offering* is obviously inflected by religion. The intersecting categories of religion and childhood are just beginning to be examined in detail. Allison Giffen and Robin L. Cadwallader have observed that, although '[s]cholarship in both childhood studies and religion is currently undergoing a renaissance of interest ... thus far these two terms are rarely brought into conversation with each other'.[13] Moreover, as Marcia Bunge

62   Philanthropy in Children's Periodicals, 1840–1930

explains, scholars of religion have typically ignored its impact on children despite the fact that '[r]eligious traditions, for better or worse, shape the lives of children in a variety of ways'.[14] Hugh Morrison and Mary Clare Martin take up the question of how religion and childhood can be mutually constitutive while also asserting how 'religion can potentially recede to the scholarly margins with respect to understanding historical aspects of children's and young people's development and identity'.[15] Scholars from a variety of disciplines, including literary studies, history, and religious studies, are developing a more nuanced understanding of how religion and religious practices can inform understandings of childhood and the complexities of adult–child relationships.

The religious practice of particular interest here is the religious periodical. Kirsten Drotner observes that the Christian evangelical revival of the late eighteenth century, 'with its emphasis on obedience, orderliness, spiritual piety, and bodily cleanliness', became part of 'the dominant ethic of Victorian society' that first manifested through cheap repository tracts and evolved into inexpensive periodicals.[16] The religious periodicals that were published throughout the nineteenth century, including those for children, were aimed at increasing literacy, promoting religious feeling, and encouraging charity. Religious philanthropy, Drotner explains, 'expanded its activities into new areas such as tract and temperance societies, missionary associations, and Sunday School organizations' that agreed on the importance of reading for the 'moral edification of the young'.[17] Michelle Elleray accounts for how mid-Victorian adventure novels can be read alongside missionary culture, which included periodicals and children's fundraising efforts, 'to investigate how empire was conveyed to children'.[18] Her examination of the relationship between various forms of children's print culture and representations of Christian Pacific Islanders offers an opportunity to explore 'a key site of intercultural engagement'.[19] She considers how 'the agency of the socially marginal is manifested in the imperial context . . . to support evangelical goals rather than social change'.[20] She concludes that the London Missionary Society used its *Juvenile Missionary Magazine* to position the child 'as a direct intervener in missionary efforts'.[21] Children's print culture of this period has a profound influence on children's charitable behaviours and thus their agency in charitable settings.

The importance of literacy for the evangelical movement meant the rapid introduction of periodicals aimed specifically at young people. At the same time, the periodicals became the vehicle by which the organisation's objectives – both religious and charitable – could be explicitly laid out in print. Prochaska writes that '[n]owhere in the charitable world did the young play a more important part than in the evangelical missionary movement', which 'recruited, organised, and sent children to every corner of the country as collectors and tract distributors'.[22] The first decades of the nineteenth century saw the development of juvenile associations and Sunday Schools that regularised children's giving. The rapid expansion of these associations 'made it imperative that their operations be rationalised and co-ordinated', which was done through the establishment of 'the paraphernalia of organisation' such as subscription rates and collection protocols.[23] As discussed in the previous chapter, the parent societies, anxious to increase the amounts raised by the juvenile associations, began publishing children's periodicals to promote their progress.

These periodicals had a two-fold purpose. They not only provided updates about the tangible monies being raised by children, but they were also designed to instruct children in the habits of charity such that they would become charitable agents. Diana Dixon observes that '[r]eaders of the religious press were ... constantly reminded of the plight of the poor and needy, and the virtues of charity were extolled'.[24] Children's literature was written to mould children into 'charitable beings who would consider the poor, give generously and learn lifelong lessons in order to become charitable adults'.[25] One significant aspect of this charitable behaviour was specific action to alleviate the plight of the poor. Margot Hillel explains that '[i]t is not enough ... for the child reader simply to understand about poverty'.[26] Instead, these children were being 'asked to actively engage in charity as a matter of course' as part of their daily lives.[27] While Hillel is predominantly referring to nineteenth-century children's novels and promotional literature, children's periodicals also include the fictional and promotional materials she discusses. They also contain explicit editorial content calling children to action alongside – eventually – correspondence, essay contests, and subscription lists that contribute to our understanding of the extent to which evangelical religious ideas about charity operated for children and were part of the dominant ethos of the period.

64   Philanthropy in Children's Periodicals, 1840–1930

This set of expectations for children was based on an implied readership of generally middle-class readers, yet the pricing and availability of these magazines indicate an actual readership that was likely much wider, as it included working-class children. Although the first issue was presented to each collector at no cost, each subsequent number, 'with which you may be supplied through any Bookseller or Wesleyan Ministers, *will be sold for One Penny*'.[28] From the outset, the dual purpose of this magazine as an inspiration for and a record of children's fundraising efforts is clear. It required that children make a one-penny donation to the organisation, which then became part of their monthly contribution, while also reinforcing the value of this work through descriptions of missionary activities. Tract literature was 'inseparable from charity, and charity, as practiced in Victorian times, involve the rubbing in of class distinctions', where 'class interest' is evident beneath 'the veneer of altruism'.[29] Importantly, the poor were not the only intended audience for these religious texts.[30] The children of evangelical families, predominantly middle-class, were a substantial part of the periodicals market. Indeed, the *Wesleyan Juvenile Offering* is primarily focused on the potential of middle-class readers to raise significant funds and to become charitable adults. By the end of the nineteenth century especially, the discourses of charity operating in the magazine focus on fashioning 'benevolent children . . . who would grow into benevolent adults'.[31] The future potentiality of these child readers as donors and charitable workers was vital to the ongoing success of these charitable institutions.

The *Wesleyan Juvenile Offering* was launched in January 1844, but this did not mark the beginning of Wesleyan Missionary Society interest in children as fundraisers. Prochaska notes that 'evangelical missionary societies began to report the financial contributions of children' from the first decade of the nineteenth century.[32] In the first issue of the magazine, 'To Our Young Readers', the editor comments on the 'happy results' of the interest 'our young friends' have had in the missions of the society.[33] The Christmas and New Year's Offering, a campaign that began in 1841, had become sufficiently successful that the society had decided to share information about its missionary activities with its juvenile subscribers and collectors through a monthly magazine, which became the vehicle through which this information was disseminated, and children were encouraged to raise money for the society.

The magazine contents were intended to demonstrate the range of activities in which the society was involved and how the children's fundraising was enabling the conversion of children from non-Christian countries. This sixteen-page monthly magazine contains a variety of content related to the various missionary activities, including letters from the missionaries and their wives, reports about missionary experiences, stories about children who had been influenced by their religious instruction, and letters from the editor relating fundraising progress. The connection between charitable fundraising by child readers assumed to be located in Britain and the valuable work conducted in foreign locales was implicit in every issue.

Narrative strategies for religious giving

The narrative strategies in the *Wesleyan Juvenile Offering* were designed to encourage children's charitable work in a religious context. This narrative work produces and reinforces the idea of charitable agency that children were expected to adopt. As discussed in the previous chapter, seriality is an important aspect of the construction and dissemination of the charitable model of childhood. Linda Hughes and Michael Lund explain how the serial novel published in the press is 'a whole made up of parts that at once function as self-contained units and as building blocks of a larger aesthetic structure'.[34] While neither the *Wesleyan Juvenile Offering* nor *At Home and Abroad* contains serialised fiction, they nonetheless created a charitable ethos 'through the individual monthly parts that stand alone, but which are also part of a greater whole'.[35] The narrative strategies embedded in the magazine are evident not only in individual issues but also its overall run. In particular, the *Offering* encourages children to perform charitable work (which may require sacrifice) includes evidence of its missionary activities through letters contributed by missionaries and their wives, and explains the religious benefits to both the child contributors and the child recipients of charity.

The child readers of the magazine were inducted into its ethos of charity through narrative strategies that conveyed its religious and charitable ideologies. The direct address of the first article, 'To Our Young Readers', tells readers that '[w]e shall also tell you about various other things which you may like to know, in order that you love the Missionaries, and encourage you to

66   Philanthropy in Children's Periodicals, 1840–1930

continue and increase your efforts for them, that they may have the opportunity of preaching to the ignorant and lost.'[36] The implied reader – 'you' – is encouraged to continue to support the missionary efforts of the organisation. This strategy is employed consistently across the issues of the magazine to create the charitable public defined in Chapter 2. Yet this community, implied through the direct address, was more than simply imagined. Instead, the children reading this magazine were assumed to share the objectives of the organisation, and the evidence of this came from the children's ongoing – and hopefully increasing – financial support.

Charitable agency for young magazine readers is modelled regularly through examples of British children working for the missionary cause. 'Juvenile Sympathy' relates the story of eight-year-old Emily, who requested permission from her parents to beg for donations of clothing for the 'many distressed widows and fatherless children in Newfoundland', where one of her aunts lives as a missionary's wife. Emily went 'from house to house' and 'succeeded in obtaining many useful articles of clothing'.[37] The author uses this example to encourage other young people to 'do the same among their friends and neighbours' since the 'poor little children on Mission Stations' will be 'thankful' to receive these presents from 'thoughtful little boys and girls in England'.[38] Articles such as these provide tangible examples of how children are working to support the missionary cause and directly address the child readers to encourage them to perform similar work.

Articles like 'Juvenile Sympathy' make visible the discourses of charitable agency operating in the *Wesleyan Juvenile Offering*. British children are giving gifts to the mission children, who are expected to be thankful to receive them and who will likely 'pray to God to bless their kind friends every time they put on the frock, or shoes, or stockings'.[39] As I discussed in the Introduction, giving behaviours can be understood as a system in which '[d]onors and recipients formed reciprocal relationships in which each was obliged to perform both functions of giving and receiving, to create a gift cycle'.[40] In this case – and indeed in the majority of the examples of charitable giving discussed in this book – the relationship between the donors and the recipients is indirect. The child donors rarely met the individual recipients of their charitable work. Nonetheless, their agency as charitable donors is reinforced through these depictions of giving behaviours.

The reciprocity of the gift cycle was likewise indirect, insofar as the donor was unable to individually display altruism toward a specific recipient, nor was the recipient able to display their gratitude. Young Emily would never meet those people in Newfoundland who received the donated clothes she collected, and the recipients similarly never met Emily. Instead, her specific actions to solicit, collect, and send the clothing were made on behalf of the Wesleyan Missionary Society, and one might anticipate that the recipients would be grateful to the society, rather than the individual donors, for these goods. Yet the article encourages readers to think that the child recipients will be 'thankful' and will 'pray to God to bless their kind friends'.[41] These actions form the basis of the reciprocal gift expected from the recipient. To be deemed 'deserving' of this charity, they must demonstrate their understanding of their relative status as 'poor' and indicate their gratitude in receiving money or goods to help alleviate their subordinate position.

According to Kidd, the charity relationship is 'fundamentally unequal' since the 'inequalities between donor and recipient are likely to be more or less permanent' and thus 'the potential for reciprocity is slight'.[42] In these missionary magazines, one of the ways in which recipients can demonstrate their gratitude is through their religious practice. In 'Juvenile Sympathy', the author uses conditional phrasing about how the poor children 'would be' thankful and how they are 'likely' to pray for the children who had donated the clothing. The author invites the child readers to imagine the emotional and religious response that their charitable work would inspire in the grateful recipients to complete the gift cycle. The strong connections between affect and faith 'suggest that religious belief is both intensely personal and yet a universal ideal that can and should be embodied by child readers and protagonists'.[43] Child readers of the magazine are led to understand that their charitable donations will produce an affective response that will result in prayer, a point that is discussed further in the next chapter.

To encourage the charitable religious ethic of the magazine, child readers are informed about the inadequate conditions in which children live in other parts of the world. Missionary literature was designed to make sure 'that the children celebrated their Englishness while encouraging them to a state of missionary zeal, with the intention of converting the "other" to something like

68   Philanthropy in Children's Periodicals, 1840–1930

them'.[44] In the 'Letter of a Missionary's Wife, in New Zealand, to the Readers of the "Juvenile Offering"', the material differences between these children are explicitly stated. The author writes that British children owe a great deal 'to your heavenly Father for your birth and education in a Christian country' and describes the supposedly inadequate care received by 'native' children in New Zealand.[45] She describes how Indigenous mothers 'have no nice little clothes for their babies', who are 'laid down on a bit of old dirty native mat, or a piece of old dirty rag'.[46] Within a day or two of their birth, babies have their ears pierced to enable the display of decorative ornaments of 'smoothed green stone' or 'a shark's tooth',[47] a tradition which the writer evidently feels is barbaric. Moreover, the 'poor children are brought up naked' and rarely receive baths, 'so that they smell so foul, that you could not nurse them'.[48] The children eat with their hands since they have 'no knives, forks, or spoons, nor would they know how to use them if they had'.[49] The parents 'seldom correct their children' but 'when they do chastise them, they do it cruelly, by pinching and angry blows'.[50]

The lens through which this woman understands the material circumstances of the Māori children ignores the cultural differences operating within this Indigenous community. As she describes it, these children are poorly cared for and receive 'very little bodily comfort'.[51] Yet, in a shared relationship with God, they are not much different from the British children reading the *Wesleyan Juvenile Offering*. The author describes how the children are taught to read the Bible and how 'I have been astonished to hear the little creatures, so filthy, and almost naked, joining with the old people and elder children in repeating their Catechism'.[52] Regardless of their material circumstances, these poor children are equally as capable as the British readers of demonstrating their religious knowledge. Nonetheless, despite the similarities in religious devotion, the British child readers are the ones expected to be 'ever grateful for the privileges you enjoy' and to 'increase your sympathy' for the New Zealand children, presumably in the form of financial donations.[53]

The community developed in the magazine is based on a shared understanding that readers are united in their charitable agency as fundraisers. The implied readership is explicitly British, but other articles demonstrate how the shared community of implied white child readers can be found around the world. In an 1857 article,

Charitable Agency   69

'A Letter from a Friend in Melbourne to the Children in England', Elizabeth Draper writes that

> As the children in the 'Southern World' appear to be interested in the varied information contained in the 'Juvenile Offering', and especially in that which relates to young people, I have thought that the children of Great Britain would like to know, through the same medium, something of the young people in Victoria.[54]

Unlike much of the other content in the magazine, in which British readers are informed about children being assisted in missions, this letter offers an introduction to Australian children who are engaged in similar activities as their British counterparts. Draper describes the eighty-two Wesleyan Sabbath-schools in the colony of Victoria, with 5,227 children receiving religious instruction and encouraged 'to pursue the path that leads to happiness and heaven'.[55] Each school has a good library, and Bible-classes are conducted regularly. Some of the teachers, she explains, were taught in their local Sabbath-school before taking on educational responsibilities within the Wesleyan Missionary Society, indicating the longevity and reputability of the society and its schools.

The activities in which the Victorian children participate are similar to those that occupy British children. At the 1857 anniversary services, Victorian children sang hymns and anthems, an exercise in which they were said to 'greatly excel'.[56] In the previous year, they collected £460 towards the repairs of the 'John Wesley' missionary ship, which had been funded through juvenile collections since the society first announced that it was being built in 1846. This year, Draper explains, the children have collected an equal amount for the missions. Such facts are 'encouraging to persons emigrating to Australia' since they show that the Wesleyan church in Victoria is 'intent on supplying the children of our people, and others, with the benefits of Sabbath-school instruction, from which the youth of Britain have derived such incalculable advantages'.[57] These children, like those in Britain, are learning about God and raising funds to help support Wesleyan missionary activities in Australia and abroad. Although in this case these connections are presumably primarily imperial in origin and rationale, they are also based on shared expectations of children who support the society. Nationality is subsumed by mutual care for and interest in the Wesleyan missionary cause.

70   Philanthropy in Children's Periodicals, 1840–1930

This shared missionary ethos becomes even more evident when we consider the entirety of the July 1857 issue in which the 'Letter' from Melbourne appears. This issue contains the list of the 'Juvenile Christmas Offerings for 1856' by district and circuit, but it begins with a sketch of the Wesleyan Wayside Preaching-Place in Bangalore, India and an accompanying article by Wesleyan missionary Thomas Hodson discussing the town and the mission. He describes the town and its inhabitants as well as the features of the mission, including a large printing establishment where Scriptures, tracts, and schoolbooks are prepared for the local inhabitants speaking Canarese. Missionaries speak at the preaching-place three times a week and occasionally publicly examine some of the school classes. Hodson concludes with his hope that 'we may soon see thousands of Bangalore people, young and old, truly converted to God, and that at last all the "Juvenile Offering" readers may meet them in heaven'.[58] Even though the readers of the magazine will never visit the Bangalore mission, they can meet other supporters of the Wesleyan missionary cause in death because they are united by their religious conversion.

The article following the 'Letter' from Melbourne is a discussion of 'How the Little Children in America Get Money for the Missions', and it, too, promotes the shared missionary ethos across the issue. Reprinted from *Youth's Dayspring*, an American missionary magazine published between 1850 and 1855, it relates a true story about how some American children earned money to support the Wesleyan missionary ship.[59] The Sabbath-school member who forwarded the money writes, 'Enclosed you will find the sum of eighty cents, contributed by five little children who do not attend our Sabbath-school, but who wish very much to assist in sending the Mission ship on its way to the poor Heathen, with the words of eternal life.'[60] The poor children gave up their leisure time to run errands and do small tasks to earn their money. They were inspired and motivated by the mission ship and one boy, the son of Roman Catholics, explains that '[w]hen I am a man, I am going to be a Missionary, and perhaps I shall go out in that very ship.'[61] These children are remarkable not only because they are fundraising for a cause that is outside their own religious background, but also because they embody the model of childhood depicted in the *Wesleyan Juvenile Offering*. Children in the magazine are consistently inspired by the society's efforts to convert others to the word of God and are willing to sacrifice both money and time to support the evangelical cause. They are embodying the missionary ideal when they regularly reflect on the importance of their work to help others to obtain eternal life. One little girl, who has been hemming pocket-handkerchiefs for her father to earn a small allowance, explains that '[i]t is so pleasant to work when you think you are doing it for the Good Missionaries who go away so far to teach the Bible to the poor Heathen.'[62] Even tedious work can be transformed with the proper religious attitude, and this attitude is available to anyone who is open to the word of God.

A common narrative strategy in the magazine is the depiction of a child whose charitable agency is made visible through sacrifice to encourage child readers to do the same. One such example appears in the April 1844 issue. The opening article, 'A Child's Self-Denial for the Mission Cause', describes the Swedish Missionary Society, which formed an auxiliary in 1840. The author, George Scott, was a Methodist Scotsman ordained in Edinburgh and working in Sweden from 1830.[63] By the time of this article, Scott had returned to England, but he describes an 'interesting conversation' between a six-year-old Swedish girl and her mother, in which the girl offers to give up her daily morning biscuit so that the money can be put towards her missionary society membership.[64] Scott uses this example to encourage child readers to perform the same kinds of sacrifices: 'British children, British mothers, emulate this spirit, and then our Mission work shall not languish from want of funds!'[65] British children were expected to be inspired by the example of others and to consider how their sacrifices might enable further contributions to the missionary society.

In its early years, the magazine depended heavily on missionary reports and correspondence as it sought to educate child readers about the organisation's activities. While it might be tempting to assume the missionaries were united in the specifics of their charitable messaging, Anna Johnson asserts the need to 'maintain a kind of sceptical double-vision' about missionary textuality.[66] She concludes that, when letters appear in magazines, they 'rarely remain unexpurgated or unedited'.[67] Her point reflects the often-times unremarked influence of the editor in the production and dissemination of ideologies of childhood. In the *Wesleyan Juvenile Offering*, content was selected and edited to reinforce for child readers that charitable work was important and might require sacrifices.

Collective agency through children's fundraising

Having laid out the framework for charity work and the expectations of charitable agency for child readers, in this section I turn to the specifics of their fundraising activities. The limited amounts raised by individual children could be collected together to provide substantial support for missionary activities, and they indicate significant agency on the part of young readers. Elleray explores how the coral insect used in mid-nineteenth-century evangelical writing 'manifests itself culturally as the narrative of a humble being small and insignificant in itself but that working collectively is able to produce a result disproportionate to its size, in turn provoking admiration and wonder'.[68] She discusses this in relation to the London Missionary Society and especially the children's financial support for the John Williams ship. The coral insect 'figures the sublimation of the individual to the social, rendering what is ordinary, small, and unprepossessing into a structure renowned for its beauty and purpose'.[69] About the child contributors she explains how 'the children, like the coral insect, manufacture through a process of accretion a spectacular product that bears witness to the individual labours of many'.[70]

The relationship between the individual and the collective is apparent in the central role that fundraising played in the *Wesleyan Juvenile Offering*. The children's religious giving is simultaneously individual and collective since individual agency is essential in creating collective action that enables the coral insects Elleray describes to produce the charitable fundraising that was necessary and valued by the organisation. Prochaska writes that many of the children raising funds for the missionary societies were from working-class homes, and this accords with Joseph Blake's description of the circumstances leading to the formation of the Wesleyan Juvenile Missionary Society in *The Day of Small Things* (1849).[71] He describes the establishment of 'systematic arrangements of employing the *many*, instead of the *few*' to raise funds and train the young.[72] The premise was to encourage many children to raise small amounts that would eventually grow into substantial sums. By providing updates on children's activities, the funds raised, and the importance of continuing to raise yet more money, the magazine reinforced the need for children's charitable giving to support missionary activities through money or goods that could be sold.

Charitable Agency   73

The religious imperative for this charitable agency is at the forefront of much of the magazine's messaging. In the annual announcement about the Christmas Offerings, readers are reminded about the importance of their work and how charitable giving is a recurring demand. The editor writes that

> The time is now approaching when our young people are accustomed to make their yearly offering to the Missionary cause. It is now almost a form to remind you of it; because, I dare say, most of you are looking forward to the time with great satisfaction, and are forming plans by which you may get more money than you did last year. Your help is wanted as much as ever, nay, more than ever; thousands upon thousands are gasping for the words of eternal life, waiting for us to send the Gospel to them, eager to receive Missionaries to teach them the way to heaven. You will, I am sure, do your very utmost this Christmas, and try to collect more money than you did last year. O, my dear young friends, you know not how much good you are doing by your Christmas Offerings! By your means souls are saved from hell; and you never will know the full value of this your united effort, till you can estimate the worth of immortal souls.[73]

The language in this article emphasises the regularity of children's giving, since it is 'now' the time in which children are 'accustomed to make their yearly offering'. This annual giving will provide 'satisfaction' because it will help to save the immortal souls of non-Christian children. Child readers are encouraged to collect even more money than they did the previous year, since each penny will help to save a soul.

The children's contributions are reported each year in the January issue of the *Wesleyan Juvenile Offering* as well as in the annual reports. This coincides with the end of the financial year as well as the society's focus on encouraging children to raise funds at Christmas. The 'Juvenile Christmas Offerings' campaign, launched in 1841, raised more than £7,000 in its first two years.[74] Table 3.1 shows the amounts collected as part of the Christmas offerings between 1841 and 1876, as identified in the annual reports. From 1877, the children's contributions were divided into the Christmas Offerings and the money raised separately through the Juvenile Associations via subscriptions.[75] Between 1841 and 1914, children were responsible for £519,268 (Christmas Offerings) and £645,256 (Juvenile Association), totalling over £1.1 million and

Table 3.1 Juvenile Contributions to the Wesleyan Missionary Society (1841–1919).

Christmas Offering   Juvenile Association

Charitable Agency   75

equalling about 13% of the society's domestic fundraising.[76] These amounts represent the significant contribution made by children through either personal contributions or collections.

The development of the Juvenile Associations emerged over time, with the magazine gradually devoting more pages to sharing association news. In December 1867, the editor writes, 'As we set very great value upon the help rendered by our young collectors, in these Associations ... we propose to set apart a portion of each number ... specifically for Association purposes'.[77] This marked a significant shift in the magazine as it reflects the need to formalise and support the Juvenile Associations. The split in the annual reports of the collected amounts beginning in 1877 between the Christmas giving and the Juvenile Associations makes this explicit. While the Christmas offerings remain relatively stable after this point, the amounts attributed to the Juvenile Associations continued to increase.

The importance of children's fundraising cannot be underestimated, and the Wesleyan Missionary Society clearly paid close attention to the amounts being raised. In a February 1844 circular aimed at adults, the society writes that 'we are just now *painfully anxious. We are distressed. We are alarmed*' at the financial situation at the end of 1843, where a deficit of ten to twelve thousand pounds was anticipated.[78] Of the two strategies designed to redress this shortfall, the Juvenile Christmas or New Year's Offerings is the main hope. The treasurers write: 'We own, that on this Juvenile Effort our hopes of averting a New and heavy Debt materially repose'.[79] The children's ability to solicit additional donations is vital to the society's fundraising efforts since, as the treasurers observe, whereas 'Juvenile Efforts were before *needed*; they are now become *essential*'.[80] The organisation depended on children's agency as charitable donors to keep it solvent.

The reward for the child contributors is the emotional satisfaction gained through the knowledge that their money is helping others, a point discussed further in the next chapter. This knowledge is obtained by reading 'as much as you can about Missionaries and their work, and when you see how much good they are doing, and how glad the Heathen are to receive them, and to be taught by them, you will have a rich reward for all your labour'.[81] The magazine encourages the fundraising and then provides information about the good work that is being done by missionaries as a result of this financial support. The knowledge that other children

76   Philanthropy in Children's Periodicals, 1840–1930

are being converted is assumed to be sufficient to motivate and inspire children to raise funds and pray for the mission's success.

The annual amounts raised by children represent a significant contribution to the society, which is why the *Wesleyan Juvenile Offering* drew attention to their accomplishments each year. John Pritchard concludes that about 20 per cent of the society income came from the Juvenile Missionary Association by the end of the nineteenth century.[82] Children are praised for their 'truly laudable' exertions at fundraising, while also being reminded that more can always be done. Mary Batchelor, the wife of the Rev. Peter Batchelor, was running a school in Negapatam, India, and her letter appears in the *Wesleyan Juvenile Offering* in 1845, reminding child readers of the ever present need to raise more money:

> [Y]ou may do still more; redouble your exertions; make greater sacrifices; offer yourselves upon the Missionary altar; and though you may not all be called into the field where the contest is actually going on between Heathenism and Christianity, yet you may, by your prayers, by your augmented subscriptions, by your more diligent collecting from house to house, aid those who are bearing 'the burden and heat of the day'.[83]

Children's charitable activity may lead to them becoming missionaries themselves, but their fundraising is equally important in supporting missionary efforts. Batchelor speaks with the authority of one who is bearing 'the burden' of this urgent 'contest' to convert children to Christianity. She exhorts the child readers to 'do still more' to support her efforts and those of the other missions. In addition to the fundraising activities, she also encourages her 'little Missionary friends' in England to pray that God will convert 'the hearts of the little girls' in the Negapatam mission school. Financial support must be accompanied by religious work, which in this case comes through prayer by the child readers.

This religious work involves fundraising alongside Christian love and devotion. Children's religious fiction published in the 1840s often features a child on their deathbed. In evangelical texts, the knowledge that the child will be rewarded in heaven is intended as a consolation to assuage grief. In the *Wesleyan Juvenile Offering*, the motifs of sacrifice and child mortality appear in some of its articles. 'The Little Missionary Collector' relates the story of a little girl, not yet six, who was desperate to receive a collecting card. Although she finally receives one, she returned home 'sad and penniless' because she was unable to convince people to contribute.[84] Her father 'cheered and encouraged her, put his own name down on her paper, and promised to take her under his patronage'.[85] She returned the completed collection card and received an orange and a picture of the missionary ship for her efforts. That same day, however, she was struck by a dangerous illness and died less than a week later. The story concludes, 'She never was able to eat her orange; but that, and the Missionary ship, were . . . the last things she noticed in this world'.[86] Her religious devotion and her love for Jesus are the basis of her reward in heaven. The child readers are asked directly: 'Dear little Missionary Collectors, do you love Jesus? Do you wish to work in his vineyard because you love him? Otherwise you have no reward of your Father.'[87] Without a true heart, children's labour is useless. This story highlights the difficulty in determining how much of the money was contributed by children themselves. In certain ways, however, this question is irrelevant. Whether the children contributed the funds directly or collected them from others, they were responsible for this fundraising. The child's individual activity – through donation or collection – contributed to the collective financial goals of the society.

That the children were engaged in collective activity is an important distinction to be made about their mid-century charitable work. In contrast to the predominantly individual subscription lists published in *Aunt Judy's Magazine* that were discussed in the previous chapter, the Wesleyan Missionary Society subscription lists were published at the district level, subdivided into local circuits and then into branches. Consequently, money collected by individuals received no acknowledgement in the *Wesleyan Juvenile Offering* (although they were sometimes listed in the annual reports) and were instead amalgamated within a collective goal for a local area. For instance, the annual report for April 1856 (see Fig. 3.1) includes the contributions from each branch within a circuit. The City Road branch details the individual contributions made to the Christmas Offerings collection, including £1 4s contributed by each of five children in the Ingoldby family. It also lists contributions from Radnor Street, divided into the 'small sums' collected by the Sunday School boys and girls as well as individual donations. The City Road branch

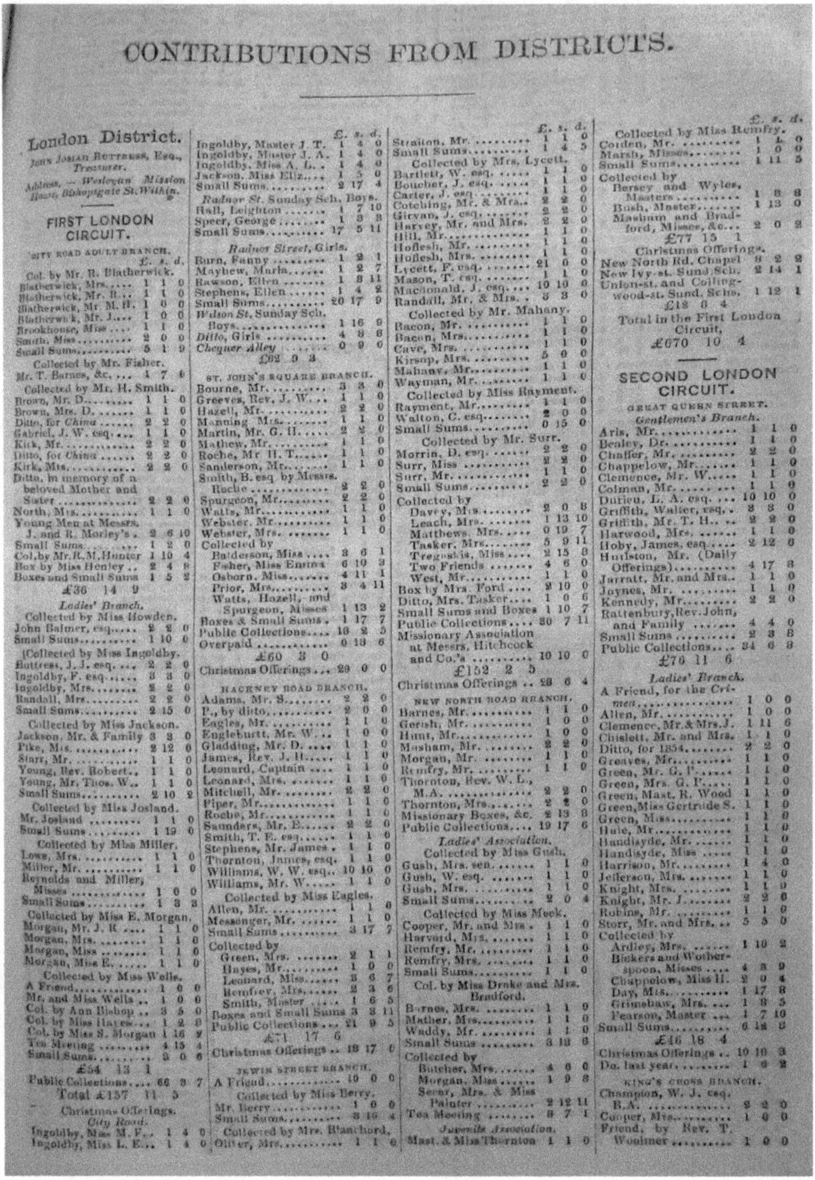

CONTRIBUTIONS FROM DISTRICTS.

London District.

John Josiah Buttress, Esq., Treasurer.

Address, — Wesleyan Mission House, Bishopsgate St. Within.

FIRST LONDON CIRCUIT.

CITY ROAD ADULT BRANCH.

£. s. d.

Col. by Mr. R. Blatherwick.
Blatherwick, Mrs. 1 1 0
Blatherwick, Mr. R. .. 1 1 0
Blatherwick, Mr. M. H. 1 0 0
Blatherwick, Mr. J. 1 0 0
Brookhouse, Miss 1 1 0
Smith, Miss 2 0 0
Small Sums.......... 5 1 9
Collected by Mr. Fisher.
Mr. T. Barnes, &c. ... 1 7 6
Collected by Mr. H. Smith.
Brown, Mr. D.......... 1 1 0
Brown, Mrs. D. 1 1 0
Ditto, for *China* 2 2 0
Gabriel, J. W. esq. ... 1 1 0
Kirk, Mr. 2 2 0
Ditto, for *China* 2 2 0
Kirk, Mrs. 2 2 0
Ditto, in memory of a beloved Mother and Sister 2 2 0
North, Mrs. 1 1 0
Young Men at Messrs. J. and R. Morley's . 2 6 10
Small Sums.......... 1 2 0
Col. by Mr. R. M. Hunter 1 10 4
Box by Miss Henley .. 2 4 8
Boxes and Small Sums 1 5 2
£36 14 9

Ladies' Branch.
Collected by Miss Howden.
John Balmer, esq..... 2 2 0
Small Sums.......... 1 10 0
Collected by Miss Ingoldby.
Buttress, J. J. esq. ... 2 2 0
Ingoldby, F. esq...... 3 3 0
Ingoldby, Mrs. 2 2 0
Randall, Mrs. 2 2 0
Small Sums.......... 2 15 0
Collected by Miss Jackson.
Jackson, Mr. & Family 3 3 0
Pike, Mrs. 2 12 0
Starr, Mr. 1 1 0
Young, Rev. Robert.. 1 1 0
Young, Mr. Thos. W.. 1 1 0
Small Sums.......... 2 10 2
Collected by Miss Josland.
Mr. Josland 1 1 0
Small Sums 1 19 0
Collected by Miss Miller.
Lowe, Mrs. 1 1 0
Miller, Mr. 1 1 0
Reynolds and Miller, Misses 1 0 0
Small Sums.......... 1 3 3
Collected by Miss E. Morgan.
Morgan, Mr. J. R. 1 1 0
Morgan, Mrs. 1 1 0
Morgan, Miss 1 1 0
Morgan, Miss E. 1 1 0
Collected by Miss Wells.
A Friend............. 1 0 0
Mr. and Miss Wells .. 1 0 0
Col. by Ann Bishop .. 3 5 0
Col. by Miss Hayes.... 1 2 0
Col. by Miss S. Morgan 1 16 9
Tea Meeting 4 15 4
Small Sums.......... 3 0 6
£54 13 1
Public Collections.... 66 3 7
Total £157 11 5

Christmas Offerings.
City Road.
Ingoldby, Miss M. F... 1 4 0
Ingoldby, Miss L. E... 1 4 0
Ingoldby, Master J. T. 1 4 0
Ingoldby, Master J. A. 1 4 0
Ingoldby, Miss A. L. . 1 4 0
Jackson, Miss Eliz.... 1 5 0
Small Sums.......... 2 17 4
Radnor St. Sunday Sch. Boys.
Hall, Leighton 1 7 10
Speer, George 1 3 3
Small Sums.......... 17 5 11
Radnor Street, Girls.
Burn, Fanny 1 2 1
Mayhew, Maria....... 1 2 7
Rawson, Ellen 1 8 11
Stephens, Ellen 1 4 2
Small Sums.......... 20 17 9
Wilson St. Sunday Sch. Boys.............. 1 16 9
Ditto, Girls 4 8 6
Chequer Alley 0 9 0
£62 9 3

ST. JOHN'S SQUARE BRANCH.
Bourne, Mr. 3 3 0
Greeves, Rev. J. W. .. 1 1 0
Hazell, Mr. 2 2 0
Manning Mrs. 1 1 0
Martin, Mr. G. H. 2 2 0
Mathew, Mr. 1 1 0
Roche, Mr. H. T...... 1 1 0
Sanderson, Mr....... 1 1 0
Smith, B. esq. by Messrs. Roche 2 2 0
Spurgeon, Mr......... 2 2 0
Watts, Mr........... 1 1 0
Webster, Mr......... 1 1 0
Webster, Mrs. 1 1 0
Collected by
Balderson, Miss 3 6 1
Fisher, Miss Emma 6 10 3
Osborn, Miss....... 4 11 1
Prior, Mrs.......... 3 4 11
Watts, Hozell, and Spurgeon, Misses 1 13 2
Boxes & Small Sums . 1 17 7
Public Collections.... 16 2 5
Overpaid 0 18 6
£60 3 0
Christmas Offerings ... 29 0 0

HACKNEY ROAD BRANCH.
Adams, Mr. S......... 2 2 0
P., by ditto,.......... 2 0 0
Eagles, Mr. 1 1 0
Englebürtt, Mr. W. .. 1 0 0
Gladding, Mr. D. 1 1 0
James, Rev. J. H..... 1 1 0
Leonard, Captain 1 1 0
Leonard, Mrs. 1 1 0
Mitchell, Mr. 2 2 0
Piper, Mr............ 1 1 0
Roche, Mr............ 1 1 0
Saunders, Mr. E...... 2 2 0
Smith, T. E. esq...... 1 1 0
Stephens, Mr. James . 1 1 0
Thornton, James, esq. 1 1 0
Williams, W. W. esq.. 10 10 0
Williams, Mr. W...... 1 1 0
Collected by Miss Eagles.
Allen, Mr. 1 1 0
Messenger, Mr. 1 1 0
Small Sums.......... 3 17 7
Collected by
Green, Mrs. 2 1 1
Hayes, Mr......... 1 0 0
Leonard, Miss...... 3 6 7
Remfrey, Mrs...... 2 3 6
Smith, Master 1 6 5
Boxes and Small Sums 3 3 11
Public Collections ... 21 9 5
£71 17 6
Christmas Offerings .. 18 17 0

JEWIN STREET BRANCH.
A Friend............. 10 0 0
Collected by Miss Berry.
Mr. Berry............ 1 0 0
Small Sums.......... 3 16 4
Collected by Mrs. Blanchord.
Oliver, Mrs.......... 1 1 0
Straiton, Mr. 1 1 0
Small Sums.......... 1 4 5
Collected by Mrs. Lycett.
Bartlett, W. esq. 1 1 0
Boucher, J. esq. 1 1 0
Carter, J. esq. 1 1 0
Cotching, Mr. & Mrs.. 2 2 0
Girvan, J. esq. 2 2 0
Harvey, Mr. and Mrs. 2 2 0
Hill, Mr. 1 1 0
Hoflesh, Mr. 1 1 0
Hoflesh, Mrs. 1 1 0
Lycett, F. esq. 21 0 0
Mason, T. esq. 1 1 0
Macdonald, J. esq. ... 10 10 0
Randall, Mr. & Mrs. . 3 3 0
Collected by Mr. Mahany.
Bacon, Mr. 1 1 0
Bacon, Mrs. 1 1 0
Cave, Mrs. 1 1 0
Kirsop, Mrs. 5 0 0
Mahany, Mr......... 1 1 0
Wayman, Mr......... 1 1 0
Collected by Miss Rayment.
Rayment, Mr......... 1 1 0
Walton, C. esq....... 2 0 0
Small Sums.......... 0 15 0
Collected by Mr. Surr.
Morrin, D. esq. 2 2 0
Surr, Miss 2 2 0
Surr, Mr. 1 1 0
Small Sums.......... 2 2 0
Collected by
Davey, Mrs........ 2 0 8
Leach, Mrs. 1 13 10
Matthews, Mrs. 0 19 7
Tasker, Mrs........ 5 9 11
Tregaskis, Miss 2 15 8
Two Friends 4 6 0
West, Mr.......... 1 1 0
Box by Mrs. Ford 2 10 0
Ditto, Mrs. Tasker.... 1 0 6
Small Sums and Boxes 1 10 7
Public Collections 30 7 11
Missionary Association at Messrs. Hitchcock and Co.'s 10 10 0
£152 2 5
Christmas Offerings .. 28 6 4

NEW NORTH ROAD BRANCH.
Barnes, Mr. 1 1 0
Gerish, Mr. 1 0 0
Hunt, Mr............ 1 0 0
Masham, Mr. 2 2 0
Morgan, Mr. 1 1 0
Remfry, Mr. 1 1 0
Thornton, Rev. W. L., M.A. 2 2 0
Thornton, Mrs........ 2 2 0
Missionary Boxes, &c. 2 13 8
Public Collections.... 19 17 6
Ladies' Association.
Collected by Miss Gush.
Gush, Mrs. sen. 1 1 0
Gush, W. esq. 1 1 0
Gush, Mrs. 1 1 0
Small Sums.......... 2 0 4
Collected by Miss Meek.
Cooper, Mr. and Mrs. . 1 1 0
Harvard, Mrs. 1 1 0
Remfry, Mr. 1 1 0
Remfry, Mrs. 1 1 0
Small Sums.......... 1 1 0
Col. by Miss Drake and Mrs. Bradford.
Barnes, Mrs. 1 1 0
Mather, Mrs.......... 1 1 0
Waddy, Mr. 1 1 0
Small Sums 3 13 8
Collected by
Butcher, Mrs....... 4 0 0
Morgan, Miss 1 9 8
Searr, Mrs. & Miss Painter 2 12 11
Tea Meeting 8 7 1
Juvenile Association.
Mast. & Miss Thornton 1 1 0
Collected by Miss Remfry.
Corden, Mr. 1 1 0
Marsh, Misses....... 1 0 0
Small Sums.......... 1 11 5
Collected by
Bersey and Wyles, Masters 1 8 8
Bush, Master....... 1 13 0
Masham and Bradford, Misses, &c... 2 0 2
£77 15 1
Christmas Offerings.
New North Rd. Chapel 8 2 2
New Ivy-st. Sund. Sch. 2 14 1
Union-st. and Collingwood-st. Sund. Schs. 1 12 1
£12 8 4
Total in the First London Circuit,
£670 10 4

SECOND LONDON CIRCUIT.

GREAT QUEEN STREET.
Gentlemen's Branch.
Aris, Mr. 1 1 0
Bealey, Dr. 1 1 0
Chaffer, Mr. 2 2 0
Chappelow, Mr....... 1 1 0
Clemence, Mr. W..... 1 1 0
Colman, Mr. 1 1 0
Durieu, L. A. esq. ... 10 10 0
Griffith, Walter, esq. . 3 3 0
Griffith, Mr. T. H.. .. 2 2 0
Harwood, Mrs. 1 1 0
Hoby, James, esq..... 2 12 6
Hurlston, Mr. (Daily Offerings).......... 4 17 8
Jarratt, Mr. and Mrs.. 1 1 0
Joynes, Mr. 1 1 0
Kennedy, Mr......... 2 2 0
Rattenbury, Rev. John, and Family 4 4 0
Small Sums 2 3 8
Public Collections.... 34 6 8
£70 11 6
Ladies' Branch.
A Friend, for the *Crimea*.............. 1 0 0
Allen, Mr. 1 0 0
Clemence, Mr. & Mrs. J. 1 11 6
Chislett, Mr. and Mrs. 1 1 0
Ditto, for 1854........ 2 2 0
Greaves, Mr.......... 1 1 0
Green, Mr. G. P...... 1 1 0
Green, Mrs. G. P..... 1 1 0
Green, Mast. R. Wood 1 1 0
Green, Miss Gertrude S. 1 1 0
Green, Miss.......... 1 1 0
Hale, Mr............ 1 1 0
Handisyde, Mr. 1 1 0
Handisyde, Miss 1 1 0
Harrison, Mr......... 1 4 0
Jefferson, Mrs. 1 1 0
Knight, Mrs. 1 1 0
Knight, Mr. J........ 2 2 0
Robins, Mr. 1 1 0
Storr, Mr. and Mrs. .. 5 5 0
Collected by
Ardley, Mrs. 1 10 2
Bickers and Wotherspoon, Misses 4 8 9
Chappelow, Miss H. 2 0 4
Day, Mrs. 1 17 8
Grimshaw, Mrs. ... 1 8 5
Pearson, Master ... 1 7 10
Small Sums.......... 6 18 0
£46 18 4
Christmas Offerings .. 10 10 3
Do. last year......... 1 0 2

KING'S CROSS BRANCH.
Champion, W. J. esq. B.A. 2 2 0
Cooper, Mrs.......... 1 0 0
Friend, by Rev. T. Woolmer 1 0 0

Fig. 3.1 First page of 'Contributions from Districts' in *Wesleyan Missionary Society Annual Report*, 1856, 27.

Charitable Agency   79

total for the Christmas Offerings is £62 9s 3d. In contrast, the adults raised £157 11s 5d, making the children's contributions almost 40 per cent of the annual total. The City Road branch evidently strongly supported the Christmas Offerings in the 1840s and 1850s, raising the most money each year, beginning with £35 5s in 1842, a much smaller amount (£14 8s) in 1843 (the year in which the treasurers were '*alarmed*' by the prospective deficit) and then between £19 and £36 over the next decade. The 1856 amount is a significant increase, suggesting that perhaps more children had joined the City Road branch and were contributing to its coffers. The other branches in the 1856 annual report do not contain a detailed list of children's contributions, indicating that the society did not require branches to provide that level of detail, although some – like City Road – may have chosen to submit it to the head office. While the adult contributions are all listed individually, the children's could be amalgamated, suggesting a different understanding of children as charitable agents in which the small individual amounts were less significant than their collective efforts.

The collective nature of children's agency is similarly evident in the *Wesleyan Juvenile Offering*, which typically included only the total funds raised through the Juvenile Christmas Offerings. The magazine regularly featured an annual editorial discussing the children's success in raising funds for the Christmas collection. For instance, in the May 1859 issue, the editor congratulates 'our young friends . . . upon having collected for their Christmas Offering a larger sum by a thousand pounds than they ever did before'.[88] This amount of £8,355 12s 2d reflects children's dedication and determination, for it could not have been collected

> without a great deal of labour, perseverance, and exertion on the part of our young friends. Some of you have worked early and late, have gone out in the cold and wet, in the dark, and perhaps in roads that were not safe, that you might get as many subscriptions as you could for the Missionaries. You have been persevering, courageous, self-denying, and merciful.[89]

The editorial concludes by reminding children how their funds are being used to support missionaries, who 'esteem no labour or sacrifice too great for the sake of the Heathen'.[90] The children's efforts were extensive, but the missionaries suffer even greater challenges in their work. Yet they are cheered by thoughts of the 'many children in England thinking of them, working for them, and praying for them'.[91] The individual efforts of children result in collective efforts by the Wesleyan Missionary Society and its missionaries to bring the word of God to people all around the world.

Although the children's success is typically seen as collective action, occasionally the success of individual circuits is highlighted. Throughout the 1850s, the magazine provided more detail about district and circuit fundraising. In May 1856, for instance, the magazine published the totals for each circuit so the breakdown for the districts and the achievements of each circuit was more visible (see Fig. 3.2).[92] While still eliding individual contributions, this strategy promotes a collective charitable ethos in which the small amounts collected by children were combined over the course of a year to form a significant donation. Well-established branches, like the one at City Road, made substantial donations to the Christmas Offering. Since this data elides the size and socioeconomic status of each circuit, it can be difficult to draw meaningful conclusions about the child contributors' charitable agency, yet even small collections indicate at least a degree of charitable interest.

The details behind these collective efforts are occasionally shared in the magazine to show readers what other children are doing to support the missionary cause. The secretaries of the Whitefield Road branch in Liverpool write in 1895 that '[i]t has been suggested to us that some account of our recent work may be useful to readers.'[93] They explain that they 'varied the character of our annual festival . . . by rendering the Missionary Cantata' twice in 1894, in which 'the various addresses and native hymns were capitally rendered' by branch members.[94] The branch also held their half-yearly school missionary meeting, which resulted in six new members and a collection of £2 1s; their quarterly receipts were up £4 19s from the corresponding quarter in 1893.[95] This report demonstrates not only the continuity of these fundraising activities in which they report on the financial success over the previous year, but also how these endeavours are repeated. Children's participation in activities like these indicate their willingness to contribute to the missionary cause through performances that extol the benefit of this missionary work.

JUVENILE CHRISTMAS OFFERINGS FOR 1855,

AS RECEIVED OR ADVISED UP TO MARCH 31st, 1856.

LONDON DISTRICT.

	£	s.	d.
City-Road	62	9	3
St. John's-Square	29	0	0
Hackney-Road	18	17	9
Jewin-Street	28	6	4
New-North-Road	12	8	4
Great Queen-Street	12	4	5
King's-Cross	9	4	2
Camden-Town	6	10	6
Kentish-Town	4	9	8
Highgate	2	10	10
Spitalfields	5	8	6
St. George's	9	3	1
Limehouse	10	0	4
Poplar	7	0	0
Globe-Road	3	10	0
Southwark	7	7	3
Grove and Union-Street	7	12	0
Silver-Street	3	1	2
Albion-Street	0	3	3
Peckham	9	2	0
Lambeth	15	0	0
South Lambeth	2	18	11
Walworth	19	2	5
Vauxhall	7	0	5
Brixton-Hill	13	14	6
Southville	1	18	4
Waterloo-Road	6	9	8
Sydenham	3	3	9
Norwood	3	1	10
Hinde-Street	10	10	8
Stanhope-Street	7	2	11
Bayswater	1	17	0
Milton-Street	4	6	3
St. John's-Wood	9	14	10
Chelsea	12	11	3
Westminster	8	13	4
Islington	36	0	2
Hackney	13	16	1
Stoke-Newington	20	4	4
Tottenham	3	11	1
Edmonton	2	0	0
Hornsey-Road	3	3	2
Dalston	6	0	0
Leyton	2	1	4
Deptford	11	3	6
Blackheath	2	14	5
Greenwich	7	11	2
Lewisham	3	5	10
Bromley	2	3	7
Woolwich	10	9	2
Richmond	8	9	0
Hammersmith	11	12	6
Croydon	3	9	0
Barking, &c.	6	18	0
Hertford, &c.	10	18	1
Cambridge	13	0	7
Windsor	6	6	0
Uxbridge	2	7	3
Chelmsford	13	11	6
Leigh	2	9	3
Colchester	8	13	3
Manningtree	10	8	0
Ipswich	11	11	0
Hastings	11	2	3
Sevenoaks	5	2	11
Tunbridge-Wells	13	13	2
Tunbridge	5	2	9
Lewes, &c.	5	17	0
Brighton	9	9	6
St. Alban's	7	9	4
Guildford, &c.	8	14	7
Dorking, &c.	4	9	6

BEDFORD AND NORTHAMPTON DISTRICT.

	£	s.	d.
Bedford	17	2	6
Leighton-Buzzard	12	0	7
Luton	28	0	3
Dunstable	23	17	11
St. Neot's	15	8	7
Biggleswade	10	12	4
St. Ives, &c.	6	16	8
Northampton	8	2	11
Towcester	4	6	10
Daventry	4	2	6
Rugby	3	6	8
Newport-Pagnell	8	4	0
Higham-Ferrers	5	12	0
Wellingborough	8	17	2
Kettering	4	7	5
Market-Harborough	2	18	4
Chatteris	10	9	0
Oundle	3	11	8

KENT DISTRICT.

	£	s.	d.
Canterbury	9	6	7
Faversham	4	18	1
Rochester	11	18	3
Gravesend	6	12	11
Sheerness	1	14	3
Margate	15	14	6
Dover	18	5	3
Deal	9	4	9
Rye	7	5	7
Tenterden	13	13	4
Ashford	4	9	4
Sandhurst	13	14	10
Maidstone	11	8	5
Sittingbourne	3	5	0

NORWICH AND LYNN DISTRICT.

	£	s.	d.
Norwich	7	10	4
Bungay	8	0	11
North Walsham	6	0	11
Yarmouth	7	7	3
Lowestoft	4	4	0
Framlingham, &c.	6	3	8
Diss	12	11	10
Attleborough, &c.	5	5	10
Bury St. Edmund's	6	11	7
Holt	1	9	8
Lynn	9	2	5
Swaffham	3	8	6
Downham	8	18	3
Walsingham	4	12	0
Wisbeach	5	2	0
Thetford	9	9	6
Mildenhall	4	15	0
Ely	8	3	7

OXFORD DISTRICT.

	£	s.	d.
Oxford	7	0	0
High-Wycombe	5	0	8
Aylesbury	8	3	5
Witney	6	16	8
Banbury	8	17	4
Kineton	4	3	1
Newbury	18	7	4
Reading	5	16	4
Hungerford	12	14	10
Watlington	3	15	0
Thame	3	3	0
Brackley	8	5	6
Chipping-Norton	7	0	10
Swindon	6	18	9
Wantage	6	0	2

PORTSMOUTH DISTRICT.

	£	s.	d.
Portsmouth	21	14	0
Gosport	3	9	0
Salisbury	19	3	1
Poole	14	7	6
Wimborne	9	10	0
Southampton, &c.	23	18	3
Christchurch	1	8	10
Andover	3	17	3
Chichester	5	4	0

CHANNEL ISLANDS DISTRICT.

	£	s.	d.
Guernsey (English)	8	8	8
Guernsey (French)	12	3	3
Alderney (English)	1	12	3
Jersey (English)	8	13	2

DEVONPORT DISTRICT.

	£	s.	d.
Devonport	14	6	0
Plymouth	25	17	1
Launceston	15	17	4
Holsworthy	11	3	4
Kilkhampton	11	16	1
Liskeard	11	4	0
Callington	3	14	5
Camelford	14	0	0
Kingsbridge	6	0	2
Brixham, &c.	3	0	2
Ashburton	18	3	0

CORNWALL DISTRICT.

	£	s.	d.
Redruth	8	7	3
Camborne	12	9	0
Falmouth	6	14	4
Truro	16	0	0
St. Agnes	5	6	6
St. Austle	10	13	0
St. Mawes	3	13	10
Bodmin	7	7	1
St. Columb	4	18	11

Fig. 3.2 'Juvenile Christmas Offerings for 1855', *Wesleyan Juvenile Offering*, May 1856, 2.

Moreover, by formalising the process of fundraising, the society hoped to encourage children to remain interested, thereby reducing the risk of children abandoning the missionary cause in the present or in the future. As Blake explains, training children in

82 Philanthropy in Children's Periodicals, 1840–1930

the practice of charity 'must not be estimated solely by the present amount of money which it brings to the Missionary Society, but must also be considered in its bearing upon their future character, and upon every branch of the Wesleyan Economy'.[96] The potentiality of these child contributors for the future of the organisation and the development of their charitable characters was of equal importance to the amount of money that could be collected in the present moment.

Supporting individual charitable agency

This final section discusses the structural shifts in the magazine that signal its interest in rewarding individual charitable agency from the turn of the twentieth century. To encourage child readers in their fundraising efforts, the society occasionally presented one-off rewards to young contributors. In the January 1849 issue, for instance, readers are informed that 'young Collectors' for the Christmas and New Year's Offering are to be gifted with 'a beautiful engraving' of the 'John Wesley' missionary ship. It was planned that the ship would travel between the missions in New South Wales, New Zealand, and the Pacific Islands and would provide 'a final opportunity for our young friends ... to send any thing they may be able to contribute for the natives of these Stations'.[97] 'Our young friends,' the editor writes, 'will no doubt feel much pleasure in employing some of their money and time towards helping the Heathen children, who need their assistance so much.'[98] Once again, the emotional satisfaction of supporting these 'Heathen children' is an important part of the rationale for young readers to contribute to the charitable cause. Regular features in the magazine provided updates on the ship's progress. A short paragraph in November 1846 describes the ship's launch, which was followed up with a longer article in February 1847 including an illustration and a longer description of the ship itself.[99] In November of the same year, the ship is reported to have stopped in Sydney before travelling to New Zealand, the Friendly Islands (Tonga), and the Feejee islands (Fiji).[100] The charitable giving that has enabled the successful voyage is rewarded, with a copy of an engraving of the ship provided to everyone who collected funds for the Christmas Offering in 1848, thereby encouraging further giving through its symbolic value as a physical manifestation of the financial contributions. A child pinning the illustration to their wall would be inspired to think

Charitable Agency   83

of the ship and the missionary efforts and would presumably be expected to redouble their efforts to raise more money.[101]

Individual fundraising achievements were also rewarded at annual meetings. In April 1882, *At Home and Abroad* includes a report from the Pontefract Juvenile Missionary Society about their annual meeting. They hosted a public tea 'which was partaken heartily of by about 360 children from the town and district'.[102] At the meeting which followed, the Rev. J. C. Sowerbutts 'read the annual report of the society', confirming the sum collected of £89 12s 8d.[103] In addition to identifying the branches that contributed to this amount, the society then distributed unspecified book prizes to the children, 'many of whom were so young that they could scarcely climb on the platform unassisted'.[104] Specific individuals were recognised for their contributions, including Master John Crofts, who received 'a handsome white banner which bore the motto "Victory" as a recognition of his industry in having collected the sum of £2 18s 3d during the past year, which was the largest sum collected' by an individual.[105] The next three individuals, having each collected more than £2, were each presented with a white rosette. These rewards were designed to encourage individual charitable agency alongside collective activity, and they would have inspired children to attempt to maximise the amounts they collected on their own.

The magazine's use of photographs and the introduction of a dedicated editorial persona in the form of 'Uncle Ned' reflects changes in print technologies and differing expectations of child readers. These strategies were designed to continue to encourage children not only to engage with the magazine but also to redouble their efforts to raise more money for the missionary cause. Towards the end of the century, and corresponding to new photographic reproduction techniques, missionary children's periodicals began including more photographs of the missions and of child contributors. In 1901, for example, *At Home and Abroad* contains a review of 'Our Juvenile Associations', a frequent and longstanding column in the magazine. A picture of a young boy (see Fig. 3.3) is printed between two columns of text, with a caption reading 'Head of the List, Fern Street, Bolton'.[106] The district report for Fern Street, Bolton is on the following page and it identifies Master Stanley Heaton as heading the list of juvenile collectors with £5 14s for a total of £23 11s 5d.[107] His Western dress is in contrast to a later photograph of the juvenile collectors (see Fig. 3.4) at

Fig. 3.3 'Head of the List, Fern Street, Bolton', *At Home and Abroad*, 1901, 11.

Bethesda, Cheltenham, who gave speeches at the annual meeting 'dressed in Chinese, South African, Indian (Mohammedan) and Indian (Pariah) costumes, kindly lent by the Mission House, and which added additional interest'.[108] The accompanying report explains that the children raised £26 11s 8½d in 1900, well above the £12 4s 11½d the previous year. The secretaries also identify the three highest collectors, where they are standing in the photo, and their individual collection totals. Both images demonstrate how charitable agency has shifted since mid-century. While fundraising is still communal, high achievers receive recognition that draws attention to their individual efforts and makes them identifiable and recognisable.

Fig. 3.4 'Collectors at Bethesda, Cheltenham', *At Home and Abroad*, 1901, 45.

Images were increasingly employed to promote fundraising over the years. Pritchard observes that the magazines published by the Methodists in the twentieth century 'were lavishly illustrated with photographs. They were much more attractive than the Missionary Notices of old, and more effective at putting readers "in the picture".'[109] In 1900, 'More Successful Collectors' includes portraits of four children, and a brief article on the following page explains that '[w]e give opposite the photographs of four collectors whose achievements are worthy of record'.[110] The editor encouraged the branch secretaries to submit photos of successful collectors for publication in the magazine. However, in June 1901, he announced that the plan had become altogether too successful. The original intent was 'to give recognition to eager, zealous young helpers in the missionary cause, which at the same time might act as a stimulus to others less eager and zealous'.[111] However, the circumstances made the plan untenable, since 'the applications are too numerous, and frequently include groups of office bearers and former collectors, who scarcely come within the category of juveniles'.[112] Thus the rules for publishing photos were formalised to clarify that children must have raised at least £2 in the previous year to have their por-

86   Philanthropy in Children's Periodicals, 1840–1930

trait published and must have a current portrait accompanied by age, name, address and circuit to which they belong, and amount raised. Children are required to meet certain financial commitments in order to have their pictures published in the paper, and those who do not meet these criteria, including former collectors and groups of circuit officials, cannot be accepted. The rules also note that if there are too many photos submitted for publication in any given month, which is limited to six, the magazine is not obligated to print them in a subsequent month, which means that some children may end up missing out. The realities of the publishing business and a fixed number of pages in each monthly issue meant that not all charitable agents could be acknowledged in the magazine.

However, these rules failed to limit the number of portraits that were expected to be published. The opening article in August 1902 on 'Our Juvenile Associations' explains that 'we have been gratified to find ... how many collectors there are who exceed the £2 limit', but, with a rule of publishing just six portraits a month, the number of children whose photos should be published exceeded the capacity of the magazine, for 'our readers would not like it if *At Home and Abroad* were full of report of Juvenile Associations and portraits of collectors, and there were no news in it from the mission field!'[113] Readers are reminded that the '*chief* purpose' of the magazine 'is to tell our young readers about the work of God in the world, and about the need of the Saviour in all lands'.[114] Indeed, children are gently reminded of the importance of the work without the prize:

> And we should like to whisper also that we shall feel specially glad when we hear of collectors who have worked for the cause without the stimulus of prizes. When the mission cause is served from love to Jesus and pity for the heathen ... then the service is most precious in the eyes of the Saviour and in our eyes.[115]

In addition to reminding children that they should be collecting for the good of the society and the benefits it can provide to others, the magazine also increased the amount to £3 to reduce the number of children eligible to have their portraits published. This amendment, along with reminding children to do the work for its own sake, had the practical outcome of reducing the number of portraits that must be published. By 1904, the amount had been raised again, this time to £4, suggesting the ongoing popularity of the scheme.[116] It also indicates that individual charitable activity was important to both the Wesleyan Missionary Society and the readers. With less focus on collective efforts, children were rewarded for their individual charitable work.

In response to the volume of photos, an index of 'Our Juvenile Collectors' was introduced in the 1903 annual so that children could easily find themselves in the pages of their magazine.[117] Importantly, however, the index includes both individuals and groups, meaning that group collections remained important alongside individual effort. Yet the index does not include the contribution amounts like those found in earlier publications such as *Aunt Judy's Magazine*. Readers were still expected to browse through the magazine to find the photographs, read the update about the branch, and find out how much money had been collected. Thus, whether the photo depicted an individual or a group, these Juvenile Associations were expected to be communal, in which boys and girls of various ages were all working together to raise money for the society.

As photography was employed to reward individual fundraising efforts, it was also used to support the charitable cause more widely. At the turn of the century, the magazine began including group photos. Also appearing in the 1901 volume are a range of photos depicting adults and children who are receiving assistance from the missions. An article on 'Famine Waifs' by the Rev. Joseph Reed is accompanied by two photos, one of the girls at the Hawa Bagh orphanage in Jabalpur, and one of the boys. Reed explains how the recent famine of 1900 has resulted in thirty-eight children joining the orphanage, some of whom appear in the photographs. He describes the circumstances of some of the children not pictured, including a boy who was terribly emaciated on his arrival but who had 'picked up wonderfully' and two girls afflicted with paralysis from eating a noxious kind of pulse.[118] He concludes by explaining that '[o]nly one of these children is supported; the others are a charge upon general orphanage funds'.[119] The cost of upkeep is either £3 for food and clothing or £5 for complete upkeep and education per annum, and he expresses hope that 'the worry of this additional financial burden may be shared or wholly removed by our friends at home'.[120] The need for financial support from the readers at home remains a consistent focus, even as the magazine employed new strategies such as photographs to encourage charitable effort.

Individual charitable agency was further developed in the magazine through the introduction of a new column called 'Notes by

88   Philanthropy in Children's Periodicals, 1840–1930

Uncle Ned' in June 1903. Stanley Sowton, a banker who was 'influential in transforming the Juvenile Missionary Association into a dynamic children's movement', authored the column under the by-line 'Uncle Ned' for almost half a century.[121] Addressed to 'My dear boys and girls', his introductory letter explains that he has been invited to 'write you a letter once a month . . . about our work as Collectors', which he hopes will be 'of some service to the missionary cause by encouraging and stimulating both you and me to do more for Jesus than we have ever done before'.[122] Accompanying the column is a line drawing of 'Uncle Ned', depicting an older, portly man dressed in a bow tie and waistcoat, with glasses perched on his nose. While not smiling, he is clearly intended as an avuncular, welcoming presence to child readers, a sentiment reinforced in his letter. 'As a rule,' he writes, 'I get on pretty well with boys and girls . . . and you may be quite sure that I shall be very anxious to get on well with you, so let us be friends from the very start.'[123] Like Aunt Judy in *Aunt Judy's Magazine* and consistent with Siân Pooley's analysis of children's columns in English provincial popular newspapers between 1876 and 1914, the editor wrote under a familial *nom-de-plume* and maintained 'an affectional style' that 'was essential to [the] appeal and the creation' of a community of readers.[124] Uncle Ned draws on the familial relationship and declares 'all you Missionary Collectors [are] my nephews and nieces, and . . . I want you to try to get as many more as you can to become the same relation'.[125] He wants his child readers to find other children to join the Juvenile Association and promises a return letter to anyone who writes to say that they will be looking out for his column. This correspondence between Uncle Ned and his readers transforms the charitable public being developed through the magazine into a real community comprised of actual children and adults who correspond about ideas raised through the printed pages of the magazine.

The importance of individual charitable agency continues to be highlighted in the twentieth century. Through a variety of strategies, including an indication of future content and competitions, Uncle Ned encourages his readers to return to his column each month to obtain news and advice about being a collector, thereby creating a community of child readers who are committed to the missionary cause and are working to raise funds to support it. He writes that he hopes to start a 'J. M. C. D. S. O.' and wonders who can guess what the initials stand for, offering six prizes to the first children who write to him with the correct meaning.[126] In September 1903, he lays out the details of the Juvenile Missionary Collectors' Distinguished Service Order, which is intended to 'give still further recognition' to children who have 'distinguished themselves by their successful efforts' as collectors by raising £5 during the year.[127] They will be awarded a badge 'very much like the Victoria Cross in shape and colour with a special ribbon attachment' to which additional clasps for subsequent successful years can be added.[128] These badges will be presented in public to the recipients to make visible the success of these young people and to inspire others. This list becomes explicitly visible in the March 1904 issue, when the magazine dedicates more than two full pages to the names of collectors raising more than £5. As with *Aunt Judy's Magazine*, this list includes their locations and amounts, making the collectors and their accomplishments identifiable. Uncle Ned also includes a brief summary of these new members to the Order, explaining that the decoration has been awarded to sixty-four girls and thirty-seven boys, who have collected 'the handsome sum' of £661 15s 7d.[129]

Despite the strategy of attracting children to specific fundraising targets through awards and badges, Uncle Ned writes that he does not want children to work hard 'from such a base motive' of receiving a badge. Instead, they should be motivated 'for the sake of their love for Jesus, for the sake of the poor heathen, and for the sake of the many blessings we enjoy in Christian England'.[130] This language echoes narrative work done elsewhere in the magazine and over the decades, in which the privileges of being Christian and being English should be sufficient to motivate children to support the missionary cause. He was undoubtedly thrilled to read the letter from Evelyn Hall of the Chadlington Juvenile Missionary Association, which was printed on the first page of the October 1903 issue. She writes that the members 'all belong to the [Chadlington] "Children's Home", so that we cannot give much of our own money', and yet she adds that the sixteen of them raised twelve guineas last year, and this year, with twenty-two members, they hope to raise twenty guineas.[131] She concludes that '[w]e have worked for nearly two years without prizes, because we do not want to rob the Missionary Society. We write because we see in the August number of *At Home and Abroad* that you would like to know this.'[132] Child readers of the magazine are persuaded about the need for collective charitable agency and

90   Philanthropy in Children's Periodicals, 1840–1930

eschew the promised individual rewards. Moreover, as a member of the Children's Home, Evelyn indicates her status as a charitable recipient who is interested in supporting foreign missionary work.

Another similar article highlights the dedication of child readers regardless of class. In a series of extracts from letters to Uncle Ned, child writers indicate the work they have done to raise funds for the organisation. Dorothy Darby explains that, while on a holiday at Rhyl, she came across a group of children who had created some sand decorations and were collecting funds for Dr Barnardo's, Dr Stephenson's Homes, and the Life Boat fund. However, 'none seemed to have remembered the Missionaries'.[133] After decorating her own sand hole, she collected 5s 7d and on her next holiday hoped to do even better. This brief extract highlights one type of child reader who contributed to the missionary fundraising. This presumably middle-class child comes from a family who is able to holiday and anticipates another such holiday at a later date. She is aware of other charitable causes and both notes the absence of the missionaries and is motivated to support it. Another extract mentions how Alice Bartrupt of the Chadlington Children's Home has collected 5s 6d from two concerts. Other activities at the Children's Home 'have been made to contribute to the object [of the missionary cause], which is evidently kept well in view'.[134] The children in this home, likely orphaned or temporarily abandoned, would have been markedly different from young Dorothy on a holiday. Yet, as Uncle Ned observes, the inhabitants of the home are well aware of the missionary cause and are doing their bit to collect funds despite very different material circumstances. Both Dorothy and Alice received prizes for their submissions to the August 'Holiday' Competition.

The motivation behind the charitable agency was as important as the fundraising itself, as is evident in one of the earliest competitions introduced by Uncle Ned. Each month, he posed a question to which children were encouraged to write a response. In the July 1903 competition, he asks: 'If you had a subscriber who gave you a halfpenny a week with a pleasant smile, and another who gave you a penny a week as if it hurt him to part with the money – which of the two would you prefer and why?'[135] The three best answers to the question will be given a handsome book as a prize, and he tantalisingly indicates that '[i]f any of the answers deserve it', they will be printed in the magazine.[136] Uncle Ned provides a summary of the 239 letters he received, in which the overwhelming majority (230) give preference to 'the ha'penny and the smile, rather than to the penny and the frown'.[137] He writes how glad he is 'to see so many of my nieces and nephews know the text 2 Cor. ix, 7; I hope that they will not forget it when they grow up and are giving money instead of collecting it'.[138] This passage from the Bible refers to the need for cheerful, not grudging, giving and indicates Uncle Ned's belief that his child readers will either be sufficiently familiar with this passage or look it up. The winning entry, by Julia Smith of Gosport, reflects the charitable ideal of giving that is promoted throughout the magazine. She explains the reasons for preferring the half-penny contribution, including that 'God loves a *cheerful giver*' and that the 'smile from the subscriber calls forth an answering smile in the heart of the collector' that 'will awaken fresh energies, and renew flagging spirits'.[139] Moreover, she writes, 'A freewill offering carries its own blessing with it', as a deed done with the right spirit will be blessed by God.[140] Those who are donating money should be doing so with cheer and goodwill to both inspire the collector and to be blessed by God.

A range of competitions are included in the magazine to encourage children to regularly read and share the magazine. The July 1903 column includes a different image of Uncle Ned seated on a bench, surrounded by a number of children who are watching him intently, emphasising his appeal to young readers. Readers are informed that these pictures should be saved, as they will be needed for a competition in the future. In the accompanying article, he describes his missionary experiences and relates how he became a missionary collector and 'have remained so . . . from that day to this'.[141] In his first year as a collector, he was seventeenth on the list, 'but the second and every following year I was No. 1'.[142] His comments indicate a competitive edge to the collecting, yet he acknowledges that his accomplishment is not entirely owing to his own work. He says further that 'it is only fair to add that just as much of the credit for this belonged to my mother as to me . . . Some of the best workers for the Juvenile Missionary Society are the fathers and mothers of the boys and girls who get all the credit.'[143] This observation signifies the shared – and often overlooked – responsibility the child collector's family sometimes undertook to assist with fundraising.

Conclusion

This chapter has demonstrated the significance of the *Wesleyan Juvenile Offering* and later *At Home and Abroad* in developing and reinforcing ideologies of charitable agency for child readers. These children were vital contributors to the Wesleyan Missionary Society since even before the magazine published its first issue. Yet its contents reflect the ongoing campaign to inform readers about mission activities and encourage charitable giving. These activities were regularly reiterated over the decades as generations of readers grew up and left their local Juvenile Association. The organisation was always looking to attract contributors whose interest in missionary activities would be matched by their religious belief and a willingness to work and sacrifice for the charitable cause.

The financial contributions made by Wesleyan children formed a substantial portion of the annual monies raised by the organisation. This fundraising was supported by specific magazine strategies to encourage individual and collective activities. This collective behaviour is clearly evident through the *Wesleyan Juvenile Offering* and yet, at the turn of the twentieth century, the magazine also sought to recognise the achievements of high-performing children through individual rewards that took advantage of new print technologies and responded to cultural shifts that encouraged personal interactions between the magazine and its readers through correspondence and essay contests.

Notes

1. 'Letter from an old missionary', *Wesleyan Juvenile Offering*, February 1844, 17.
2. 'Letter from an old missionary', 17.
3. 'Letter from an old missionary', 18.
4. In 1974, *At Home and Abroad* was renamed *Windows*.
5. David F. Lancy, 'Unmasking Children's Agency', *AnthropoChildren* 2 (2012): 3, 5.
6. Kristine Alexander, 'Agency and Emotion Work', *Jeunesse* 7.2 (2015): 120; Mona Gleason, 'Avoiding the Agency Trap', *History of Education* 45, no. 4 (2016): 447.
7. Lynn M. Thomas, 'Historicizing Agency', *Gender and History* 28, no. 2 (August 2016): 335.

Charitable Agency 93

8. Thomas, 'Historicizing Agency', 328.
9. Susan A. Miller, 'Assent as Agency in the Early Years of the Children of the American Revolution', *Journal of the History of Children and Youth* 9, no. 1 (2016): 49.
10. Miller, 'Assent as Agency', 49.
11. Miller, 'Assent as Agency', 50.
12. Anna Johnston, *Missionary Writing and Empire, 1800–1860* (Cambridge: Cambridge University Press, 2003), 15.
13. Allison Giffen and Robin L. Cadwallader, 'Introduction', in *Saving the World: Girlhood and Evangelicism in Nineteenth-Century Literature*, ed. Allison Giffen and Robin L. Cadwallader (London: Routledge, 2018), 1.
14. Marcia Bunge, 'The Child, Religion, and the Academy: Developing Robust Theological and Religious Understandings of Children and Childhood', *Journal of Religion* 86, no. 4 (2006): 551.
15. Hugh Morrison and Mary Clare Martin, 'Introduction: Contours and Issues in Children's Religious History', in *Creating Religious Childhoods in Anglo-World and British Colonial Contexts*, ed. Hugh Morrison and Mary Clare Martin (London: Routledge, 2017), 4.
16. Drotner, *English Children and Their Magazines, 1751–1945* (New Haven: Yale University Press, 1988), 23.
17. Drotner, *English Children and Their Magazines*, 24.
18. Elleray, *Victorian Coral Islands*, 2.
19. Elleray, *Victorian Coral Islands*, 3.
20. Elleray, *Victorian Coral Islands*, 3.
21. Elleray, *Victorian Coral Islands*, 45.
22. Prochaska, 'Little Vessels', 103, 104.
23. Prochaska, 'Little Vessels', 105.
24. Diana Dixon, 'Children and the Press, 1866–1914', in *The Press in English Society from the Seventeenth to Nineteenth Centuries*, ed. Michael Harris and Alan Lee (London: Associated University Presses, 1986), 143.
25. Margot Hillel, '"Nearly all are supported by children": Charitable Childhoods in Late-Nineteenth- and Early-Twentieth-Century Literature for Children in the British World', in *Creating Religious Childhoods in Anglo-World and British Colonial Contexts, 1800–1950*, ed. Hugh Morrison and Mary Clare Martin (London: Routledge, 2017), 163.
26. Hillel, '"Nearly all"', 168.
27. Hillel, '"Nearly all"', 168.

94 Philanthropy in Children's Periodicals, 1840–1930

28. 'To Our Young Readers', *Wesleyan Juvenile Offering*, January 1844, 1. Emphasis in original.
29. Richard D. Altick, *The English Common Reader: A Social History of the Mass Reading Public, 1800–1900* (Columbus: Ohio State University Press, 1957), 107.
30. Altick, *The English Common Reader*, 108.
31. Hillel, '"Nearly all"', 164.
32. Prochaska, 'Little Vessels', 104.
33. 'To Our Young Readers', *Wesleyan Juvenile Offering*, January 1844, 2.
34. Hughes and Lund, 'Textual/Sextual Pleasure and Serial Production', 149.
35. Moruzi, 'Serializing', 169.
36. 'To Our Young Readers', 2.
37. W. C. 'Juvenile Sympathy', *Wesleyan Juvenile Offering*, 1844, 192.
38. W. C., 'Juvenile Sympathy', 192.
39. W. C., 'Juvenile Sympathy', 192.
40. Kidd, 'Philanthropy and the "Social History Paradigm"', 183.
41. W. C., 'Juvenile Sympathy', 192.
42. Kidd, 'Philanthropy and the "Social History Paradigm"', 187.
43. Kristine Moruzi, 'Charity, Affect, and Waif Novels', in *Affect, Emotion, and Children's Literature: Representation and Socialisation in Texts for Children and Young Adults*, ed. Kristine Moruzi, Michelle J. Smith and Elizabeth Bullen (New York: Routledge, 2018), 49.
44. Margot Hillel, '"Give us all missionary Eyes and missionary hearts": Triumphalism and Missionising in Late-Victorian Children's Literature', *Mousaion* 29, no. 3 (2011): 183.
45. 'A Friend'. 'Letter of a Missionary's Wife, in New Zealand, to the Readers of the "Juvenile Offering"', *Wesleyan Juvenile Offering*, January 1849, 2.
46. 'A Friend', 'Letter', 2.
47. 'A Friend', 'Letter', 2, 3.
48. 'A Friend', 'Letter', 3–4.
49. 'A Friend', 'Letter', 4.
50. 'A Friend', 'Letter', 4.
51. 'A Friend', 'Letter', 4.
52. 'A Friend', 'Letter', 4.
53. 'A Friend', 'Letter', 4.
54. Susan Draper, 'A Letter from a Friend in Melbourne to the Children in England', *Wesleyan Juvenile Offering*, July 1857, 80.

Charitable Agency   95

55. Draper, 'A Letter', 80.

56. Draper, 'A Letter', 80.

57. Draper, 'A Letter', 81.

58. Thomas Hodson, 'Bangalore', *Wesleyan Juvenile Offering*, July 1857, 31.

59. 'American children's periodicals, 1841–1850', accessed 15 January 2021, https://www.merrycoz.org/bib/1850.xhtml#06.1842.04.

60. 'How the Little Children in America Get Money for the Missions', *Wesleyan Juvenile Offering*, July 1857, 32.

61. 'How the Little Children', 32.

62. 'How the Little Children', 32.

63. Carol M. Noren, 'Origins of Wesleyan Holiness Theology in Nineteenth-Century Sweden', *Methodist History* 33, no. 2 (1995): 112.

64. George Scott, 'A Child's Self-Denial for the Mission Cause', *Wesleyan Juvenile Offering*, April 1844, 49.

65. Scott, 'A Child's Self-Denial', 50.

66. Johnston, *Missionary Writing and Empire*, 32.

67. Johnston, *Missionary Writing and Empire*, 33.

68. Elleray, 'Little Builders', 224.

69. Elleray, 'Little Builders', 226.

70. Elleray, *Victorian Coral Islands*, 44.

71. Prochaska, 'Little Vessels', 108; Blake, *The Day of Small Things*, 7.

72. Blake, *The Day of Small Things*, 7.

73. 'To Our Juvenile Collectors', *Wesleyan Juvenile Offering*, November 1847, 132.

74. 'Juvenile Missionary Offerings for the Year 1843, made at Christmas, or early in January, 1844', *Wesleyan Juvenile Offering*, 1844, 2.

75. These figures come from the Wesleyan Missionary Society annual reports from 1841–1914. Figures are missing for 1857–62, 1865, 1867, 1879, and 1909.

76. This figure is based on the total of the annual income from the annual reports until 1863, after which it includes 'Home Receipts' only. The domestic total excluded foreign contributions.

77. 'Our Juvenile Missionary Associations', *Wesleyan Juvenile Offering*, December 1867, 144.

78. 'Circular. To the Wesleyan Ministers, the Local Missionary Officers, Committees and Collectors, and other Friends of the

96   Philanthropy in Children's Periodicals, 1840–1930

Wesleyan Missions', *Wesleyan Missionary Notices*, February 1844, 481. Emphasis in original.

79. 'Circular', 481.
80. 'Circular', 481. Emphasis in original.
81. 'Christmas and New Year's Juvenile Offering', *Wesleyan Juvenile Offering*, 1846, 11.
82. John Pritchard, *Methodists and Their Missionary Societies 1900–1996* (London: Taylor & Francis Group, 2014), 46.
83. M. Batchelor, 'To the Juvenile Friends of Missions', *Wesleyan Juvenile Offering*, 1845, 21.
84. Margaret, 'The Little Missionary Collector', *Wesleyan Juvenile Offering*, February 1850, 16.
85. Margaret, 'The Little Missionary', 17.
86. Margaret, 'The Little Missionary', 17.
87. Margaret, 'The Little Missionary', 17.
88. 'Income of the Wesleyan Missionary Society for 1858', *Wesleyan Juvenile Offering*, May 1859, 51.
89. 'Income', 51.
90. 'Income', 51.
91. 'Income', 52.
92. 'Juvenile Christmas Offerings for 1855', *Wesleyan Juvenile Offering*, May 1856, 2–4.
93. 'Our Juvenile Associations', *At Home and Abroad*, February 1895, 33.
94. 'Our Juvenile Associations', 33.
95. 'Our Juvenile Associations', 33.
96. Blake, *The Day of Small Things*, 7.
97. 'The "John Wesley" Missionary Ship', *Wesleyan Juvenile Offering*, September 1846, 103.
98. 'The "John Wesley" Missionary Ship', 103.
99. 'Launch of the "John Wesley"', *Wesleyan Juvenile Offering*, February 1847, 15–16.
100. 'The "John Wesley" Missionary Ship', *Wesleyan Juvenile Offering*, November 1847, 123–4.
101. See Chapter 1 in Elleray's *Victorian Coral Islands* for a detailed discussion of a similar campaign conducted by the London Missionary Society.
102. 'Our Juvenile Associations', *At Home and Abroad*, April 1882, 78.
103. 'Our Juvenile Associations', 78.
104. 'Our Juvenile Associations', 79.
105. 'Our Juvenile Associations', 79.

Charitable Agency 97

106. 'Our Juvenile Associations', *At Home and Abroad*, 1901, 11.
107. 'Our Juvenile Associations', 12.
108. 'Our Juvenile Associations', *At Home and Abroad*, 1901, 45.
109. Pritchard, *Methodists*, 61.
110. 'More Successful Collectors', *At Home and Abroad*, 1900, 100–1.
111. 'Our Juvenile Associations: Important Notice to Secretaries', *At Home and Abroad*, 1901, 86.
112. 'Our Juvenile Associations', 86.
113. 'Our Juvenile Associations', *At Home and Abroad*, 1902, 113.
114. 'Our Juvenile Associations', 113. Emphasis in original.
115. 'Our Juvenile Associations', 113.
116. 'Our Juvenile Associations', *At Home and Abroad*, 1904, 27.
117. 'Our Juvenile Collectors', *At Home and Abroad*, 1903, np.
118. Rev. Joseph Reed, 'Famine Waifs', *At Home and Abroad*, 1901, 21.
119. Reed, 'Famine Waifs', 23.
120. Reed, 'Famine Waifs', 23.
121. Pritchard, *Methodists*, 46.
122. 'Notes by Uncle Ned', *At Home and Abroad*, 1903, 88.
123. 'Notes', 88.
124. Pooley, 'Children's Writing', 79.
125. Pooley, 'Children's Writing', 88.
126. Pooley, 'Children's Writing', 88.
127. 'Notes by Uncle Ned', *At Home and Abroad*, 1903, 134.
128. 'Notes', 134.
129. 'J. M. C. D. S. O. First List', *At Home and Abroad*, 1904, 40–2.
130. 'Notes', 135.
131. 'We Don't Want Prizes!', *At Home and Abroad*, October 1903, 144.
132. 'We Don't Want Prizes!', 144.
133. 'How I Managed to Get Some Extra Money for Missions During My Holidays', *At Home and Abroad*, 1903, 155.
134. 'How I Managed', 155. The National Children's Home opened a branch at Chadlington in 1900, which was relocated to Chipping Norton in 1904. See http://www.childrenshomes.org.uk/ChadlingtonNCH/.
135. 'Notes by Uncle Ned', *At Home and Abroad*, 1903, 104.
136. 'Notes by Uncle Ned', *At Home and Abroad*, 1903, 104.
137. 'Notes by Uncle Ned', *At Home and Abroad*, 1903, 135.
138. The verse Uncle Ned refers to is 'Every man according as he purposeth in his heart, so let him give; not grudgingly, or of necessity: for God loveth a cheerful giver' (*King James Bible*, 2 Corinthians 9:7).

98 Philanthropy in Children's Periodicals, 1840–1930

139. 'Notes by Uncle Ned', *At Home and Abroad*, 1903, 136. Emphasis in original.
140. 'Notes by Uncle Ned', 136.
141. 'Notes by Uncle Ned', *At Home and Abroad*, 1903, 103.
142. 'Notes by Uncle Ned', 103.
143. 'Notes by Uncle Ned', 103.

4

Charitable Motivation

Thomas Barnardo's charity was founded in 1868 with the establishment of the East End Juvenile Mission and the purchase of Stepney Causeway, a building intended to house destitute boys until 'employment or foster homes were secured'.[1] Although admission to the home was initially limited, the tragic death of 'Carrots', a young boy who had been denied entrance and was later found dead from exposure, prompted a new policy in which 'No Destitute Child Ever Refused'. It took over two decades for Barnardo to begin to specifically capitalise on the potential of young people to assist with the organisation's fundraising by developing a charitable infrastructure. In the 1893 annual report, Barnardo describes the establishment of the Young Helpers' League, in which habitations comprised of at least twenty-four Companions under the age of eighteen undertake 'to collect sufficient money to support a Cot in Her Majesty's Hospital for a year' by raising £30 per annum.[2] Each Companion pays an annual one shilling membership fee, 'in return for which each receives for the year a prettily printed and illustrated *quarterly* magazine'.[3] He is pleased to emphasise that forty out of the seventy cots in the hospital are already supported, and '[t]hus there is established a link of sympathy and perennial interest between these young people from happy homes and the children of sadness and suffering – a link which undoubtedly proves of the highest value as an educational and moral factor'.[4] In this relatively brief mention of the league, Barnardo explicitly links together sympathy and the financial support of over half of the hospital cots. Child readers' 'perennial interest' is enabled through the publication of a magazine and is manifested through their fundraising efforts.

100   Philanthropy in Children's Periodicals, 1840–1930

As Barnardo summarises, by the close of the year, the contributions made by the 10,729 members of the Young Helpers' League total £4,186 2s 5d.[5]

The previous chapter explored the strategies used in the *Wesleyan Juvenile Offering* to develop and reinforce readers' agency as charitable donors. Most charitable magazines deployed similar strategies to mobilise children as active fundraising participants, and the regular reporting on fundraising totals indicates the success of these efforts. The question about why children were motivated to perform this work still needs to be answered. In this chapter, I explore the narrative and editorial strategies in Barnardo's *Young Helpers' Magazine* (1892–1929?) that deployed emotions to depict poor children in need, encourage middle-class child readers to help others, and produce emotional and affective responses that were expected to be translated into actions directly assisting others or, more often, resulting in fundraising that would help others. The 'educational and moral' feelings engendered by the magazine would produce actions whereby readers were expected to sympathise with those less fortunate and then to be motivated to mitigate those circumstances through charitable activity.

Formations of middle-class childhood in the nineteenth century were highly dependent on Romantic conceptions of childhood. Wordsworth's *Ode on Intimations of Immortality from Recollections of Early Childhood* (1807) is central to the emergence of a nineteenth-century middle-class ideal in which childhood 'was transformed from being a preparatory phase in the making of an adult to being the spring that should nourish the whole life'.[6] Alongside the consolidation of childhood as a time of happiness, innocence, and purity was a growing sense that children were to be pitied when their reality did not reflect this ideal. This idea did not typically apply to working-class children, who were 'economically useful from a young age . . . and by twelve were likely to enter fulltime work'.[7] However, poor and neglected children, who were often the 'victims of rapid urbanization and the effects of irregular employment, early adult death-rates and acute poverty', were subject to child rescue campaigns to improve their living conditions.[8] The terminology used to describe such children, such as 'waif' and 'street arab', points to not only the pity that such figures might inspire, but also 'the fear which such children evoked, and to their threatening outsider status'.[9] These children were nonetheless typically featured as 'objects of pathos' in the literature that emerged in the last decades of the century.[10]

The materials appearing in *Young Helpers' League Magazine* reflect the concern for the loss of childhood innocence and the shift in missionary efforts from conversion to rescue, which 'spawned a literature and a set of visual images with immense propaganda potential'.[11] In her discussion of child rescue literature, Shurlee Swain argues that the 'stories, poems, and vignettes that filled the magazines issued by the key child rescue organisations consistently constituted the state of the neglected child as one of "lack"', where innocence, purity, and protection had all been lost.[12] Swain and Hillel make a related point about the significance of this bifurcation of childhood models, observing that '[n]ineteenth-century children's literature reinforced the tropes of the vulnerable child, needing to be taken from a life of poverty and degradation, and the charitable child, who needed to learn life-long lessons of selflessness and support for others'.[13] They emphasise the 'long tradition of writing for children' that intertwines ideas of 'charity, class and Christianity'.[14] The religious doctrine of charity to others is embedded in literature of this period. In Anna Davin's discussion of waif novels written by evangelical women writers between the 1860s and the 1890s, she observes that most were written after reformers had already begun to establish rescue organisations, and thus these novels were depicting 'old solutions' to 'new problems'.[15] As Gillian Avery notes, the 'ministering child' began to replace the ideal evangelical child who achieved salvation and then died.[16] Nonetheless, the message that 'action should be taken to protect vulnerable children' was a clear and consistent one in which the 'emotional force of the stories is tied up with the Christian narrative, yet transcends it'.[17] Davin argues that waif novels encourage action to protect young people, but young readers are not necessarily the ones who are encouraged to take action.[18]

However, in magazines like *Young Helpers' League Magazine*, children's charitable activity was specifically encouraged. This chapter argues that *Young Helpers' League Magazine* published material in its pages that aimed to produce an affective response among its readers and then directed that response towards charitable aims that manifested in material ways. In the sections that follow, I begin by discussing how charitable motivation has been theorised and how reading in the nineteenth century was intertwined with this charitable work. I then discuss the

102   Philanthropy in Children's Periodicals, 1840–1930

narrative strategies appearing in the magazine and how emotion is used to create a charitable ethos and motivate implied readers to perform charitable work. In the highly visual *Young Helpers' League Magazine*, these narratives are often accompanied by illustrations that work together to motivate children towards charitable acts. In the final section, I discuss the significance and ubiquity of these narrative strategies by exploring how stories written by child contributors followed similar narrative arcs. Together the examples in this magazine provide a case study of how children were motivated to be charitable through an editorial strategy that juxtaposed negative emotions associated with pitiful children against the positive potential of the cause to effect change through material support.

Charitable motivation and the importance of reading

The mechanisms that produce charitable behaviours can be difficult to pin down since this behaviour can be motivated by multiple factors, both internal and external. Does a child decide to donate money to a charitable cause because they are distressed about ill children and believe their donation will help or because they will derive some benefit (recognition, status, satisfaction) from it?[19] C. Daniel Batson explains that proponents of universal egoism claim that 'everything we do, no matter how noble and beneficial to others, is really directed toward the ultimate goal of self-benefit'.[20] While advocates of altruism do not deny the egoistic motivation, they claim 'that at least some of us, to some degree, under some circumstances, are capable of a . . . motivation with an ultimate goal of benefiting someone else'.[21] The extent to which children's work for and contributions to a particular charitable cause can be attributed to egoistic or altruistic motivations is unclear. Even a seemingly altruistic act may result in forms of self-benefit. As previous chapters discussed, children sometimes received material rewards like badges or public recognition by being named in subscription lists or having their photos published. Even in the 'absence of obvious external rewards', however, children can still receive 'self-rewards' by congratulating themselves for doing charitable work or by avoiding self-censure.[22]

The Introduction discussed how charity permeated the social fabric of Victorian England.[23] Kidd explains how the utilitarian concepts of self-interest are only part of a larger picture of

Charitable Motivation 103

understanding charitable acts since '[c]hoices are made in a social, political, cultural and ethical context' in which 'voluntary co-operative behaviour, including charity, cannot be rationalized as a mechanism of self-interest without the intervention of an internalized social ethic to impel voluntary action'.[24] This internalised social ethic is crucial to understanding how children saw themselves as people who should help others. The '"field" of charity', drawing on Pierre Bourdieu's field of cultural production,

> could be conceived as a semi-autonomous territory the contours of which are determined by both its agents (the charitable) and its own objective structures: its rules, conventions and hierarchies; its external relations with other 'fields' (e.g. business, politics, religion); and its grounding in the class system.[25]

The field of charity is a point which is discussed further in Chapter 7 on 'Charitable Habits'. Middle-class child readers come to magazines like *Young Helpers' League Magazine* and other charity magazines like those from the Junior Red Cross because they are already part of the charitable field but are also helping to define its contours as they relate to young people and charitable work. The magazine establishes the rules, conventions, and hierarchies of its specific field through its charitable infrastructures, which contribute to the charitable public defined in its pages.

The norms of beneficence and social responsibility are part of the charitable field, and child readers are presumably already versed in its language.[26] Historian Gertrude Himmelfarb explains that while the government might intervene in a limited fashion 'to alleviate misery ... the immediate responsibility and the primary moral obligation belonged to individuals and private associations'.[27] The role of reading is a central constituent of the field in which young readers are informed about the value and importance of this particular charitable work. Because philanthropy is so 'thoroughly embedded' in social and material conditions, the 'question of motive' is relevant for 'the ways it restates the concerns of nineteenth-century writers who engaged the relation between self-interest and sympathy as they shaped the representation of philanthropy for ... observers and participants'.[28] The multiple representations of philanthropy that appear in texts for young people are both helping to shape and are shaped by the charitable field. According to Kelly J. Mays, reading in the nineteenth

104   Philanthropy in Children's Periodicals, 1840–1930

century 'was threatening not only individuals but also ... the entire social fabric', and writers were deeply engaged in trying to answer 'the question of how, why, and what readers were and should be reading'.[29] The recurring question about what children were reading, from fairy tales at the end of the eighteenth century to penny dreadfuls in the 1850s, meant that adults were deeply engaged in ensuring quality texts were available for young people since they would influence children's moral development. In writing for children, then, the child reader was 'positioned through reading for their future place in the world as morally upstanding, hard-working adults who [understood] their responsibilities'.[30]

The transformative potential of reading has been a persistent question for literary studies scholars, and one that is intertwined with affective response. Martha Nussbaum argues that literature cultivates 'power of imagination' in order to enable readers to see the lives of others 'with sympathetic understanding'.[31] Narrative is essential, she believes, 'for moral interaction'.[32] Yet whether reading changes readers' 'ability to become more empathetic, tolerant, and better people' remains an open question.[33] Suzanne Keen likewise wonders whether 'empathetic reading experiences can contribute to changing a reader's disposition, motivations, and attitudes'.[34] Importantly, we cannot assume that readers' responses to a text will be identical.[35] The timing and the context of the reading experience inform how the young reader responds. The extent of their emotional response may also be 'contingent on the ... historical, economic, cultural, or social circumstances in which a text is written or read'.[36] Nonetheless, in the nineteenth century, readers were expected to sympathise with the circumstances of the poor waifs depicted in child rescue literature. The language of pity and sympathy was deployed consistently to produce an affective response in which child readers were expected to feel sadness and distress at these unfortunate circumstances.

Yet the emotional response was only the first step in the process since it did not, on its own, produce charitable behaviours. The need to act was a result of the moral impetus that those who could act should do so. The content in charity magazines like *Young Helpers' League Magazine* directed young readers to take on charitable activities at a young age as part of their current and future obligations and emerging from their emotional responses to distressing stories about poor and sick children. Karen Vallgårda, Kristine Alexander, and Stephanie Olsen define the term 'emotional formation' as 'a set of emotional structures' that are organised into a *'pattern'* and supported through a *'process* that depends on each individual learning the imparted codes of feeling'.[37] Child readers learned the appropriate 'codes of feeling' through the magazine and in other forms of everyday life and were instructed through their reading about the expectation that they would act. Narratives featuring emotional responses and resulting in charitable behaviour were part of the charitable pattern appearing in magazines like *Young Helpers' League Magazine*, and they were expected to induct young readers into patterns of charitable giving. In contrast to waif novels that were intended to produce feelings of pity for the poor among readers but not necessarily material support, the contents of this magazine were intended to produce an emotional response and motivate young people to support the cause.[38]

Narrative strategies

As Chapter 2 briefly described, the Young Helpers' League was launched in 1891 to encourage children to learn about and support Barnardo's charitable efforts. 'To give definiteness to the work of the League', the endpaper for *Young Helpers' League Magazine* explains, members would support cots in Her Majesty's Hospital for Waif Children or the Home of Little Incurables.[39] Each habitation raising the required annual amount would be allocated a cot, which would be named after it. Companions are 'permitted to visit their own Cot in the afternoon of any day'.[40] Barnardo thus establishes a specific, achievable, financial goal for the young people joining a habitation that is clearly identified from the outset. That the children sought to meet this goal is unsurprising, yet it also raises questions about how the magazine content furthered this goal. This section explores how emotion is deployed in the fictional content and argues that highly emotive language is used to encourage readerly identification in multiple ways. In some cases, readers are invited to align themselves with an ideological position in which assisting poor waifs is urgent, essential, and a moral responsibility. In other cases, this identification is with middle-class characters who can and do understand their responsibility to help those less fortunate, despite 'the limits of sympathy produced and mediated via the imagination'.[41]

106   Philanthropy in Children's Periodicals, 1840–1930

Emotion is an important aspect of the serialised story beginning in the first issue of *Young Helpers' League Magazine*. In 'Waif and His Friends', Barnardo employs the allegorical character names of Waif, Sister, and Scavenger to relate the story of a poor boy living on the streets, the nursing sister who cares for him, and Barnardo himself, who scavenges the streets for poor children in need of assistance. The description of Waif is designed to produce a feeling of pity. This 'queer' boy has 'a very big head', but his body is 'very small' with a lump on his back.[42] One leg is crooked and much shorter than the other. Waif is pitiable, which the reader learns as Barnardo explains how, '[o]ther folks, if they looked at Waif more closely, wanted to cry'.[43] The invisibility of people like Waif on the streets of London means that they often go unnoticed and uncared for. The narrator remarks that 'it is perhaps not surprising that [Waif] grew thinner and thinner . . . and his eyes sadder and sadder'.[44] Not only do others feel sorry for Waif, but he too is saddened by his wretched circumstances. The story suggests no other reading than pity and dismay over poor Waif.

This pitiful situation is juxtaposed to the positive emotions generated when Scavenger trips over Waif, gives him sixpence, and invites him to the Home in Stepney Causeway for 'some dinner by the fire'.[45] The possibilities of the sixpence bring tears to Waif's eyes, and his feelings of cold, hunger, tiredness, and illness are temporarily banished, for 'it seemed as if the sun had shone out!'[46] When Waif discovers the coin is actually half a crown instead, his brief vision of 'untold warmth and rest and food' disappears as he mutters that he 'aren't no prig'.[47] He collapses at the Barnardo's Home, but before falling unconscious returns the coin and informs Scavenger that he is not a thief. The honesty and integrity of Waif shine through in this interaction as he forsakes self-interest by refusing to accept the coin as a boon and instead insists on returning it to its owner.

When Waif awakens, the changes in his circumstances are designed to produce positive emotions in him and in the implied readers. The 'lovely' scene in the hospital ward with white beds and pretty pictures on the walls makes him forget his pain, and Sister smiles at him as she puts a cool hand on his forehead. Waif falls asleep with 'a reflection of the smile' he received from her on his face and, as he recovers, readers are told that his frown 'would not again return'.[48] The tension of the story is resolved through Sister's tender care and the knowledge that Waif is now happy and content within the Home. The hopeful conclusion to Waif's story provides an archetypal pattern of the main characters and the emotional register for this type of narrative. A downtrodden, unhappy Waif is saved from the dire circumstances of the street by the Philanthropist and placed under the care of suitable, loving caregivers like Sister. From the despair and sadness of Waif's original situation, the charity enables hope, optimism, and happiness.

Lest readers are unclear about how to help the charity produce the positive emotional response, surrounding materials remind them of their obligations in both figurative and literal terms. In 'What One Little Sunbeam Did!' by Eva Travers Evered Poole, some aspects of the desired charitable behaviours are laid out. The sunbeam is a metaphor for how young people can spread joy and light to people around them as part of the Young Helpers' League. Mother-sun explains to her child that '[w]e have all our work to do. Life is not meant only for play'.[49] The baby sunbeam wonders if 'perhaps there is work for me to do', and the wise mother says that '[s]urely there is ... in kindness and love to light up the path of the sick or the sad'.[50] What follows is a series of encounters as the sunbeam seeks work to do. It first shines through an attic window, where it encounters an 'ill-clad and hungry-looking baby' whose mother had gone out to work to earn money for food: 'Alone, hungry, weary, unable to do more than kick or cry on the bare floor where it had been placed, it missed the mother's face and the mother's voice'.[51] When the sunbeam arrives to play, the poor baby 'forgot to cry', and the narrator explains to the reader that '[y]ou would have laughed to see the fun had you been there'.[52] The sadness of the baby's circumstances is mitigated by the sunbeam, who leaves the baby tired and happy. The sunbeam is pleased with its accomplishments as well; it 'danced with glee' before seeking its next job.[53] The valuable charitable work performed by the sunbeam is emphasised through the emotional shift from sadness and pity through to happiness and even glee. The baby's circumstances have been improved, all through the sunbeam's efforts. The implied readers, too, are invited to feel the sunbeam's joy at helping others.

The religious overtones of doing good are made explicit in the next encounters. In the first of these, the sunbeam visits a sickroom inhabited by a woman 'wearied out with long wakefulness and pain'.[54] The sunbeam transports her in her dreams to the woodland scenes from her past that she 'loved so well' and were

108   Philanthropy in Children's Periodicals, 1840–1930

far away from the 'dim, darkened room that was her prison'.[55] When she wakes, the sunbeam 'rested lovingly upon the open Bible' and this reminds the woman that 'The Lord God is a *sun and a shield*' and 'The Lord is my *light* and my salvation'.[56] These two lines, from Psalms 84 and 27 respectively, with the italicised emphasis on the sun imagery, connect charitable work with religious faith and duty. Yet again the sunbeam transforms a sad and pitiful existence into one of hope. In the final two visitations, to a suffering girl in a hospital ward and a blind boy on the street, the children's pitiful circumstances are laid out. The girl's eyes are 'full of mute sorrow' and she has 'never known what joy and happiness meant; kicked and buffeted, sworn at and abused, the poor child's only thought was one of mistrust and fear'.[57] The sunbeam, with whom the implied reader is expected to identify, is 'full of pity', and goes 'straight to her heart'.[58] It kisses the eyes of the little boy 'so softly, so warmly, so lovingly' that he 'forgot all his darkness' and 'sang of the day when his blind eyes should see' in heaven.[59] Pity is the dominant emotion in these encounters, yet they too are transformed into hope and optimism even if the material circumstances remain much the same. In some ways, the sunbeam's ability to spread joy even as it makes minimal improvements in the waifs' circumstances aligns with middle-class children's ability to enact change. Nonetheless, children are expected to respond to the emotional transformation from sadness to hope and be inspired to make similar attempts.

The impact of the charitable work remains even after the sunbeam has gone to rest. Poole explains that 'the light and happiness it gave *did not die with it*'.[60] The long-lasting impact of this emotional work is why boys and girls, 'the *living sunbeams*', should be thinking about how they can assist others. She describes children in the Romantic sense as 'full of the joy of living, happy, innocent and glad' and asks how they might be able to do the work that the sunbeam has done.[61] The metaphorical is refigured in practical terms after the narrative produces the affective response. 'If a child's heart is filled with God's love, and a real desire to do good,' she remarks, 'it will not long be left idle'.[62] The work children can do is 'sunbeam work: to comfort, to help, to sympathize. You cannot *say* much, but you can *shine* a great deal; you can be bright, joyous, helpful, and the magic of your happiness will drive trouble away'.[63] This emotion work demands little except for care and kindness and is situated by Poole as a precursor for assisting the Young Helpers' League, which is concerned with the care of a wider group of people.

The final section of the article is focused on how children can contribute to the Young Helpers' League. Poole asks readers to consider what they can do 'for their poorer suffering brothers and sisters'.[64] By describing those in need in familial terms, she brings them into the circle of those who should be cared for, despite and because of their 'poorer' material circumstances. They are 'sad-faced, sad-hearted children ... whose poor little lives have been terribly darkened by cruelty and by suffering ... and shadowed for want of love's sunshine and cheer'.[65] The emotional terms of this description are designed to encourage implied readers to sympathise with the poor children and to motivate them:

> To *you* God has given true sunbeam work to do for these little ones. You may, by loving thoughts *of* them, loving prayers *about* them, loving work *for* them, flood their lonely hearts with a wonderful gladness and help them to forget the dark past.[66]

Vallgårda, Alexander, and Olsen write about how considering emotions in relation to children allows us 'to explore how childhood emotional formation [is] tied in with the marking of social identities'.[67] The emotional formation in Poole's article connects love with care and the production of happiness for others. The emphasis on loving thoughts, prayers, and work to clear away loneliness and darkness indicates the importance of children's altruistic motivations to help others rather than thinking of any self-interest. A series of short, declarative sentences remind readers of the positive emotional aspects of their role to offset the negative emotions experienced by those who are less fortunate. As Poole writes,

> Work away, dear little living sunbeams! Do your bright part in cheering darker lives than your own! Think of our Homes and Hospitals, with their blind, crippled or sick inmates. Remember every young Companion is working for one purpose – that of brightening these sorrowful lives.[68]

In this article, the child is unquestionably constructed as a charitable worker who both understands their role and the urgency of

110   Philanthropy in Children's Periodicals, 1840–1930

the need to help others through their participation in the Young Helpers' League. Their sunbeam work will brighten sad lives.

The narrative focus on transforming sadness to hope is embedded throughout *Young Helpers' League Magazine* and was at the heart of Barnardo's charity. In Susan Ash's detailed exploration of Barnardo's charitable efforts, she asserts that he deployed many similar strategies in materials aimed at adults and at children, one of which is his concept of 'the open door ... as a multifaceted metaphor both to characterize and to promote his version of philanthropy in a crowded charity market'.[69] She also argues that Barnardo's storytelling practices are deployed 'as a form of direct appeal' in his 'true fiction'.[70] One story included in the magazine that employs this emotional arc comes from Barnardo himself. In '"My First Arab", or How I Began My Life's work', Barnardo relates the story of opening his first home for children.[71] He describes meeting a boy who had no home or family and wished only to spend the night at Barnardo's Ragged School. The boy has 'a small, spare, stunted frame, clad in miserable rags – loathsome from their dirt – without either shirt, shoes or stocking ... I could see he was far poorer' than any of the other children attending the school.[72] His appearance causes an 'acute sense of pain' for his listener and his truthful sharing of his unfortunate circumstances are a revelation for Barnardo, a point to which he returns repeatedly. Young Jim's orphan status is established early; he has never known his father, and his mother died five years earlier. He also knows nothing of God, for he is a 'poor little heathen child ... needing as much as any other child of Adam the solace and comfort' of religious faith.[73] Jim takes Barnardo to find other boys like him, where he soon realises 'the terrible fact that they were all *absolutely homeless and destitute*'.[74] The first-person narrative encourages reader identification with Barnardo as he explains the pain of this discovery and how his heart beats 'with compassion for these unhappy lads'.[75] He urges Jim not to wake the others because to hear their stories – 'of misery, of destitution, of suffering, of loneliness, of cruelty, perchance of crime and sin' – is more than he can bear to think of.[76]

Barnardo's pain comes from being unable to help, but the situation is different for the readers of *Young Helpers' League Magazine*. The temporal shift of this story from the past – in which nothing had yet been done to solve this suffering – is juxtaposed with the readers' knowledge that the magazine is the embodiment of the

Charitable Motivation   III

support that Barnardo has provided over the years. His story concludes with the facts related to this charitable work, announcing that the Home in Stepney has been enlarged to accommodate 400 boys and the Village Home for girls shelters nearly 1,000 girls; a total of 26,000 children have been 'snatched from positions of privation or danger, and brought under the potent sway of Christian love'.[77] Although he is confident that God will 'supply the wants of the ever-growing family' of nearly 5,000 children currently under his care, the subtext is that the child readers of the magazine will come to his aid. The emotional journey that Barnardo relates, from his pain and sadness at the terrible circumstances of Jim's life to the happiness and satisfaction of establishing a successful charity to assist poor children, is a model for the young readers. Although their charitable efforts might begin, as Barnardo's did, '[i]n a small way', they too can make a big impact on other children's lives.[78]

These types of narratives were not always factually correct, although they contributed to the feelings of pity that Barnardo was hoping to produce among young readers. As Lydia Murdoch explains,

> The common phrases used to describe poor children accented their alleged separation from parents and lack of connection to established, stable communities. They were 'waifs and strays', or 'nobody's children', or 'street arabs' who wandered nomadically through the urban landscape without homes or any kind of domestic life.[79]

By telling a particular kind of story about the waif in need of charitable assistance, Barnardo could hope to inspire his young middle-class readers to feelings of pity in ways that were consistent with late nineteenth-century ideas about social welfare and that encouraged specific actions that would help others. A protagonist's background in a narrative, then, 'was not simply a fictional representation separate from social reality, but a tool for ordering and understanding society'.[80] Although I make an argument for children's agency as charitable donors in the previous chapter, this agency is only within clearly defined boundaries that assert the individual's responsibility to help while never suggesting structural change to alleviate the causes of poverty. As Murdoch suggests, philanthropists 'produced narratives that focused on individual and family pathologies' instead of broader structural causes.[81]

112   Philanthropy in Children's Periodicals, 1840–1930

'My First Arab' mobilises the tropes and narrative structures that Murdoch identifies as melodrama, which involved 'a stark division between unambiguously good and evil forces'.[82] This melodrama serves 'as a tool to structure the details of child poverty in a manner that would resonate with the public'.[83] Seth Koven makes a related point in his discussion of the arbitration hearing prompted by rumours impinging Barnardo's integrity. At the heart of these rumours was a critique of Barnardo's 'artistic fictions' consisting of a small number of staged photographs depicting a waif before and after entering the Home, in which the images were not entirely accurate.[84] Barnardo's photography has been discussed in detail elsewhere, and these types of photographs do not appear in *Young Helpers' League Magazine*.[85] They are mentioned here because they are relevant to the point this chapter makes about the emotional impact of the narratives and illustrations that do appear in the magazine. According to Koven, Barnardo anticipated that these comparative images 'would evoke different responses among the rich and poor' in which the rich 'would make generous donations to assist the work' and the poor would be encouraged about the possibilities for 'moral and physical elevation'.[86] Brian Maidment and Aled Jones suggest that the images were understood by editors and proprietors to assist 'in negotiating social values' to reinforce 'such cherished ideas as the domestic, temperance, and self-improvement through a range of visual tropes and codes available even to barely literate readers'.[87] *Young Helpers' League Magazine* was unlikely to have been read by poor children, but the implied middle-class readers were expected to respond positively and generously to these kinds of contrasting depictions in which the poor waif is transformed through their interactions with the charity. Ubiquitous in the press at this time, these images would have been understood by poor and well-to-do readers of any age. Ash argues that Barnardo 'used a repertoire of images and narrative, structured particularly around a fraught configuration of work and play', to recruit child workers.[88] While I concur that charitable activities are often figured as work, a point to which I return below, and indeed the 'Sunbeam' article is evidence of this, my interest in the emotional and affective registers of the magazine contents is equally important. The emotional impact of the content inspired young people's charitable giving.

Using illustrations

From its first numbers, *Young Helpers' League Magazine* was highly illustrated, featuring numerous line drawings and eventually black-and-white photographs, but by 1897 it includes multiple full-page colour plates in each issue. These plates always depict an element from one of the accompanying stories and are intended to bring the narrative to visual life. These colourful illustrations reinforce the emotional language of the story, which is typically written to direct readers towards specific interpretations of the image/text pairings that reinforce both the privileged middle-class position of the implied reader and the need for both Barnardo's and the reader's charitable efforts.

'Houseless and Homeless', appearing in the 1902 volume, interpolates the implied reader into the emotion of need and the reality of charitable giving. The story begins with the word 'EV-ICT-ED' and the imagined reader wondering about the meaning of the word. According to the narrator, 'It has nothing to do with any part of your life ... The only place you are likely to learn of it is in the dictionary.'[89] The middle-class reader will never know anything about being evicted from their home, so the narrator invites them to 'please look at the illustration' (see Fig. 4.1) and directs them to '[s]ee the chain and padlock on the door [where] once that little family lived'.[90] The 'few things that helped to make the house a home have been bundled out to the pavement', and the illustration depicts the small number of belongings sitting on the street. The mother, looking haggard, holds the youngest child while two older children stand around her. Only the father is criticised; he is 'not worthy of the name' as he has deserted the family.[91] Poverty 'was increasingly read as a moral failure', and accordingly the reader is encouraged 'to search for the moral failings and vices to which this suffering might be attributed'.[92] Blame is attributed to the father, as the mother is homeless 'through no fault of her own' and is now 'an outcast on the weary streets of dreary London'.[93] The language used to describe the mother emphasises her unfortunate, and hopeless, circumstances.

The intent of this story and illustration are not solely to depict 'such sad cases of destitution and misery', although readers may wonder about its purpose.[94] Barnardo explains that 'it would have been heartless to produce this picture' merely to explain the meaning of eviction and then invites readers to consider the

Fig. 4.1 'Turned Out!', *Young Helpers' League Magazine*, 1901–2, 93.

Charitable Motivation   115

question of why it has been included. His answer – '[i]n order to show the value of applied sympathy' – informs readers of the meaning that they are supposed to take away.[95] On discovering the eldest boy begging, an image of which is inset in the larger illustration, Barnardo found that the mother could just manage to support herself if he was able to take the three children, 'So what else could he do but increase the largest family in the world by three?'[96] The story is resolved, with Barnardo posing yet another rhetorical question: '[I]s it not satisfactory to know that he is enabled to do the right thing at the right time?'[97] The reader is reminded that 'without friends' such as Young Helpers' League Companions, this assistance would not be possible. Thus, dismay and sadness are transformed in the narrative to satisfaction about doing the right thing. It may be Barnardo himself who discovered and saved the family, but this action is enabled by the contributions made by Young Helpers' League friends who are never at risk of eviction and homelessness.

While the image in 'Houseless and Homeless' is focused on the circumstances prior to receiving assistance from Barnardo's, on the next page is another story, 'In the Gordon Ward, Her Majesty's Hospital', with an accompanying illustration depicting poor children who are currently patients in the hospital. The central image (see Fig. 4.2) features Jimmy sitting up in a bed with crisp, white sheets, tiny toy soldiers on top of a book lying on his lap, and a bird resting on his hand. At the head of the bed is a sign reading 'Young Helpers' League Wellington Cot'.[98] The narrator once again uses second-person address to ask, 'Would you [like to] know Jimmy's story?'[99] 'Not long ago,' the narrator continues, 'he was rescued from a poor home, where he lay sick and ill, and devoid of proper care and nursing.'[100] After he 'became a *protégé* of the Young Helpers' League all this was changed ... [S]urrounded by love and tenderness, his pain and weakness lessened day by day, until a faint rose flush of returning health chased away the pallor of sickness.'[101] Jimmy is 'as happy as the day is long' with his return to health, and soon comes the 'glad day' when he can dress and play about in the ward.[102] In the illustration and the story, the successes of the charity are explicitly stated. Even the caption of the illustration, 'What Our Leaguers Work For', situates this narrative as a goal for the charity, in which the poor and sick are transformed into healthy, happy children through the Young Helpers' League support of the hospital.

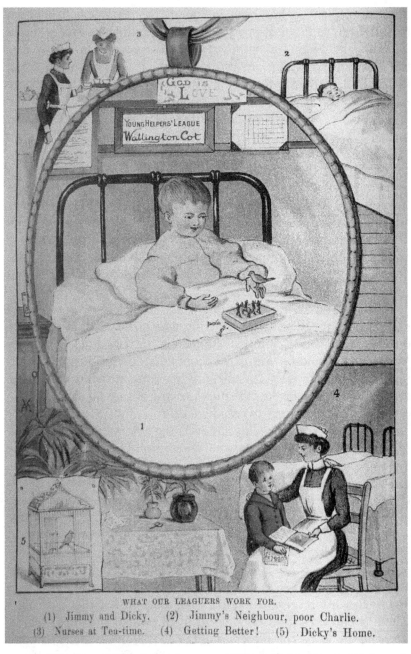

Fig. 4.2 'What Our Leaguers Work For', *Young Helpers' League Magazine*, 1901–2, 96.

The material support provided by members of the league is evident on the facing page. Between the story 'In the Gordon Ward' and its illustration is the first of five pages of the 'Cot Chronicle'. Like the reports of the inhabitants of the 'Aunt Judy's Magazine Cot' that were discussed in Chapter 2, the 'Cot Chronicle' reports on the patients currently being assisted through the Young Helpers' League Habitations. Unlike *Aunt Judy's Magazine*, which raised funds for a single cot (in perpetuity) at a time, the 'Cot Chronicle' provides evidence of a different kind of charity work, in which each habitation was required to raise at least £30 per annum to continue funding their named cot. By 1902, the magazine contains details of the inhabitants in 339 cots in multiple institutions, including Her Majesty's Hospital, the Babies' Castle, the girls' Village Home in Ilford, and homes in Felixstowe, Bradford, and Birkdale.[103]

Cot inhabitants are described in consistent ways that emphasise, where possible, their improving health and sunny dispositions. In Cot 195, named for the Gravesend Habitation and located at Babies' Castle, is a young boy whose situation is getting better:

> Alfie goes on his happy way, improving and developing as a small boy should, but though quite strong looking he takes cold easily, and Sister never allows herself to forget what manner of little men were the twins in their miserable early infancy.[104]

Alfie's twin brother Duggles occupies another cot, Nottingham No. 2, at Babies' Castle and is 'growing rather fast, and ... is a living witness to the wonders that Castle care and tending can accomplish'.[105] These reports hearken back to an earlier one in 1901, in which 'Alfie and Duggles are still at the Castle, as much alike as ever, and a wonderful little pair, considering what they were at times'.[106] Their situation was evidently quite poor when they first arrived in Barnardo's care. Other reports suggest the transitory nature of this care, such as Cot 206, the Bickley cot at Her Majesty's Hospital, where Billy

> is so far better that he is now under the care of a country foster-mother. His place here is occupied by Percy Robinson, who has undergone an operation on his troublesome knee that seems likely to leave him as active as a fifteen-year-old, healthy lad should be.[107]

118   Philanthropy in Children's Periodicals, 1840–1930

Not only do these reports emphasise the quality of the care and its potential to restore good health to poor children through the careful attention of nursing sisters, fresh air and food, companionship, and improved circumstances, but they also provide evidence of the hope provided to young patients and the charity's success. The magazine committed multiple pages to the 'Cot Chronicle' in each issue in addition to the time it would have taken to write, consolidate, and typeset the reports. By 1905, the 'Cot Chronicle' was published by location rather than being sorted numerically by cot number, which was presumably a more efficient reporting method.

Nonetheless, publishing the 'Cot Chronicle' alongside illustrated stories provides direct examples of how a young person inspired by these reports or by other content in the magazine might be able to contribute. One such example is an illustrated story entitled 'How Alice Helped'. The didacticism of the story and illustration are explicit. Captioned 'A Hint for Companions', the illustration is a collage of four images beginning in the top left with Alice Grey gesturing towards a poster for a Young Helpers' League meeting announcing an address by Barnardo (see Fig. 4.3). The main image, with a rectangular border to make it stand out, is in the bottom left and features Alice at the bazaar she has helped organise as she sells a doll to a well-dressed woman. Extending across the top-left corner is a string of coins to indicate the money raised by Alice through her participation in the Young Helpers' League. On the bottom corner is a portion of a bank cheque in the amount of £10 6s 3d written out to Barnardo.

The accompanying story describes Alice's encounter with the Barnardo's charity as the beginning of her 'life work'.[108] She already had 'a desire to do some good for others' but had not yet found 'a particular outlet for her energies'.[109] When her mother agrees to take her to hear Barnardo speak at a league meeting, 'so keenly was [Alice's] heart touched by the sorrows of the sick and crippled Waif Children, that she was filled with longing to aid them'.[110] The narrative depicts the transformation from emotional response to charitable activity that lies at the heart of this chapter. It helps, perhaps, that Alice is already seeking an outlet for her charitable work, yet the story demonstrates the direct connection between emotion and action. Even if the connection between emotion as a motivation for action can be unclear, the Victorians believed in the connection between them and mobilised these rhetorical strategies

Charitable Motivation 119

Fig. 4.3 'A Hint for Companions', *Young Helpers' League Magazine*, 1901–2, 101.

120   Philanthropy in Children's Periodicals, 1840–1930

to encourage charitable behaviours. The money that Alice raises is 'destined to bring sunshine and happiness into the life of many a little prisoner of pain'.[111] Like the sunbeam, money can also create joy for the poor and sick. Moreover, Alice's charitable work is designed to encourage others. Like some of the other stories appearing in the magazine, this one also includes a call-to-action question. The author Clarissa asks: 'Does not Alice's example inspire you to go and do likewise?'[112] The implied middle-class reader is able to do the same charitable work that Alice has done and, like her, will be thanked for this 'loving service' through God's acknowledgement.[113]

Middle-class children are regularly shown how their privileged upbringing offers opportunities for charitable work. In another similar story, a much younger girl, Dora, receives a shilling from her father and considers how she will spend it. Her mother reminds her of what she recently learned about 'pleasing the King of Heaven', although Dora remarks that '*my* little hands couldn't do much'.[114] Her worries about her inability to perform charitable work are soon replaced by pleasure as her mother proposes a 'delightful plan' in which Dora shares her league collecting box with some visiting women.[115] The narrator explains that, 'To the child's delight, each visitor dropped some coin into her little box', and Dora is asked to explain about the league.[116] Her response, that 'Mother says it is for boys and girls in happy homes, to help the poor little children who are sick and crippled', foregrounds the maternal role in establishing the charity as a cause in ways that are somewhat at odds with the magazine's overall objectives to motivate children to take action.[117] The story places responsibility for identifying the cause and doing work on its behalf with adult caregivers, and it culminates with the visitors agreeing to run a bazaar. Unlike in the previous story, when Alice was the instigator of the charitable work, here the younger girl is directed by adults. Nonetheless, Dora is the inspiration for and the voice of the charitable cause, and she is pleased at the success of her 'childish efforts'.[118] The accompanying image emphasises Dora's young age. She wears a pretty, white dress with a blue sash and matching blue ribbon in her blond curls and holds a small box with the letters 'Y. H. L.' inscribed on the front. Her mother sits next to her, and the three well-dressed ladies are watching her intently, with one leaning forward to put a coin into the box. Dora's work as an agent of the charity is sufficient since by sharing its goals and asking others with the means to support it, she can indirectly fundraise.

The reward for charitable work is provided through God's blessing. The religious ideology that '[i]t is more blessed to give than to receive' underpins many of the stories in the magazine.[119] 'Giving and Receiving' begins with Laura Maynard memorising a hymn:

> Little deeds of kindness,
>   Little acts of love,
> Make this world an Eden
>   Like the Heaven above.[120]

Although she knows the words by heart, her mother is concerned that she may not fully understand their meaning since, as the narrator explains, although Laura is 'sweet and loveable', her one weak point is *'selfishness'*.[121] Later that day, Laura and a friend ignore the 'little bare-footed waif' sitting on the doorstep of a baker's shop and pay little attention to the 'hungry plea' in his eyes. Suddenly, however, she recalls the verse she learned earlier and retraces her steps to give the boy one of her cakes. The accompanying colour illustration depicts the young, well-dressed girl handing a cake to the poor, shoeless boy wearing a torn shirt. She pauses long enough to discover the boy's story of his sick, widowed mother who is unable to work and the family's destitution. The story concludes by explaining that '[b]righter days have dawned' for Jack and his mother since, '[t]hanks to Mrs. Maynard's kindness and care, the poor widow grew strong and well again, and able to work for herself and her little lad'.[122] Like Dora in the previous story, Laura is thrilled to have been able to help: 'Oh, mother! . . . how happy it makes one to do things for others!'[123] Mrs Maynard is thankful that Laura has learned the lesson that it is better to give than to receive. Laura's charity is more direct than Dora's insofar as she has specifically helped a young boy and his mother, but both girls have learned the importance of sharing their wealth to help others and the happiness that results from such efforts.

Children's contributions

Children's fictional contributions to *Young Helpers' League Magazine* also contain a similar narrative arc that begins with an

122   Philanthropy in Children's Periodicals, 1840–1930

emotional response and ends with charitable work. In Barnardo's request for contributions, he explains that he is seeking original stories that are 'marked by good literary style and a decidedly Christian tone'.[124] Each month the winning story will be awarded one guinea, with a consolation prize of ten shillings. Within a few months, the winning story was also being published in the magazine, offering children the opportunity to see their contributions in print. These contributions are an important vehicle through which readerships are created in children's periodicals. Pooley describes the efforts of regional newspapers to attract child readers through 'participatory columns' in which children were actively encouraged to submit articles.[125] Likewise, in her examination of New Zealand children's columns, Anna Gilderdale argues for a new type of social network in which the distinctions 'between real and imagined connection, between public and private, and between the competing meanings of anonymity, pseudonymity, and celebrity' are blurred.[126] The prizing of children's contributions produced a competitive environment and ensured the quality of the submissions printed on the page while also reflecting the ideological complexities of framing and administering competitions for young readers.[127]

In *Young Helpers' League Magazine*, the child writers adhered to submission guidelines, and the winning entries reflect their ideas of storytelling and capacity to deploy appropriate and engaging narrative strategies. They also offered an opportunity to display the charitable emotion appearing elsewhere in the magazine's pages. Yet the types of content they were reading elsewhere limited the child writers as well. The waif story was seemingly so ubiquitous that Barnardo inserts an important corrective to his instructions when he explains to potential contributors some months later that, although stories 'should be *bright* and *lively*, and definitely *Christian* in tone ... we do *not* want Stories necessarily about Waif children'.[128] This strong wording suggests that the pervasive narrative arc that appears throughout the magazine and elsewhere in children's print culture had such a significant influence on child readers that they, consciously or otherwise, were repeating narrative structures already present in its pages. Moreover, given that the writers likely had minimal first-hand knowledge of poor children, these stories presumably lacked originality.

'Lady Rosamund' by Theodora may have won a prize, then, because it focused not on waif children but on the charitable

Charitable Motivation   123

motivations of a young girl. This story reflects on the need for true sacrifice in charitable work after Dorothy brings half a crown from her father for the church collection plate. In the week's sermon, the clergyman spoke about giving and sacrifice, such that Dorothy had tears in her eyes as she dropped the coin in the plate '[f]or the bright piece of money had cost her nothing to give'.[129] She later decides to sacrifice her most beloved doll, Lady Rosamund, to 'some poor little girl who had no toys, or anything to make her happy'.[130] Inspired by her sacrifice of something that means so much to her, Dorothy's parents also consent to their older daughter's 'great wish' to become a missionary.[131] The story concludes by relating how, '[i]n a miserable attic, a little crippled girl is made happy all day long by the presence of "Lady Rosamund"', while in 'far away India, the face of many a poor girl wife brightens at the sight of the sweet-faced Englishwomen'.[132] Back in 'a happy English home a father and mother, and their little girl "rejoice, in that they offered willingly"'.[133] This line from 1 Chronicles 29:9 emphasises the importance of giving because of necessity rather than for convenience, a sentiment consistent with the magazine's ethos. In addition, it offers a hopeful conclusion in which charity has helped to improve people's lives.

The children's written contributions reflect the importance of being of good character. Two of the stories discussed in the previous section emphasise the importance of giving as a form of God's work. In the readers' contributions, emotion is also intertwined with charity. In 'Lena's Lesson', a prize-winning story by Carissima, 'spoiled, wayward' Lena refuses to do any plain sewing for the local bazaar because she prefers fancy work. Her guardian Mrs Brown is concerned because young people who do as they please 'grow up selfish and arrogant, unloveable and horrid'.[134] The sixteen-year-old girl is perhaps beginning to see that 'life [is] a responsibility, which ought not to be taken lightly', yet she fails to act in a charitable manner when a young girl falls and breaks her arm at a garden party. Lena balks because little Elsie is 'so dirty . . . and sticky'.[135] Miss Bright, the new schoolteacher, comes to the rescue, and the young curate transfers his affection to the more capable and charitable young woman. Mrs Brown is outspoken in her condemnation of Lena:

[Y]ou have lost the love of a good man through want to those qualities which he admires . . . he does not want only a pretty face, but the

124 Philanthropy in Children's Periodicals, 1840–1930

character which abides when the face is faded. This has been a hard lesson for you . . . but I am not sorry it has happened, since I trust God will . . . open your eyes to your lack of him.[136]

In the brief conclusion, Lena's eyes are opened and 'now she is filling her life full of useful deeds and helping words. But she ever regrets the years she wasted in her youth in selfish frivolity.'[137] Emotion and charity are operating differently in this story. Lena's regret for her lack of charitable outlook is the dominant motif that hearkens back to earlier mid-nineteenth-century ideas about women and charity.[138] Yet the idea of selfishness as anathema to a charitable perspective is consistent with many of the stories in *Young Helpers' League Magazine*.

Conclusion

This chapter has attempted to grapple with the question of charitable motivation by exploring how stories and illustrations work together to provide an emotional framework for charitable work. It has shown how children were part of a charitable field in which charity work is understood and expected from readers of the magazine. The editorial strategy was to consistently depict middle-class children who were expected to feel pity for poor, neglected children and happiness when the poor children are provided with charitable support that relieves their circumstances. The colour illustrations accompanying many of the stories reinforce the binary between pitiful and benevolent children and directs readerly attention to the expectations that well-to-do children will do appropriate charitable work. Aimed at middle-class children with the money or the connections to raise more funds, *Young Helpers' League Magazine* explicitly identified its charitable objectives, used emotion to motivate young people, and recorded its charitable successes through regular reports about cot inhabitants. The types of stories included in the magazine were so consistent in their use of emotion that child writers incorporated similar narrative strategies exploring the transformation from sadness to hope through charitable activities.

Notes

1. Corbett, *Nation Builders*, 16.

Charitable Motivation   125

2. *Dr. Barnardo's Homes for Orphan and Destitute Children of the Waif Class Annual Report*, 1893, 27.

3. *Annual Report*, 27. Emphasis in original.

4. *Annual Report*, 27–8.

5. *Annual Report*, 28. Portions of this chapter were first published by Kristine Moruzi, 'Charity, Affect, and Waif Novels', in *Affect, Emotion, and Children's Literature: Representation and Socialisation in Texts for Children and Young Adults*, edited by Kristine Moruzi, Michelle J. Smith, and Elizabeth Bullen. © 2018, Taylor & Francis. Reproduced with permission of The Licensor through PLSclear.

6. Hugh Cunningham, *Children and Childhood in Western Society Since 1500* (London: Taylor & Francis, 2020), 55.

7. Anna Davin, 'Waif Stories in Late Nineteenth-Century England', *History Workshop Journal* 52 (2001): 67.

8. Davin, 'Waif Stories', 70.

9. Davin, 'Waif Stories', 70.

10. Davin, 'Waif Stories', 69.

11. Cunningham, *Children of the Poor*, 133.

12. Shurlee Swain, 'Sweet Childhood Lost: Idealized Images of Childhood in the British Child Rescue Literature', *Journal of the History of Childhood and Youth* 2, no. 2 (Spring 2009): 201.

13. Shurlee Swain and Margot Hillel, *Child, Nation, Race and Empire: Child Rescue Discourse, England, Canada and Australia, 1850–1915* (Manchester: Manchester University Press, 2010), 4.

14. Swain and Hillel, *Child, Nation, Race and Empire*, 4.

15. Davin, 'Waif Stories', 92.

16. Gillian Avery, *Childhood's Pattern: A Study of Heroes and Heroines of Children's Fiction, 1770–1950* (London: Hodder and Stoughton, 1975), 112.

17. Davin, 'Waif Stories', 92.

18. See Moruzi, 'Charity, Affect, and Waif Novels', 33–51.

19. See Richard S. Lazarus, *Emotion and Adaptation* (New York and Oxford: Oxford University Press, 1991), especially Chapter 3, for his discussion of the connection between emotion and motivation.

20. C. Daniel Batson, *The Altruism Question: Toward a Social-Psychological Answer* (New York: Psychology Press, 1991), 2.

21. Batson, *The Altruism Question*, 2.

22. Batson, *The Altruism Question*, 2.

23. Kidd, 'Philanthropy', 180.

24. Kidd, 'Philanthropy', 184.

25. Kidd, 'Philanthropy', 191.
26. Kidd, 'Philanthropy', 184.
27. Gertrude Himmelfarb, *Poverty and Compassion: The Moral Imagination of the Late Victorians* (New York: Vintage, 1991), 183.
28. Frank Christianson, *Philanthropy in British and American Fiction: Dickens, Hawthorne, Eliot, and Howells* (Edinburgh: Edinburgh University Press, 2007), 62–3.
29. Kelly J. Mays, 'The Disease of Reading and Victorian Periodicals', in *Literature in the Marketplace: Nineteenth-Century British Publishing and Reading Practices*, ed. John O. Jordan and Robert L. Patten (Cambridge: Cambridge University Press, 1995), 165.
30. Michelle J. Smith and Kristine Moruzi, 'The Child Reader: Children's Literary Culture in the Nineteenth Century', in *Literary Cultures and Nineteenth-Century Childhoods*, ed. Michelle J. Smith and Kristine Moruzi (Cham: Palgrave Macmillan, 2023), 55.
31. Martha Nussbaum, *Cultivating Humanity: A Classical Defense of Reform in Liberal Education* (Cambridge: Harvard University Press, 1997), 85, 88.
32. Nussbaum, *Cultivating Humanity*, 90.
33. Kerry Mallan, 'Empathy: Narrative Empathy and Children's Literature', in *(Re)Imagining the World: Children's Literature Response to Changing Times*, ed. Yan Wu, Kerry Mallan, and Rod McGillis (Berlin: Springer, 2013), 105.
34. Suzanne Keen, 'A Theory of Narrative Empathy', *Narrative*, 14, no. 3 (2006): 214.
35. See Patrick Colm Hogan, *What Literature Teaches Us About Emotion* (Cambridge: Cambridge University Press, 2011).
36. Elizabeth Bullen, Kristine Moruzi, and Michelle J. Smith, 'Children's Literature and the Affective Turn: Affect, Emotion, Empathy', in *Affect, Emotion and Children's Literature: Representation and Socialisation in Texts for Children and Young Adults*, ed. Kristine Moruzi, Michelle J. Smith, and Elizabeth Bullen (New York: Routledge, 2017), 9.
37. Karen Vallgårda, Kristine Alexander, and Stephanie Olsen, 'Emotions and the Global Politics of Childhood', in *Childhood, Youth and Emotions in Modern History: National, Colonial and Global Perspectives*, ed. Stephanie Olsen (Houndmills: Palgrave Macmillan, 2015), 20. See also Stephanie Olsen, 'Children's Emotional Formations in Britain, Canada, Australia, and New Zealand Around the First World War', *Cultural and Social History* 17, no. 5 (2020): 643–57.

38. Moruzi, 'Charity, Affect, and Waif Novels', 36.
39. Endpaper, *Young Helpers' League Magazine*, np.
40. Endpaper, np.
41. Christianson, *Philanthropy*, 54.
42. Thomas Barnardo, 'Waif and His Friends', *Young Helpers' League Magazine*, January 1892–December 1894, 4.
43. Barnardo, 'Waif', 4.
44. Barnardo, 'Waif', 6.
45. Barnardo, 'Waif', 15.
46. Barnardo, 'Waif', 15.
47. Barnardo, 'Waif', 16.
48. Barnardo, 'Waif', 49, 50.
49. Eva Travers Evered Poole, 'What One Little Sunbeam Did!', *Young Helpers' League Magazine*, January 1892–December 1894, 53.
50. Poole, 'Sunbeam', 53.
51. Poole, 'Sunbeam', 53.
52. Poole, 'Sunbeam', 53.
53. Poole, 'Sunbeam', 53.
54. Poole, 'Sunbeam', 53.
55. Poole, 'Sunbeam', 54.
56. Poole, 'Sunbeam', 54. Emphasis in original.
57. Poole, 'Sunbeam', 54.
58. Poole, 'Sunbeam', 54.
59. Poole, 'Sunbeam', 54.
60. Poole, 'Sunbeam', 54. Emphasis in original.
61. Poole, 'Sunbeam', 54.
62. Poole, 'Sunbeam', 55.
63. Poole, 'Sunbeam', 55. Emphasis in original.
64. Poole, 'Sunbeam', 55.
65. Poole, 'Sunbeam', 55.
66. Poole, 'Sunbeam', 55. Emphasis in original.
67. Karen Vallgårda, Kristine Alexander, and Stephanie Olsen, 'Emotions', 12.
68. Poole, 'Sunbeam', 55–6.
69. Susan Ash, *Funding Philanthropy: Dr. Barnardo's Metaphors, Narratives and Spectacles* (Liverpool: Liverpool University Press, 2016), 4.
70. Ash, *Funding Philanthropy*, 5.
71. Lindsay Smith explores how 'discourses of race and class are played out on the homespun scale of the East End of London',

128   Philanthropy in Children's Periodicals, 1840–1930

where they 'rehearse and modify other versions of colonial encounter in the period' in 'The Shoe-Black to the Crossing Sweeper: Victorian Street Arabs and Photography', *Textual Practice* 10, no. 1 (1996): 29.

72. Thomas Barnardo, '"My First Arab", or How I Began My Life's Work', *Young Helpers' League Magazine*, January 1892–December 1894, 3.

73. Barnardo, '"My First Arab"', 23.

74. Barnardo, '"My First Arab"', 37. Emphasis in original.

75. Barnardo, '"My First Arab"', 37.

76. Barnardo, '"My First Arab"', 37.

77. Barnardo, '"My First Arab"', 38.

78. Barnardo, '"My First Arab"', 38.

79. Murdoch, *Imagined Orphans*, 1.

80. Murdoch, *Imagined Orphans*, 16.

81. Murdoch, *Imagined Orphans*, 14.

82. Murdoch, *Imagined Orphans*, 15.

83. Murdoch, *Imagined Orphans*, 17.

84. Seth Koven, *Slumming: Sexual and Social Politics in Victorian London* (Princeton: Princeton University Press, 2004), 122.

85. See Clare Rose, 'Raggedness and Respectability in Barnardo's Archive', *Childhood in the Past: An International Journal*, 1, no. 1 (2009): 136–50, Smith, 'The Shoe-Black to the Crossing Sweeper', and Koven, *Slumming*. Monica Flegel also discusses how the National Society for the Prevention of Cruelty to Children used photography to provide 'evidence of its effectiveness in combating cruelty to children' ('Changing Faces: The NSPCC and the Use of Photography in the Construction of Cruelty to Children', *Victorian Periodicals Review* 39, no 1 (Spring 2006): 7).

86. Koven, *Slumming*, 123.

87. Brian Maidment and Aled Jones, 'Illustration', in *Dictionary of Nineteenth-Century Journalism*, ed. Laurel Brake and Marysa Demoor (London: Academia Press and the British Library, 2009), 305.

88. Ash, *Funding Philanthropy*, 133.

89. 'Houseless and Homeless', *Young Helpers' League Magazine*, January 1901–December 1902, 91 [91–2].

90. 'Houseless and Homeless', 91.

91. 'Houseless and Homeless', 91.

92. Lori Merish, 'The Poverty of Sympathy', in *Philanthropic Discourse in Anglo-American Literature, 1850–1920*, ed. Frank

Q. Christianson and Leslee Thorne-Murphy (Bloomington: Indiana University Press, 2017), 15.

93. 'Houseless and Homeless', 92.
94. 'Houseless and Homeless', 92.
95. 'Houseless and Homeless', 92.
96. 'Houseless and Homeless', 92.
97. 'Houseless and Homeless', 92.
98. 'In the Gordon Ward, Her Majesty's Hospital', *Young Helpers' League Magazine*, January 1901–December 1902, 96.
99. 'In the Gordon Ward', 94.
100. 'In the Gordon Ward', 94.
101. 'In the Gordon Ward', 94.
102. 'In the Gordon Ward', 94.
103. By 1902, the high number of cots meant that the report was lengthy. Rather than dedicating all of a single issue to the report, it was divided into three sections and printed over three months. Her Majesty's Hospital provided medical care for Barnardo's children and was opened in 1888 in Stepney Causeway. The Village Home first opened with 1876 with thirteen cottages, eventually growing to include more than sixty cottages and housing approximately 1,500 girls. Babies' Castle was opened in 1884 in Kent and housed babies and children under the age of six. Felixstowe opened in 1886 for convalescents. Two homes in Bradford and Birkdale were opened in the 1890s for permanently disabled children. See Peter Higginbotham, *Children's Homes: A History of Institutional Care for Britain's Young* (Barnsley: Pen & Sword Books, 2017).
104. 'Cot Chronicle', *Young Helpers' League Magazine*, January 1901–December 1902, 95.
105. 'Cot Chronicle', 95.
106. 'Cot Chronicle', *Young Helpers' League Magazine*, January 1901–December 1902, 181.
107. 'Cot Chronicle', 95.
108. Clarissa, 'How Alice Helped', *Young Helpers' League Magazine*, January 1901–December 1902, 100.
109. Clarissa, 'How Alice Helped', 100.
110. Clarissa, 'How Alice Helped', 100.
111. Clarissa, 'How Alice Helped', 102.
112. Clarissa, 'How Alice Helped', 102.
113. Clarissa, 'How Alice Helped', 102.
114. 'The Three-Letter League', *Young Helpers' League Magazine*, January 1901–December 1902, 139, 138. Emphasis in original.

130   Philanthropy in Children's Periodicals, 1840–1930

115. 'The Three-Letter League', 138.
116. 'The Three-Letter League', 138.
117. 'The Three-Letter League', 138.
118. 'The Three-Letter League', 140.
119. 'The Three-Letter League', 140.
120. Clarissa, 'Giving and Receiving', *Young Helpers' League Magazine*, January 1901–December 1902, 140.
121. Clarissa, 'Giving and Receiving', 140. Emphasis in original.
122. Clarissa, 'Giving and Receiving', 140.
123. Clarissa, 'Giving and Receiving', 140.
124. 'Contributions Wanted!', *Young Helpers' League Magazine*, January 1899–December 1900, 177.
125. Pooley, 'Children's Writing', 79.
126. Anna Gilderdale, 'Where "Taniwah" Met "Colonial Girl": The Social Uses of the *Non de Plume* in New Zealand Youth Correspondence Pages, 1880–1920', in *Children's Voices from the Past: New Historical and Interdisciplinary Perspectives*, ed. Kristine Moruzi, Nell Musgrove, and Carla Pascoe Leahy (Cham: Palgrave Macmillan, 2019), 54.
127. For instance, Beth Rodgers argues that competitions were an important form of community building in girls' magazines in the late nineteenth century, but that they did not always successfully forge 'a coherent textual identity' for the magazine ('Competing Girlhoods: Competition, Community, and Reader Contribution in *The Girls' Own Paper* and *The Girl's Realm*', *Victorian Periodicals Review* 45, no. 3 (Fall 2012): 277). Lois Burke observes how writing professionally 'was a common ambition of girls' and opportunities to write 'were cultivated in correspondence and competition pages' ('The *Young Woman* and Scotland: The Late-Victorian Writings of Ethel Forster Heddle and Isabella Fyvie Mayor in Girls' Print Culture'. *Scottish Literary Review* 14, no. 1 (Spring/Summer 2022): 56.
128. 'To Authors and Authoresses', *Young Helpers' League Magazine*, January 1901–December 1902, 137. Emphasis in original.
129. 'Theodora', 'Lady Rosamund', *Young Helpers' League Magazine*, January 1901–December 1902, 135.
130. 'Theodora', 'Lady Rosamund', 135.
131. 'Theodora', 'Lady Rosamund', 135.
132. 'Theodora', 'Lady Rosamund', 136.
133. 'Theodora', 'Lady Rosamund', 136.
134. Carissima, 'Lena's Lesson', *Young Helpers' League Magazine*, January 1901–December 1902, 159.

Charitable Motivation 131

135. Carissima, 'Lena's Lesson', 160.
136. Carissima, 'Lena's Lesson', 161.
137. Carissima, 'Lena's Lesson', 161.
138. See Carol Dyhouse, *Girls Growing Up in Late Victorian and Edwardian England* (London: Routledge, 1981); Dorice Williams Elliot, *The Angel Out of the House: Philanthropy and Gender in Nineteenth-Century England* (Charlottesville: University Press of Virginia, 2002), and Prochaska, *Women and Philanthropy*.

5

Charitable Subjectivity

While a great deal of the charitable giving discussed in this book comes from middle-class children, working-class children were also explicitly part of the charitable infrastructure of the nineteenth and twentieth centuries. Some of their giving is elided through the literacy requirements of the periodical press and by the practice of aggregating collections adopted by some organisations, as discussed in Chapter 3. This chapter turns its attention to how working-class and impoverished children were engaged in charitable giving by examining *Ups and Downs* (1895–1914), a Canadian quarterly magazine published by Barnardo's and aimed at British children who had been emigrated to Canada. These British Home Children, as they became known, were the recipients of charity themselves, but were encouraged to send money back to Barnardo's to support other children to emigrate. This magazine reflects understandings of charity and childhood in which all children, regardless of their situation, were encouraged to consider how to help others like themselves. These children occupy multiple subject positions in these periodicals, both as the objects of charity and as charitable donors. This chapter shows how the *Ups and Downs* magazine defined the subjectivities of its child readers before turning to an exploration of the rhetorical manoeuvres employed by the boys and girls who were emigrated to Canada to show how they asserted their identities as the grateful and deserving recipients of charity while also manifesting alternate identities as agents of charitable giving.

The history of child emigration to Canada is well documented.[1] These histories relay the efforts of numerous British charities to emigrate children to Canada, where, it was believed, they would

132

Charitable Subjectivity   133

have significantly better opportunities. These children occupy multiple subject positions in periodicals like *Ups and Downs*, both as the objects of charity and as charitable donors, as they were both the recipients and the givers of financial gifts. How they navigated between these contradictory positions required them to take up what Kendall R. Phillips describes as 'rhetorical maneuvers' that allowed young people to draw upon different subject positions. This chapter explores how the *Ups and Downs* magazine defined the subjectivity of its child readers by first describing the cultural context of children's emigration to Canada and the contrasting opinions of this emigration strategy. This leads to the next section, which discusses the rationale for the establishment of the magazine and how it promoted a narrative of emigration success through its inclusion of excerpts from children's correspondence reporting on how they were adjusting to their new circumstances. These children formed a community of successful emigrants, as shown in the subsequent section, in which they were able to demonstrate their success through their ability to reciprocate the financial gifts they had received and also report on other achievements that demonstrated their acclimatisation to Canada and their growing sense of the new country as home.

The emigration scheme was a response to the increasing number of poor, neglected children in London, and the alternatives sought by British charitable agencies. At the same time, the Canadian government was eager to increase immigration rates to provide more farm hands and domestic servants to consolidate its westward expansion. Children were one stream of a multifaceted immigration strategy that resulted in the emigration of approximately 80,000 children between 1868 and 1925 'to work under indentures as agricultural labourers and domestic servants'.[2] Rural Canada was extolled as a bucolic ideal through which these urban waifs could escape the squalor and hopelessness of the slums.

Barnardo sent the first named Barnardo's party in 1882, and by the end of 1914 had sent 25,485 children to Canada.[3] It was by far the largest emigrator, greatly exceeding the numbers of children sent out by organisations like those run by Maria Rye, Annie Macpherson, Louisa Birt, and William Quarrier. Children were initially housed in a receiving home and then dispersed to farms, originally in Ontario and later in Manitoba. Farmers were invited to apply for a child, and children were typically sent by rail to situations under one of three stages: boarding out; board, clothing,

134 Philanthropy in Children's Periodicals, 1840–1930

and school; or wages.[4] Under 'boarding out', the Canadian master and mistress were paid $5 per month. As the child became more capable, the stage shifted to 'board, clothing, and school' and the master and mistress were expected to cover basic needs for the child and provide some pocket money. At the age of fourteen, the terms shifted to paid work as the child was expected to contribute to the household in significant ways. These funds were paid into a bank account held in trust by Barnardo's for the indentured child.

Although this scheme notionally might have sounded acceptable, and both Canadian and British governments agreed to it, the logistics were complex and not all children thrived in this environment. Some emigrators sent children overseas without parental consent, and children were sometimes told they were orphans despite having family connections, enabling the emigrator to sever family ties to send them overseas. The Canadian government continued to allow juvenile immigration until 1925, when it was finally prohibited after three emigrant children died by suicide.[5] These suicides are clear evidence that the children's circumstances were more complex than some positive accounts in the press might have suggested.

Defining charitable subjectivity

The contradictory positions occupied by emigrant children are defined by their dual roles. To become an emigrant with a child rescue organisation, a child must first be in need of assistance. Yet the support for emigration depended on narratives of emigrant success. How they navigated between these contradictory positions required them to take up what Phillips describes as 'rhetorical maneuvers', which are performed 'at those moments when we choose to violate the proscriptive limits of our subject position and speak differently by drawing upon the resources of another subject position we have occupied'.[6] The movement between these positions is essential for the performance, to use Butler's term, of an identity that is almost simultaneously the grateful recipient of charitable funds and the generous potential donor to the charitable cause. The tension between these two identities can be understood through Stuart Hall's explanation that '[t]he subject assumes different identities at different times, identities which are not unified around a coherent "self".'[7] Indeed, the incoherence of being both in need of and able to fund charitable

Charitable Subjectivity   135

donations can be difficult to reconcile. Within the pages of *Ups and Downs*, the children were understood to require assistance, but also frequently occupied the position of a successful emigrant who was able to help others.

The magazine's contents depict the rhetorical manoeuvres adopted by child correspondents, in which they deftly shifted between the two registers to define their charitable subjectivity. Phillips indicates that a given subject position has boundaries but that those boundaries can be transgressed in the adoption of another position.[8] The discursive nature of this transgression requires the use of language. The movement from one position to another is a form of agency, although it is not always articulated explicitly in relation to charitable activities such as fundraising. It can operate in rhetorical ways such as those described by Elizabeth Hoff-Claussen when she defines 'rhetorical agency' as 'the relative capacity of speech to intervene and effect change'.[9]

Both Phillips and Hoff-Claussen emphasise the possibility of the discursive act of 'speaking'. The rhetorical potential of print enables a shift in identity category from charitable recipient to charitable donor. By writing letters to the Canadian branch of Barnardo's to report on their success, the child correspondents are able to act in both roles simultaneously. Writing to the organisation – and having the portions of the letter printed in the magazine – is possible only because the child writer is first and foremost an emigrant who has received financial assistance to enable their move from England. Not all correspondents demonstrate their subjectivity as donors, but those that refer to their financial obligations understand they have an alternate subjectivity. Blackman et al. explain that '[s]ubjectivity . . . is the experience of the lived multiplicity of positionings. It is historically contingent and is produced through the plays of power/knowledge.'[10] As will be shown, many of the young correspondents understood their multiple positionings and how to deploy them in their letters to demonstrate their charitable subjectivity. This enables, as Phillips remarks, a 'productive tension' between the 'apparent fixity of the subject position and the seeming fluidity of the subjectivity manifested'.[11] The knowledge and expectation of editorial intervention undoubtedly also informs the tension, since the writer would have understood the limits of content and tone that would have been acceptable for publication.

Emigrant children in the press

The periodical press was pivotal in defining the subjectivity of poor children in need to charitable assistance. At its best, this emigration scheme offered hope for valuable, productive members of society. At its worst, however, the scheme was ripe for exploitation either by emigrators who failed to appropriately screen the children for their suitability or by employers who failed in their responsibilities to the young people under their care. This tension is readily apparent in the extensive coverage of juvenile immigration appearing in the Canadian press throughout the duration of the scheme, although it was initially received with some enthusiasm. A 2 October 1875 article in Toronto's *Globe*, for instance, is glowing in its discussion of Maria Rye's efforts to improve the material circumstances of children growing up in poverty. 'Great good has already been effected,' the author explains, and 'still more may reasonably be anticipated if the same course is pursued, and the same carefulness exercised'.[12] Emigration of young people was seen in some quarters as beneficial to both children and the Canadian families who took them in, provided the children were carefully screened as suitable emigrants and the families cared for them appropriately.

Government attention remained focused on the quality of child emigrants and the success of the initiative. The Select Committee of the House of Commons on Immigration and Colonization reported in 1876 that the juvenile immigrants brought out by Rye and Macpherson 'have been carefully placed and are, with very trifling exception, doing well'.[13] The report continues that

> [t]here appears to be no reasonable doubt ... that immigrant children of the class in question [orphaned, homeless, and educated in a training school], if suitably selected and properly placed, will very soon become a permanent and valuable part of the productive population of the country. The encouragement of this class of immigration is worthy of the serious consideration of the government.[14]

Once again, the need for children to be carefully selected, properly trained, and then placed in appropriate circumstances is highlighted. Their economic value to Canada is emphasised through language interpolating the child as 'valuable' and 'productive' subjects who will contribute to the Canadian economy.

Yet these government reports sit alongside allegations of misconduct by adults who were assumed to have a duty of care. Reports of neglect and abuse by those who were legally responsible for the children's care reflect the difficulties of managing children who had been removed from familiar circumstances and ensuring that they were properly treated. That the children did not always behave appropriately is hardly surprising. The reality of farming was undoubtedly far from the emigrant's imagination. As Joy Parr observes, 'No urban child could have anticipated the silence, the solitude, the daunting scale of the Canadian landscape.'[15] On 27 December 1875, the *Globe* reported on a Hamilton, Ontario case against Mr and Mrs Camidge for their treatment of fourteen-year-old Agnes Rankin, who was ill-fed and poorly clad when she was 'turned out ... on a cold night in November with little or no clothing on'.[16] Neighbours gave corroborating evidence about how Agnes had been beaten 'with a whipstock' and Mrs Camidge was found guilty of common assault.

Reports of mistreated children continued to appear in the press. Almost twenty years later, in November 1895, the *Globe* reported that Miss Ellen Findley had been arrested in her home for the murder of Barnardo boy George E. Green following an inquest into his death. Findley claimed she had 'tended him and kept him clean, and he was always healthy, and would always eat all he could get'.[17] She also claimed that she had 'never struck, beat or abused him in any way', although she was unable to explain the condition of Green's body, 'which was covered with wounds, bruises and ulcers from head to foot'.[18] Other witnesses testified that the boy had received 'unmerciful beatings' by Findley and that the boy 'had not been properly clothed, fed or cared for'.[19] The poor care and treatment of George was an indictment of the emigration system, in which the emigrating organisations were unable to effectively ensure that the children received proper care.

The Canadian press began claiming that the emigration selection process had failed. The *Ottawa Citizen* describes George as 'an innocent, simple Barnardo waif' of about sixteen years of age.[20] Barnardo rejected allegations that the medical inspection of the boy had been superficial or that the organisation was in some way to blame 'for having sent to Canada a boy manifestly unfitted for emigration'.[21] He wrote a letter to the editor of the *Times* expressing his regret about the circumstances of Greene's

138   Philanthropy in Children's Periodicals, 1840–1930

death and that unfortunately 'there are cruel people everywhere'.[22] He took issue with the claim that 'the boy was one of weak intellect, partially imbecile' and that 'the medical examination of the boy prior to sending him out was only of a superficial character', an allegation that came from the superintendent of one of the Canadian Barnardo Homes.[23] Both Canadian and British press were critical of the processes that failed to care for the boy, with the British *Evening News* reporting that '[t]he case has given rise to expressions of opinions that there should be a more rigid inspection of the boys sent out to Canada, and that the boys should be better looked after by the agents of the various homes to which they are sent.'[24] The emigrators were legally required to conduct regular inspections of each child's circumstances, but visitations could be difficult owing to poor road and weather conditions. Moreover, when an inspector did visit the child and inspect the home situation, the child may have been unlikely to share any abuse they were experiencing for fear of repercussions. In the press, children who absconded from their situation were positioned as ungrateful of the benefits of emigration to Canada. Boys travelling to new destinations were given a postcard so that they could notify the home of their safe arrival, and inspectors visited the boys annually, but Greene failed to return his card, nor had he been visited. The only communication came from Findley, that although Greene was 'stupid and slow and she was afraid he always would be so', she was willing to take him permanently.[25] As Gillian Wagner observes, this tragedy 'was the occasion for a further spate of hostile press comments' about the weakness of the medical examination system.[26]

Emigrated children were positioned as deserving children who would benefit from charitable support to enable their future success. However, some Canadians felt that their own disadvantaged children deserved this charitable support instead. For example, an 1881 article appearing in the *Globe* explains that '[i]t is high time the deportation of waifs to Canada be stopped. Until we make a reasonable effort toward solving our own "unemployed" problems we should not be burdened with the results of similar problems arising in Britain.'[27] The editorial that follows, reprinted from the Hamilton *Spectator*, is similarly dismissive of the value of child immigrants. Instead of seeing them as positive contributors to the nation, these children are 'waifs' in need of care: '[I]t is Canada's duty to first look after her own waifs, and

Charitable Subjectivity   139

there are enough of them to absorb all the money the Canadian government can afford to expend in charity right now'.[28] An article in the *Globe* on 30 March 1895 describes the Barnardo boys as coming from the 'slums of England' and being of a 'most undesirable class of immigrants', while Canadian boys are 'left to shift for themselves'.[29] The discursive register for these child emigrants shifts from being productive contributors to a drain on the country's charitable resources. These tensions between emigrant and Canadian children appeared early in discussions of the emigration scheme and remained a perennial concern as Canadians worried about providing for their own children and perceived the emigrant children to be a British responsibility.

Narratives of charitable success

The good standing of the Barnardo's charity in the community was essential to the success of a scheme that depended on Canadian farmers and other employers taking on emigrant children. While much of the criticism was aimed at the emigration scheme as a whole, Barnardo's was responsible for a significant proportion of the overall numbers of emigrants. In 1895, for instance, they sent 612 children to Canada, representing almost a third of the total 1,891 children sent out by all emigrators.[30] To combat the negative press that it was receiving, Barnardo's Canadian branch created its own magazine, *Ups and Downs*.[31] While the magazine was ostensibly intended for the young people who had been emigrated to Canada under the auspices of Barnardo, an obvious and pressing need existed to recuperate the image of the child emigrators and the quality of the children that were being sent from England. The magazine's objectives were twofold: it needed to attract readers within its child emigrant population while also demonstrating the perseverance and industry of these young people to readers who were not otherwise part of the Barnardo community as part of a marketing plan aimed at rehabilitating its reputation. The criticisms levelled at Greene as 'simple' and 'of weak intellect' demonstrate the urgency of this latter objective. The opening letter published in the magazine, written by Barnardo's Canadian agent Alfred B. Owen, reflects the magazine's desire to convince Canadian readers that Barnardo's had been responsible and thorough in identifying suitable candidates. Owen explains that

140   Philanthropy in Children's Periodicals, 1840–1930

> Many people are prejudiced against us and many more misunderstand us, and our paper will, we hope, be our organ of defense . . . We look forward to it being the means of raising materially our position and prestige . . . and to help to make us respected and to dispel some of the groundless and often very cruel and uncharitable prejudice that exists against us.[32]

The pages of the magazine provide a counternarrative to contemporary prejudices by documenting the upstanding children who have come to Canada and how successful they are (or will be) once they become acclimatised to the new country.

From the very first page of its initial issue, the intended readership of child emigrants is clearly defined. Yet the magazine also establishes its ideal reader within its pages. Since the magazine 'circulates mainly amongst the many thousand young people who have been placed out . . . with farmers and others', its main objective is to retain these readers, which it does through stories of emigrants who have persevered and succeeded in their placements.[33] Owen explains that the paper 'is the personal interest and concern of every one of Dr. Barnardo's boys in Canada, and we want all hands . . . to make it a success'.[34] He wishes both the magazine and the boys themselves to be successful, which will be enabled through personal contributions from the boys. These items will all be 'thankfully received. Send us news of yourselves, your friends, the state of business in your part of the country, what you are doing, where you have been, where you are going. Anything and everything of interest is grist to our mill and will help us to make our paper bright and acceptable.'[35] Owen's claims about accepting 'anything and everything' are clearly overstated. Given the aims of the organisation alongside the specific objectives of *Ups and Downs*, the generally upbeat tone of the magazine is easily anticipated. Indeed, Gail Corbett writes that the contents were 'highly editorialized and unfortunate experiences, sadness or loneliness deleted'.[36] While the news is typically quite positive, and thus somewhat suspect in comparison to the simultaneous counternarrative produced elsewhere in the periodical press, *Ups and Downs* nonetheless offers a productive site through which to examine the development of the rhetorical manoeuvres that editors and contributors adopted to navigate between being objects of charity and becoming potential charitable donors.

Charitable Subjectivity   141

In a section entitled 'With Our Friends', *Ups and Downs* publishes excerpts from boys' correspondence that reinforce the key ideas of steadfastness, hard work, and commitment. Notwithstanding the editorial surveillance that focused on the depiction of emigrant success, these excerpts enable the boys to position themselves within this shared community of British Home Children as hard-working, financially successful, and literate working-class boys. Pooley has demonstrated how contributions to children's columns in provincial English newspapers show children defining and embodying a literate selfhood through their written contributions. Likewise, in *Ups and Downs*, boys' letters in 'With Our Friends' both define and reflect on the Barnardo-boy ideal that appears elsewhere in the magazine. As Vipond explains in the September 1895 issue, this section offers 'so much encouragement in hearing from our friends of their contentment and progress, of their efforts to lead noble lives, and of their desire to help us'.[37] The ideal boy is content with his situation and continues to strive to improve. His 'noble life' is Christian and charitable, which leads to a desire to support Barnardo's in financial terms. At the same time, however, Vipond acknowledges that the 'trying' circumstances of emigration can be 'contagious', so that the 'best preventive for a threatened attack of dejection is an hour or two spent over letters from "our boys"', where the 'incipient despondency vanished like magic'.[38] The stories of other successful boys are, he argues, sufficient to banish homesickness and sadness.

Barnardo's encouraged boys to remain in their place of service by awarding silver or bronze medals 'in recognition of the way in which they have faithfully fulfilled their engagements and earned good characters in industry and merit'.[39] As the introduction to 'Medal Winners' explains in the second issue, 'Some of these lads have been six and even seven years in the same place, and in every case there has been an unblemished record.'[40] Emphasising their steadfastness and commitment to hard work, the article explains that these young men are now 'fairly launched in life [and] able to look after their own affairs'.[41] The magazine includes three specific examples of success. John R. Head is 'now in his fourth year' in Canada, and although he did not initially 'take kindly to farming', he was 'strenuously persuaded [to] "stick to" it and put his shoulder bravely to the wheel'.[42] His (and Barnardo's) hard work has been rewarded, as John is now 'a stalwart and energetic young farmer and realizes that there is future before

142 Philanthropy in Children's Periodicals, 1840–1930

him. He has an idea of setting up for himself before long' in partnership with another Barnardo boy.[43] William Dewbury likewise 'has not eaten the bread of idleness' during the five years he has been in Canada, and his length of service is 'highly creditable to him'.[44] George L. Swaddling is 'a good boy' with 'a good record of five years' of faithful service.[45] He now has 'the world before him and a hundred dollars in the bank at his back, and we look forward with the fullest confidence to his doing well in future'.[46] The language in these descriptions reflects Barnardo's focus on good conduct, industriousness, and perseverance. With hard work and moral fortitude, boys can learn new skills and earn enough to set themselves up for the future, where each lad will be able to 'paddle his own canoe'.[47] The emigration experience enables them to become independent, contributing members of society.

The shared expectation that the boys would remain in the positions they were assigned and would work hard while there was reinforced by the annual distribution of silver or bronze medals rewarding good conduct and length of service and acknowledgement in the magazine (see Fig. 5.1). The September 1895 issue includes facsimiles of the front and back of the medal awarded by Barnardo as well as descriptions of some boys' successes and a list of all those who have been awarded in the past month. The list identifies each boy, along with his address and the date he sailed to Canada. Moreover, for some boys at least, the medal is a motivator. Douglas Ellis writes that 'I never thought that I should ever win a medal; but I find I have. It is a great encouragement to the boys to stick to the one place; and then it is like a home to them. I know very well that I feel better now than when I first came out here.'[48] The boys are alike in that they come from impoverished backgrounds and are expected to demonstrate how much their circumstances and their attitudes have changed as a result of the opportunities afforded them in Canada. That the boys were aware of the negative press and prejudices in Canadian society can be seen in twenty-one-year-old George Moore's letter to *Ups and Downs* in February 1896, when he writes, 'I am glad to say I am not ashamed of being a Dr. Barnardo boy, for I am just as much thought of as the other young fellows.'[49]

This common refrain of not initially enjoying Canada but eventually coming to realise its possibilities appears regularly throughout the magazine and is an important aspect of the subjectivity these

UPS AND DOWNS.

MEDAL WINNERS

FAC-SIMILE OF LONG SERVICE MEDAL, AWARDED BY DR. BARNARDO.

We have the sincerest pleasure in publishing the following list of the names and addresses of boys who have recently received Dr. Barnardo's silver or bronze medal in recognition of the way in which they have faithfully fulfilled their engagements and earned good characters by industry and merit. Some of these lads have been six and even seven years in the same place, and in every case there has been an unblemished record. They are now, we consider, fairly launched in life, able to look after their own affairs, and each lad to paddle his own

FACE.

canoe, and Dr. Barnardo presents the medals as an expression of his approval and pleasure at their good conduct while they have been under his care, and of his good wishes for their future success and welfare in life.

We wish we could publish a picture and sketch of each of our prize-winners, but considerations of space will not permit of our presenting more than three. They are good representatives of the others, neither better nor worse, and the story in each case, as well

REVERSE.

as in the others, may be summed up by saying that they have done their best and done well.

JOHN R. HEAD is now in his fourth year in the country. He is an "old hand" at Stepney and had been several years in the Home before he came to Canada. John did not take kindly to farming at first and found it uphill work to begin with. But we strenuously persuaded him to "stick to" it and put his shoulder bravely to the wheel. And our advice was well bestowed. John is now a stalwart and energetic young farmer, and realises that there is a future before him. He has an idea of setting up for himself before long, and, in company with his "chum," Douglas Ellis—another of the right sort—getting a place of their own. That they will accomplish their aim, we have little doubt, and we heartily wish them God speed.

The following, taken from a letter written recently by Dr. Barnardo to the chairman of a meeting at which the Founder and Director had hoped to be present, will be read with interest by every one of our friends. From the hopeful, cheerful tone in which he writes, it is evident that Dr. Barnardo is making progress toward recovery. Though his progress is slow, it is something for which we are all devoutly thankful, and that the day of restoration to his old-time health and vigour may not be long delayed is, we are sure, the earnest prayer of every "Barnardo boy" in Canada:

". . . 'I regret to say I am *strongly advised not to attempt* to be present at the meeting on Friday, and to strictly avoid for a while all meetings of every kind, and all causes of excitement. I, therefore, very reluctantly abandon the hope I had entertained of taking some part in the meeting convened for to-morrow, and can only ask you to offer in my name *my hearty and sincere gratitude* to all the assembled friends for the great sympathy they have exhibited during my distressing illness. I never knew I had so many friends before, and my heart is full of gratitude to God as I think of the thousands of warm-hearted servants of Christ who have been raised up to support His work in your and my hands, and, for the work's sake, to think so kindly of the workers. During the last few weeks, while I have been cut off from all active share in the management of the Homes, everything has been carried on by my tried and trusty colleagues in an admirable manner, and all the arrangements for tomorrow's meeting have been in their hands. Everything that would save me from trouble or anxiety has been done with the most solicitous kindness, and, as I have often said before, I do not believe that any philanthropic or Christian work anywhere has more enthusiastic and single eyed servitors than ours; nor has any chief of a mission enterprise more loyal colleagues and comrades than I. . . .

"Before bringing this letter, already too long, to a close, I desire, for the information of all who are interested, to add that although the suddenness and alarming character of the attacks from which I have suffered during the last two months have compelled me to relinquish my share in my beloved work for a season, I am assured by each and all of the three medical men, under whose care I have been and still am, that I may confidently expect, by the blessing of God, to be able to resume my usual duties after a while, and that if certain changes are effected in my hours of daily labor and in other matters relating to the management of my health, I may hope for some years to come, if it be God's will, to continue to occupy the position it has been my privilege and joy to hold for so long.

"If spared until to-morrow I shall have reached my fiftieth year, and although deeply sensible of many wasted opportunities for serving Christ (opportunities which can never return, but are gone forever) and of much failure and imperfection in what has been accomplished, I cannot but also look back upon innumerable mercies, and upon the continued and unceasing goodness of God vouchsafed, spite of failure, to His unworthy servant; and I would ask all present at the meeting to give God thanks *alone*, the Creator rather than the creature, for what has been accomplished; to praise His name to whom alone the praise and honor are due! 'Not unto us, O Lord, not unto us, but unto Thy name give glory, for Thy mercy, and for Thy truth's sake.'"

WILLIAM DEWBURY has not eaten the bread of idleness during the past five years, and that he has kept his situation for this length of time is highly creditable to him. Year by year Mr. Griffith has brought us the same excellent report from his annual visit, and no one has better earned the silver medal we have had so much pleasure in presenting to him.

GEORGE L. SWADDLING—a good boy, and a good record of five years' faithful service. George has now the world before him and a hundred dollars in the bank at his back, and we look forward with the fullest confidence to his doing well in the future. He has earned the esteem and regard of those who know him, and the moral for our readers that we draw from George's history is, "Go and do thou likewise."

The other boys whose long service and good conduct have recently been rewarded with a medal from Dr. Barnardo are:

HERBERT C. CAVE, Box 35, Tweed P.O., who came to Canada in August, '89.
VALENTINE TURNER, care of Mr. Stewart Stinson, Mono Mills; June, '89.
CHAS. W. LEACH, care of Mr. A. Stewart, Woodbridge; April, '90.
ARTHUR H. SMITH, Mount Elgin; April, '90.
JOHN HESLOP, Warkworth; April, '90.
CHAS. E. LAWRENCE, care of Mr. F. Crossley, Jura; June, '90.
WM. LUFF, care of Mr. R. Patterson, Zimmerman; June, '90.
WM. WHEELER, care of Mr. Alva Lane, Warkworth; April, '89.
WM. C. DREWRY, care of Mr. J. B. Muir, Avonbank; April, '89.
FRANK SINCLAIR, care of Mr. J. Rainey, Cookstown; April, '88.
GEORGE HART, care of Mr. G. Lee, Chatham; June, '90.
PETER CONNELL, care of Mr. R. Jackson, Cumnock; June, '89.
JOHN ALLEN, Blackwell; April, '91.
FRANK W. STEVENS, care of Mr. A. Andrews, Watford; April, '91.
JOSEPH LEWIS, care of Mr. Henry Culver, Port Hope; June, '91.
GEORGE SUMMERSBY, care of Mr. C. Atkinson, Newport; June, '91.
WILLIAM HENRY BRAY, care of Mr. John Cropper, 464 Cannon street East, Hamilton; June, '88.
JOHN MOULDER, care of Mr. W. F. Young, Dunlop; August, '91.
WM. PICKERING, care of Mr. Alex. Morrison, Smithdale; August, '91.
DAVID A. LLOYD, care of Mr. John Shale, Exeter; March, '92.
GEORGE MANNING, care of Mr. W. T. Bowman, Ilderton; March, '92.
JOHN H. WATSON, care of Mr. J. Keats, Chatham; April, '90.
ERNEST T. ARGENT, care of Mr. W. Stewart, Cedar Mills; June, '89.
EDWARD SKENNELL, care of Mr. Edward McCracken, Rosemont; March, '92.
CHAS. E. NANSON, Thamesville; July, '92.
HORACE G. SHARPE, care of Mr. Donald Brown, Riverstown; July, '92.
ALFRED BUSH, care of Mr. A. Winger, Wardsville; March, '92.
WILLIAM HENRY STEPHENS, care of Mr. J. Bickley, Ealing; July, '92.
CHRISTMAS ASPINALL, care of Mr. J. M. Shier, Leaskdale; March, '93.
PETER ASPINALL, care of Mr. D. Walker, Leaskdale; March, '93.
ALBERT CARPENTER, care of Mr. T. Reid, Branchton; March, '93.
JOHN HAYES, care of Mr. Samuel L. Billings, Leskard; March, '93.
ALFRED HOLLYFIELD, care of Mr. W. Ramage, Droomore; March, '93.
ERNEST HAWTHORNE, care of Mr. F. W. Howe, Arnprior; March, '92.
FRANCIS ORFWOOD, care of Mr. R. Staples, Lifford; March, '93.
DANIEL BARLOW, care of Mr. C. McFadyen, Glammi; June, '93.
AS. E. DAVIS, care of Mr. John Lamb, Nassagaweya; June, '93.
DOUGLAS WILLIAM ELLIS, care of Mr. J. Stephens, Ballymote; June, '93.
CHARLES WILLIAM SMITH, care of Mr. J. C. Campbell, Melbourne; August, '93.

Fig. 5.1 'Medal Winners', *Ups and Downs*, September 1895, 5.

boys are defining for themselves, characterised by acclimatisation and improvement. A letter from William H. Mabey in November 1895 epitomises the need to adapt. He writes that 'I did not much care about it at first, but I like it now.'[50] In an accompanying editorial comment, Vipond explains, 'So it is in ninety-nine out of a hundred where a boy sticks to it and determines to make the best of his opportunity.'[51] Not only is William now content with his circumstances, but he has also saved $100. Accepting the realities of living in Canada and the willingness to work hard produces financial gain and improved circumstances.

The boys reading the magazine are guided towards qualities that define the ideal Barnardo boy. These qualities of 'Success by Perseverance, Industry and Honesty' are explicitly stated in a ribbon appearing over the top of photos of six successful young men who are being awarded with a silver medal for long service and good conduct in December 1895 (see Fig. 5.2). A corresponding ribbon at the bottom of the page reads, 'He that gathereth by Labour shall Increase'. This passage from Proverbs 13:11 emphasises the importance of honest labour to earn and retain wealth, a key to these emigrants' successes. The accompanying description uses exemplars of successful Barnardo boys to define the ideal

Fig. 5.2 'With Our Friends', *Ups and Downs*, December 1895, 5.

Charitable Subjectivity · 145

boy, explaining how these 'friends' have all been in Canada for six to ten years, and '[e]ach has made good use of his time and has before him a future which we are justified in expecting will redound still further to his credit'.[52] Two brothers, Henry and Fred C. White, 'are held in high regard by all who know them. A bank balance of several hundred dollars testifies to Henry's belief in meeting the possibilities of the future well equipped with the munitions of war.'[53] Thomas G. Wright's nine years of service has 'so thoroughly convinced' his employer of his 'ability and general trustworthiness that he has recently handed over the entire management of the farm to our friend, who is now twenty-one years old'.[54] Patrick Sullivan 'commenced his career in Canada with a very strong determination to lead an earnest Christian life' and has 'striven nobly and successfully in this direction'.[55] Charles Harlow took on responsibility for the farm when the owner, Mr Stock, was injured and 'acquitted himself in a manner eminently satisfactory to all concerned'.[56] He recently left this excellent position to join his brothers in Manitoba, and '[h]e will do well whether he remains in Manitoba or returns to Ontario' since his 'qualifications are those which always make for success'.[57] William Luke Mills 'possesses a strong tendency to "go ahead." He is a steady worker, and his six years' labours have resulted in a bank balance of more than $300 . . . He has our earnest wishes for the success to which his manly efforts entitle him.'[58] These young men are well positioned through their training at Barnardo's and have achieved individual success through steadfastness, willingness to work hard, and regular habits. Their religious and family sentiments are also celebrated as part of a masculine ideal that values sensible decision making and financial prudence.

"Our Girls"

The first issues of the magazine are exclusively focused on Barnardo boys who have emigrated to Canada. Most of the negative press pertained to boys, and many more boys than girls were sent to Canada. Between 1867 and 1897, 6,952 boys were emigrated and only 1,967 girls, for a total of 8,919 children. On an annual basis, the percentage of girls varied significantly (see Table 5.1). In some years no girls were sent out (1882 and 1890), and in others they are a more significant portion of the total (41 per cent in 1883 and 52 per cent in 1884).[59] These variances were likely

Table 5.1 Numbers of boys and girls emigrated between 1867 and 1897 ('Our Emigrants', *Ups and Downs*, January 1898, 83).

	Children Emigrated by Barnardo (1867–97)																
Year	1867–82	1882	1883	1884	1885	1886	1887	1888	1889	1890	1891	1892	1893	1894	1895	1896	1897	Total
Boys	640	51	109	120	275	390	371	395	396	291	417	596	758	635	578	490	440	6952
Girls	306	0	75	132	118	234	41	94	107	0	5	131	76	89	155	188	216	1967
Total	946	51	184	252	393	624	412	489	503	291	422	727	834	724	733	678	656	8919
Girls as % of Total	32%	0%	41%	52%	30%	38%	10%	19%	21%	0%	1%	18%	9%	12%	21%	28%	33%	22%

owing to the number of girls in England who were appropriate for emigration, the demand for placements in Canada, and the ability to care for the girls in Toronto.[60] The low total percentage of girls (22 per cent) indicates the relative importance of boys as the implied audience for the magazine.

Nonetheless, in January 1896, girls' perspectives began to be included in the magazine with the introduction of a new section entitled 'Our Girls', and here the girls demonstrate similar rhetorical manoeuvres aimed at defining an ideal Barnardo girl who is both industrious and grateful for the opportunities available in Canada. Owen makes a 'very pleasant announcement' in the preceding December number, explaining that 'Our paper is no longer to be the exclusive organ of the boys' and 'a part of each issue will be specially devoted to [girls'] interests'.[61] Miss Code, Secretary to the Barnardo's Girls' Home in Peterborough, invited the girls to become subscribers since, as with many other children's magazines, subscriber numbers remained a perennial concern. Owen reiterates his hopes that increased subscriptions will 'make our little sheet a success', and the girls responded enthusiastically to the proposal accompanied by a copy of the magazine.[62] Lizzie Adams, recently arrived in Canada, writes that 'I am just delighted with it. It seems just as if we are brothers and sisters writing to each other. You could not have commenced with anything better than the photo of Dr. Barnardo.'[63] Lizzie describes a community based on an imagined familial relationship, although at times the family connections are explicit and real. Lizzie Trott also writes positively that 'I was delighted with such a bright and newsy little journal, and I am sure it will be a huge success. I enclose my subscription.'[64] She is looking forward to seeing 'something from girls in the paper' and expresses her 'great joy' at seeing her brother's name in the magazine's pages: 'Oh, you do not know how pleased I was seeing his name there. It seemed to bring him closer; and I was also glad to see he was a subscriber.'[65] Like the boys in earlier issues, she too is convinced that the magazine's title is 'most appropriate . . . for we all have such ups and downs in this world; but it seems to apply even more to us Home girls and boys than to others'.[66] Although she does not include any detail about her own circumstances, her affinity for the title suggests that her experiences as an emigrant to Canada have been challenging at times.

Like the boys' letters, the girls' letters reinforce the need to adapt, be resilient, and work hard. In an entry specially written

148   Philanthropy in Children's Periodicals, 1840–1930

for *Ups and Downs,* a former resident of 'Wild Thyme' cottage at Barnardo's Girls' Village Home in England writes to her 'younger sisters': 'Dear Girls, – It is to those of you who have lately come to Canada, I am writing this letter; and as I write I think of the time when I was "a stranger in a strange land", and how glad I would have been to have a paper like Ups and Downs to read.'[67] Letters from older boys and girls would have been helpful to her, and thus she writes of her hopes that 'if this letter is a comfort to any of you I shall be very glad I wrote it. My hope in writing is to cheer and encourage you.' Having been in Canada for more than seven years, she recalls its strangeness and the time it took to become 'accustomed to your new life and responsibilities, but I think the longer you live here the better you will like the country and people'. The responsibilities of a girl's life are 'great', she writes, explaining that

> It is yours to make or mar your lives; yours to win a good name, to inspire respect and confidence from those around you, and as surely as you do your best for your employers, and strive day to day to live a good, pure life, just so surely you will be respected, – yes, and loved.[68]

This letter to girls who have only recently arrived in Canada emphasises the qualities of the ideal Barnardo girl who moves between the two subject positions as recipient and donor. She must work to the best of her ability and live a virtuous life to become respected and loved. Moreover, 'Wild Thyme' reminds her readers that, although 'we may think no one cares or notices what we do ... it is a great mistake, girls; we are watched, we have influenced among those around us, let it be an influence for good'.[69] Although she alludes to the positive influence girls can have on those around them, as models of virtue, hard work, and honesty, she is also referring to their position as emigrants whose behaviours are expected to be appropriate for their position as charitable subjects.

The emotional aspects of belonging are emphasised in 'Wild Thyme's' letter, unlike the industriousness, honesty, and steadfastness demanded of the boys. The ideal Barnardo girl is framed differently – both in the figurative and the literal sense – than the ideal Barnardo boy. In contrast to the rather austere image of the boys depicted in Fig. 5.2, notable girls are identified as 'faithful' in an image appearing in the first 'Our Girls' column (see Fig. 5.3). Five photos of successful girls are positioned within a crown

Charitable Subjectivity 149

Fig. 5.3 'Faithful in that which is least', *Ups and Downs*, January 1896, 11.

evoking Queen Victoria and the British empire. The religious faith signified by the cross on the top of the crown is reinforced by the Biblical passage from Luke 16:10, 'Faithful in that which is least', appearing on a ribbon below the girls. The brief descriptions of the girls' successes highlight the love and respect they have received in their placements, their steady industry through lengthy stays of between five and seven years and, in one case, teaching a Sunday School class. This service to God requires 'that we be "found faithful"'.[70] The language emphasises the community of Barnardo girls – both current and former – through the second-person narrative address and is explicit in its ideological and religious underpinnings. Other facets of the ideal Barnardo girl are apparent in the surrounding articles, including a notice about '[o]ne of Dr. Barnardo's grandchildren', a baby born to 'one of "our girls"' and an announcement of a marriage to another of 'Our Girls' held at the home of her employers, who 'bear testimony to the bride's faithful services during her residence of four years in their home,

150 Philanthropy in Children's Periodicals, 1840–1930

and have shown their appreciation in a tangible occasion on this occasion'.[71] This section of the magazine offers girl readers models of successful girlhood and the opportunities that the future might hold if they negotiate the demands of service in ways deemed acceptable to both Barnardo and their employers.

Creating a community of charitable recipients

The contributions to the magazine from both the boys and the girls echo the advice from Owen and Vipond to embrace the opportunities Canada offers while also producing a narrative for themselves that situates them within a community of other child emigrants encountering similar experiences. Many of the boys' letters comment on the shared experiences of emigrating from London and becoming established in Canada. Commenting on the launch of the magazine, Richard Wright believes the paper 'will be a good idea to keep the boys together' while Herbert Gannon explains that 'we shall know what is going on at the Homes, and how the boys in Canada are getting along'.[72] These letters reflect a desire to connect with other boys sharing their similar emigration experiences.

The girls also are keen to hear more about their friends. Emily Manning writes that the girls' page is 'a splendid idea'.[73] Her one concern is that 'if all the girls felt as I do about it, one page will not be sufficient'.[74] Given that the first issue included four pages dedicated to the girls, and that this length was a regular feature, Emily appears to have been correct that there was keen interest from the girls. Moreover, correspondence in the following month indicates that they were aware of the magazine's goals, with Louisa Maughan writing that 'the book is just lovely, and that it is worth having ... as that ought to encourage us all to be good girls'.[75] Numerous correspondents express their delight 'to see some of the girls we know' and to learn 'all that is going on in the Home, and hear from each other every month'.[76]

Boys newly arrived in Canada were keen to reconnect with friends made in London, on board the ship, and in the receiving home. The magazine responded to this desire, which was presumably also intended to reduce the need to respond to individual requests for contact details, by introducing a new feature, 'Our Old Friends Directory', in the second issue. Vipond explains that 'we intend publishing each month the names and addresses of

Charitable Subjectivity   151

one hundred subscribers, together with the dates of their arrival in Canada', since this will 'be a source of much pleasure among our friends from whom we are constantly receiving letters asking us to inform them where some of the boys of such and such a year's party are'.[77] The list (see Fig. 5.4) is a clever strategy that encourages the boys to subscribe to the magazine in order to find themselves on the list while also increasing the financial support for *Ups and Downs*. Moreover, the list enables boys who travelled together to Canada to reconnect with each other, thereby reinforcing the community that was established prior to and during their emigration. Alfred Bristow describes the directory as a 'splendid scheme'.[78] Although only a relatively short-lived feature, lasting just two years, and predating the inclusion of content for the girls, it nonetheless demonstrates the boys' engagement with the magazine and with a smaller subset of their friends.

The connection between boys is evident in Table 5.2, which shows the frequency of boys sailing on a particular date subscribing to *Ups and Downs*. The earlier sailing months in the year show that these children subscribed at a higher rate, especially striking in 1892 and 1893. This may be because they would have spent the winter in one of the Barnardo homes before sailing in the spring. In contrast, boys sailing later in the year may have had less time in the London homes before emigrating and may have had weaker ties to the other boys. The sailings within the previous two to three years (1892–4) show the highest levels of engagement with the community based on the shared emigration experience. These children were likely still working in Barnardo placements, while those who sailed in the 1880s were presumably no longer as connected to the Barnardo community, both because their experiences were less recent and because they were now older, likely in their twenties.

While the magazine defines community in an inclusive way – all boys are Barnardo boys – subscribers had a different sense of the community being defined. Henry Watts, who emigrated at eight years old in 1890, explains that 'I do not remember the names of many of the boys that came across with me, but I like to hear how boys like myself are getting along, through your paper.'[79] Although the boys may not have remembered their fellow travellers at all, or perhaps only a particular friend or two, nonetheless the shared experience of traveling on a particular sailing was enough to encourage boys to subscribe. In contrast,

OUR OLD FRIENDS' DIRECTORY.

In this column we publish each month the names and addresses of one hundred subscribers, together with the dates of their arrival in Canada. Unless otherwise stated the post offices are situated in the Province of Ontario.

NAME.	POST OFFICE.	COUNTY.	DATE OF ARRIVAL IN CANADA.
ANDERSON, WALTER R.	Thornbury	Grey	April, '91
ATKINS, ALFRED	Iona	Elgin	Aug., '91
ADAMS, JAMES	Cayuga	Haldimand	June, '91
AVERY, BERTIE	Box 110 Guelph	Wellington	Nov., '91
ASHBY, CHARLES	Box 334 Ingersoll	Oxford	July, '92
ASHBY, JNO.	St. John's, West	Welland	April, '84
ARNOLD, ANTOINE	Fox Point	Muskoka	Aug., '84
BAKER, THOS.	Leaskdale	Ontario	June, '91
BEASLEY, WILLIAM E.	Allanburgh	Welland	April, '91
BARNES, ALFRED	Oriel	Oxford	April, '85
BIRCH, GEORGE E.	Bosworth	Wellington	April, '90
BOYD, WILLIAM	Iona	Elgin	April, '91
BRICE, FRED. ROBERT	Box 22 Stayner	Simcoe	July, '88
BENNETT, FREDERICK	Cobourg	Northumberland	March, '87
CUTTRESS, CHARLES	Greenside	Grey	March, '92
COUCH, CHAS. E.	Drumquin	Halton	June, '91
COLES, CHARLES	Copetown	Wentworth	June, '89
COLLINS, JAMES	Harold	Hastings	April, '88
CLIVE, GEORGE	Chatham	Kent	June, '91
DOLLING, ALBERT	Tecumseh	Essex	April, '91
DANIELS, GEORGE HY	Fraserville	Northumberland	June, '91
DAVIS, JAS. E.	Nassagaweya	Halton	June, '91
DUNFORD, ALBERT H.	Lowville	Halton	July, '92
DENNIS, GEORGE	Burnaby	Welland	March, '93
ELINES, HENRY	Beeton	Simcoe	July, '94
EDMUNDS, ARTHUR E.	Mount Elgin	Norfolk	July, '94
ELLIS, DOUGLAS W.	Ballymote	Middlesex	June, '93
FORD, ALEXANDER	Rocklyn	Grey	July, '92
FULLER, CHAS.	Ballymote	Middlesex	July, '92
FLINT, THOS. G.	Wallacetown	Elgin	June, '93
FARROW, HENRY	Stayner	Simcoe	April, '89
FOREST, ALBERT E. H.	Copetown	Wentworth	Nov., '94
FLEETWOOD, F. A.	Verschoyle	Oxford	April, '91
GOODEN, GEORGE	Lindsay	Victoria	March '87
GRANVILLE HY. JOS.	Pickering	Ontario	March. '93
GURRELL, WILLIAM	Box 266 Orillia	Simcoe	April, '91
HOOF, JAS. JNO.	Coboconk	Victoria	Sep., '92
HURRELL, WM. H.	Bolton	Peel	March, '92
HANCOCK, JESSE	Leaskdale	Ontario	June, '91
HOWARD, ALBERT	Bonnechere	Renfrew	June, '91
HINDS, ALFRED	Innisville	Lanark	March. '92
HURLEY, ALFRED	Adelaide	Middlesex	April, '90
IBBETSON, JAMES	Schomberg	York	Aug., '91
JONES, ENOCH	Edmonton	Peel	April, '91
JONES, HENRY J.	Palgrave	Peel	March, '92

NAME.	POST OFFICE.	COUNTY.	DATE OF ARRIVAL IN CANADA.
JEWELL, CHAS.	Ingersoll	Oxford	Aug., '93
JONES, RICHARD F.	Zephyr	Ontario	March, '93
JEFFREYS, FRED'K. G.	Novar	Parry Sound Dist.	July, '92
KNIGHT, WM	Palgrave	Peel	April, '94
KNOWLES, EDGAR J.	Staffa	Perth	Aug., '93
KEEPER, CHARLES W.	Dutton	Elgin	Aug., '93
KENDRICK, JOS	Jordan	Lincoln	July, '94
LEWIS, JOSEPH	Port Hope	Durham	June, '91
LONG, BERTRAM W.	Box 90 Newcastle.	Durham	April, '90
LEONARD, HY. GEO.	Cairngorm	Middlesex	March, '93
LENSON, HERBERT S.	Black Creek	Welland	July, '92
LEWIS, ALFRED	West Meath	Renfrew	June, '93
LAWRENCE, EDWARD	Colinville	Lambton	March,
LUCAS, THOS.	Orchard	Grey	June, '91
LE GRAND, GEORGE	Cheltenham	Peel	April, '91
LANGAN, JNO.	Leaskdale	Ontario	April, '94
MOUNTAIN, CHAS	Hagersville	Haldimand	April, '91
MILES, HENRY	Plainville	Northumberland	Sep., '92
MACKEY, JOHN	Ida	Durham	June, '91
McARRAGHER, FRANK	Verschoyle	Oxford	March, '93
MIDLANE, ERNEST	Dromore	Grey	March,
MARTIN, JOS.	Brampton	Peel	Nov., '91
NOWLEN, FRED'K. GEO.	Clearville	Kent	March, '93
NASH, FRED'K HY.	Cheltenham	Peel	Aug., '91
NOAKES, JNO. W	Kinlough	Bruce	April, '94
NEWELL, ALFRED	Bolton	Peel	July, '92
OAKLEY, CHAS.	Paris.	Brant	March, '93
OWLETT, WM.	Bethesda	York	April, '90
OATES, GEORGE E.	Glen Cross	Dufferin	July, '94
OATES, HERBERT	Orangeville	Dufferin	June, '93
PEARCE, ERNEST	Haysville	Waterloo	June, '93
PARKER, FREDERICK	Drayton	Grey	April, '89
PAGE, GEO. W.	Box 585 Brantford	Brant	Aug., '91
PICKERING, W.	Smithdale	Simcoe	June, '93
POOLEY, CHARLES	Cherry Grove	Middlesex	Aug., '91
ROBINSON, MARTIN H.	Mt. Wolfe	Peel	April, '90
ROTHSCHILD, JOSEPH	Effingham	Welland	March, '93
RIST, RICHARD E	Blackheath	Wentworth	March, '92
RUSS, JAMES R.	Macville	Peel	June, '90
RELF, SAMUEL	New Lowell	Simcoe	Sep., '92
REEVES, JAS. F.	Craigvale	Simcoe	July, '94
ROBERTS, MORRIS.	Summerville	Peel	March, '92
STEVENS, FRANK W.	Watford	Lambton	June, '93
SMITH, JNO. A.	Winthrop	Huron	April, '91
SWAIN, THOS.	Adelaide	Middlesex	April, '91
STAPLES, JAS. R.	Botany.	Grey	March, '93
SHARP, HORACE G.	Yeovil	Grey	Sep., '92
STABLES, WILLIAM	Castlederg	Peel	March, '93
TOVEY, ALBERT A.	Egbert	Simcoe	April, '91
TASKER, WM. R.	Bolton	Peel	March, '92
TAYLOR GEO. A.	Allandale	Simcoe	Aug. '91
TAGGART, ALFRED	Pelham Union	Welland	Aug., '91
WOOD, ARTHUR W.	Owen Sound	Grey	Aug., '89
WILLIAMS, ERNEST	Birr.	Middlesex	March, '93
WHITE, WILLIAM H.	Goodwood	Ontario	July, '92

Fig. 5.4 'Our Old Friends Directory', *Ups and Downs*, October 1895, np.

Table 5.2 Subscribers to the Old Friends Directory published in *Ups and Downs* (1895–1896) by sailing date.

154   Philanthropy in Children's Periodicals, 1840–1930

John T. Wastell writes, 'I was glad to find some of my chums' in the magazine, whom he names explicitly and explains that 'we were all chums in the Grove Road Home' (the London children's home established in 1887). Thomas Wright, aged fourteen, similarly writes that 'I think the paper is very nice. It reminds me of a good many old chums.'[80] The Old Friends Directory was a short-lived attempt to promote boys' engagement with the magazine to not only seek out friends they had lost touch with, but also encourage them to contribute to the organisation's financial goals through monetary means.

Financial success and charitable giving

As was the case with other children's charity magazines, the financial contributions of child readers were an important aspect of the organisation's charitable objectives. Barnardo was eager to attract regular subscribers as well as encouraging them to make additional contributions to assist other children with their emigration to Canada. This narrative of hard work, acclimatisation, and success is positioned alongside a related expectation that children who benefitted from Barnardo's generosity should also be part of the financial community and repay the organisation in order to assist other less fortunate children. In principle the children had agreed to repay the £10 investment that enabled them to emigrate, but the magazine regularly reminded readers of their obligations. These financial contributions – or the lack thereof – create some of the tension informing the children's subjectivity and required their deft transition from worthy recipient to successful donor.

Having spent the first months establishing its readership of Barnardo boys – and then expanding to include Barnardo girls – the early months of 1896 are focused on donations. The January 1896 editorial by Owen reminds readers of 'a certain promise made to Dr. Barnardo by each boy who has left the Homes for Canada, to contribute, whenever it was possible, a certain small sum each year toward the support of the Homes'.[81] The next issue includes the names of sixty-six boys and young men who have contributed amounts ranging from fifty cents to ten dollars, although the majority have sent in a dollar as requested. Indeed, some correspondents were keen to demonstrate their subjectivity as charitable donors. Alfred Jolley, who arrived in June 1890, writes that '[e]nclosed you will find one dollar as I promised.

Charitable Subjectivity 155

I am sorry I cannot send more, but I will try and make up for the three years I missed'.[82] William Fery, now twenty-five, came from England ten years ago and explains, 'I now write wishing you and all connected with the Home a happy New Year; and long may Dr B live . . . I will enclose in this letter $10.00 for the benefit of the home.'[83] Although pleased with these donations, the accompanying anonymous article wonders plaintively about the rest of the contributions. Many letters 'contain feeling allusion to the writers' remembrance and appreciation of the help they have received from Dr. Barnardo in days gone by', yet their authors fail to support the organisation as they have promised.[84] The author is certain that they have been temporarily forgetful and that the next issue will contain a list 'more commensurate' with the number of those who have received help.[85] Sadly, the March issue reports that '[w]e cannot say that our expectations have been realized, but we are not without hope that next month we shall be called upon to publish a larger list' and reminds readers that '[h]e gives twice who gives quickly'.[86] The March list is, in fact, considerably shorter, containing only sixteen names.

The boys' letters suggest that, although they felt positively towards Barnardo, they did not always have the funds to be able to contribute the dollar that the organisation was hoping for. Arthur Woodgate, now twenty-two and listed among the contributors in February 1896 for his one-dollar donation, reports that he is trying to 'save as much as I can for a few years yet, so that I shall be able some day to buy a home for myself'.[87] He explains that '[y]ou will think I have quit sending money to the Home, but I have been under so much expense this last year, I could not send any, but I will make up for it when I get straightened up again'.[88] The reason for his limited circumstances might be attributed to the home he hopes to build the following summer or the news that 'I have a boy a year old'.[89] Thus, although Barnardo expected the young emigrants to make an annual contribution to demonstrate their improved circumstances, their commitment to the organisation, and their religious and charitable benevolence, the young men undoubtedly had different priorities, especially given their generally impoverished upbringings prior to emigration.

The girls were likewise encouraged to donate money, but their contributions were directed to a different cause, the Hazel Brae Cot at Her Majesty's Hospital for Sick Children, the Barnardo's hospital established in 1877. In 'Story of the Girls' Donation Fund',

156   Philanthropy in Children's Periodicals, 1840–1930

the author – presumably Code – relates the parable of young Lily, whose fortunes decline after her father's death, and her family's removal to London in hopes of better opportunities. Lily ends up in Her Majesty's Hospital suffering from hip disease, where she receives 'every needed nourishment' and 'everything that careful watching and nursing can do to alleviate pain and suffering'.[90] The money to support Lily's admission to hospital comes from the named Hazel Brae Cot in which she resides, to which the Hazel Brae girls have been donating money 'for many years'.[91] Those girls more recently arrived may not be aware of this, but they will undoubtedly 'be glad to hear about it; for we know that girls have warm, loving hearts to feel for those who are suffering, and that they are ready enough to put their hands together and help'.[92] This year they hope the girls will donate $150 to support the cot for one year since 'our girls ought very easily to make up that amount, and more' by contributing one dollar each.[93] This fundraising will enable the girls to show their 'appreciation of the work of Dr. Barnardo' for themselves and on behalf of others.[94]

The concluding language in this story expects girls to be grateful for the work Barnardo has done on their behalf while also helping him to help others. This creates a mutual obligation in which they are expected to help others because they themselves have been helped. Like the boys who are expected to pay back the charity they received so others can also be emigrated, the girls are to mobilise their 'warm, loving hearts' to help those who are suffering. While the language around the boys' giving has a certain transactional quality, the emotional register of the fable of Lily and the girls' anticipated responses are significantly different. Nonetheless, both groups are expected to donate because they have already been the recipients of charity. For the girls, though, the religious sentiment underlying charitable giving is explicitly referenced in a letter from Agnes Cutler in the same issue, where she says that each day in Canada 'we see more clearly God's blessing' as she encourages the girls to 'contribute whatever they can' and quotes from a hymn 'Oh, the good we all may do'.[95]

As with the boys, however, the girls' contributions failed to meet expectations. Emily Griffiths supports the initiative, writing that 'I think the girls ought to do as the boys do, and give a dollar a year to Dr. Barnardo. It is not very much for all he has done for us, and we would not miss it at all.'[96] She has been in Canada for three years, and so desires to have Barnardo take three dollars

Charitable Subjectivity   157

out of her bank book 'and I will send him $1 every year now'.[97] The list of contributors following her letter is relatively modest, with just nineteen names and contributions totalling $20.75. The author explains that '[w]e are waiting for our list to be increased; the sooner the better. We are very anxious to make up the hundred and fifty dollars during the month of April, and as the ocean consists of single drops, so this sum has to be composed of single dollars!'[98] They presumably hope that the girls will be inspired by an accompanying article about the Girls' Village Home that heads up the section, which includes a photo of the village and a description of its activities, reminding readers of their former home.

When the fund closed for the year, the girls had donated 100 dollars, which was sure to be valued by Barnardo 'not simply for its intrinsic worth, but as an expression of gratitude and co-operation from those who have themselves received benefits from the Institution'.[99] The article concludes with the names of all contributors for the year and a reminder not to be one of the nine: 'Were there not *ten* cleansed, but where are the *nine*?'[100] This Biblical passage from Luke 17:17 reminds readers of their duty to help others because they have already been helped. In the August 1896 issue, Barnardo's letter acknowledging receipt of the donation is published, and while he thanks 'most heartily and sincerely those girls who have contributed towards this sum of £20', he is also 'greatly disappointed that many more did not contribute'.[101] He reminds readers that '[i]f every girl now in Canada, who is doing fairly well' would contribute one dollar per year, the total amount would be enough to fund an annual cot. Alongside Barnardo's disappointment is a sense of competition as he compares the girls' efforts to those of the boys by describing how 'each individual boy sends more money than each individual girl, and the boys seem so generous and loving and thoughtful'.[102] He provides evidence of this in the form of a letter from a boy, now seventeen, who lived in the Home for three years before going to Canada:

I am now earning $48 a year and all my food and lodging, and I hope next year to be earning $70. Some day I shall have a farm of my own. But whenever that happy day comes, I will never forget that I owe it all to the dear Home in Stepney, for when I was a poor boy and my mother could not keep me I entered your Home and was trained and taught there and then sent to Canada, and since I have been out here

158   Philanthropy in Children's Periodicals, 1840–1930

> I have been looked after most carefully, and I feel just as grateful as a boy can.
>
> Please accept the enclosed order for $10, which is all I can spare this year, but I shall hope soon to send you more.[103]

This young man demonstrates his gratitude as a recipient of care, training, and emigration and also reflects on how this charity has enabled his success, which is manifest in his generous donation.

Barnardo approves of the boys' charitable subjectivity in contrast to the lacklustre contributions from the girls. He writes, 'Now, suppose that among the girls in Canada there was any deep feeling of gratitude and love for all that has been done for them, don't you think it would be easy for them to give at least $2 each per year to the Home funds?'[104] These small amounts will hardly be felt by the girls, 'but if they all gave something, and gave it from their hearts, from gratitude and love, think what a splendid gift it would be and how it would help the Home!'[105] He imagines sufficient funds to name three cots and the remainder to be contributed to the annual collection for the emigration expenses of ten or eleven girls each year:

> Thus those girls who have gone out to Canada, who have received so many favours and so much help from the Home, who have been looked after and tenderly watched over, and loved, and helped, and counselled, and careful, could show their gratitude.[106]

Barnardo emphasises the care that the girls have received and his expectation that they should be grateful for this care, which ought to be reflected in financial contributions to help sick children and other potential emigrants. Importantly, he sets specific monetary goals, with less expected from younger girls, and indicates that the contributions can be interpreted as demonstrations of gratitude. Anyone who fails to make this contribution is evidently ungrateful and potentially undeserving of the efforts to help them.

A response the following month indicates a genuine willingness to take up Barnardo's challenge to donate. Mary A. Parker writes that Canadian girls are doing '*very* little' to help the organisation: 'To think,' she explains, 'that there are over one thousand girls in Canada, and among all that number only one hundred dollars can be scraped together . . . I think it is a shame.'[107] She requests that

Charitable Subjectivity   159

four dollars be taken from her bank account because, although she is saving up for a visit to England, she can still spare '*a few dollars for the good work with which you are all connected*'.[108] Unlike the boy's letter quoted by Barnardo, Mary does not explicitly identify her gratitude to the organisation. She does, however, acknowledge the 'good work' Barnardo's does, and her financial contribution is understood to reflect the value she places on her Canadian experience.

Intermittent reports of girls' donations appear, but without much additional commentary to encourage further contributions. In April 1897, however, the list is accompanied by a comment that 'we hope for great things from April, as our fund should be completed by May 1st, but indeed the donations will have to come in quickly and abundantly to make our fund anything like what it ought to be. We are *ashamed* to say that at present we have a lamentably small sum for the number of girls out working.'[109] A letter from Barnardo acknowledging the contribution of £30 14s 9d suggests the girls fell far short of his goal of £200. This amount is sufficient to maintain the 'Hazelbrae Cot' for the year, he explains, although the required amount had not been forthcoming each year. Unlike the letter from 1896, Barnardo expresses no disappointment about the amount and instead encourages the girls to 'maintain a thoroughly good character, and retain the confidence and esteem of their employers'.[110] Given the number of articles encouraging girls to stay in their positions and letters acknowledging good girls who work hard and try their best, it may be that attention was being redirected towards ensuring that the placement system was operating smoothly rather than focusing on charitable behaviours. By October 1897, however, another editorial from Code reminds girls of 'the duty of contributing to the home'.[111] She knows the girls 'have warm, affectionate hearts' and they

> should ... think of all that has been done for them in the past to provide for their wants, as well as now to have this fresh start in life given, so that from a feeling of gratitude as well as duty the gifts ought to pour in willingly.[112]

The need to fund the Barnardo organisation remained a perennial concern and those who had been assisted were expected to contribute. That the magazine continually laments the modest contributions suggests that the boys and girls did not always – or

160   Philanthropy in Children's Periodicals, 1840–1930

even often – see themselves as responsible for paying back the funds expended on them, nor did they necessarily wish to support further activity, which perhaps speaks more loudly than the many positive letters of children's successes that appeared in the pages of the magazine.

Conclusion

The philanthropic work in the form of direct financial contributions was the culmination of the charitable public that was defined by and through the pages of *Ups and Downs*. Young children were emigrated from England to Canada to achieve successes that were likely to be impossible at home. Those who worked hard, persevered, and were careful with their money had the potential to become accomplished young men and women. Such success would enable these emigrant children to assist other children, like themselves, who would benefit from the opportunity to emigrate to Canada. The contributors to the magazine demonstrate the ideals defined by Barnardo's and reinforce the magazine's messaging that British Home Children were grateful for the opportunity to improve their circumstances and eager to help others. The letters submitted by readers reflect the initial hardships of emigration, but also the gradual acclimatisation to Canada's culture and environment.

The children's contributions to the magazine reflect their rhetorical manoeuvres in defining their charitable subjectivity, which were an essential component of the ideal Barnardo child defined in *Ups and Downs*. Their letters demonstrate their gratitude for the opportunity that was given to them and their willingness to express their gratitude in their correspondence. However, at the same time that they were positioning themselves as grateful recipients of charity, they were also required to acknowledge their obligation to help others and to demonstrate that duty through financial contributions. Although they sometimes paid their charitable dues, more often than not Barnardo's was left wondering 'where are the nine?' This suggests that the dual subjectivity as both charitable recipient and charitable donor could be difficult – and at times uncomfortable – for readers to navigate. They seemed more interested in connecting with family and friends through magazine structures like the 'Old Friends' Directory' and correspondence than in assisting unnamed children to emigrate. The relative scarcity of their monetary donations also indicates the limits of charitable giving when the contributors were required to inhabit subject positions as both recipients and donors.

Notes

1. See, for instance, Roy Parker's *Uprooted: The Shipment of Poor Children to Canada, 1867–1917* (Chicago: Policy Press, 2010), Marjorie Kohli's *The Golden Bridge: Young Immigrants to Canada, 1833–1939* (Toronto: Natural Heritage Books, 2003), Gail Corbett's *Nation Builders*, Kenneth Bagnell's *The Little Immigrants: The Orphans Who Came to Canada* (Toronto: Macmillan, 1980), and Chapter 2 in Neil Sutherland's *Children in English-Canadian Society: Framing the Twentieth-Century Consensus* (Waterloo: Wilfred Laurier University Press, 2000).
2. Joy Parr, *Labouring Children: British Immigrant Apprentices to Canada, 1869–1914* (Toronto: University of Toronto Press, 1994), 11.
3. Corbett, *Nation Builders*, 26. *49th Annual Report of Dr. Barnardo's Homes* (London: np, 1914), 33.
4. Parr, *Labouring*, 85.
5. With the change in legislation, emigrators turned their attention to Australia.
6. Kendall R. Phillips, 'Rhetorical Maneuvers: Subjectivity, Power, and Resistance', *Philosophy & Rhetoric* 39, no. 4 (2006): 312.
7. Stuart Hall, 'The Question of Cultural Identity', in *Modernity and Its Futures*, ed. Stuart Hall, David Held, and Tony McGrew (Cambridge: Polity Press, 1992), 277.
8. Phillips, 'Rhetorical Maneuvers', 312.
9. Elisabeth Hoff-Clausen, 'Rhetorical Agency: What Enables and Restrains the Power of Speech?', in *The Handbook of Organizational Rhetoric and Communication*, ed. Øyvind Ihlen and Robert L. Heath (Hoboken: John Wiley & Sons, 2018), 287.
10. Lisa Blackman, John Cromby, Derek Hook, Dimitris Papadopoulos, and Valerine Walkerdine, 'Creating Subjectivities', *Subjectivity* 22 (2008): 6.
11. Phillips, 'Rhetorical Maneuvers', 310.
12. 'Juvenile Immigration', *The Globe*, 2 October 1875, 4.

162   Philanthropy in Children's Periodicals, 1840–1930

13. 'Report of the Select Committee of the House of Commons in Immigration and Colonization', *The Globe*, 13 April 1875, 4.
14. 'Report', 4.
15. Parr, *Labouring*, 103.
16. 'Canada', *The Globe*, 27 December 1875, 3.
17. 'A Single Woman: Miss Findley Charged With Killing a Boy', *The Globe*, 14 November 1895, 1.
18. 'A Single Woman', 1.
19. 'A Single Woman', 1.
20. 'A Woman Fiend', *Ottawa Citizen*, 15 November 1895, np. Library and Archives of Canada Immigration Branch (RG 76, Volume 124, File 25399).
21. Thomas Barnardo, 'Emigration to Canada', *Times*, 25 November 1895, 6.
22. Barnardo, 'Emigration', 6.
23. Barnardo, 'Emigration', 6.
24. 'Barnardo's Boys', *Evening News*, 22 November 1895, np. Library and Archives of Canada Immigration Branch (RG 76, Volume 124, File 25399).
25. *The Globe*, 14 November 1895, np. Libraries and Archives Canada Immigration Branch (RG 76, Volume 124, File 25399).
26. Gillian Wagner, *Barnardo* (London: Eyre & Spottiswoode, 1979), 248.
27. 'Importation of Waifs', *The Globe*, 27 September 1881, 8.
28. 'Importation', 8.
29. 'What Other Papers Say', *The Globe*, 30 March 1895, 3.
30. The next largest emigrators were William Quarrier (239), the Rev. Mr Wallace (227), Louisa Birt (130), Maria Rye (121), and Annie Macpherson (102) (Frank Vipond, 'At the Editor's Desk', *Ups and Downs*, September 1895, 4).
31. By this point, Barnardo's had a lengthy history of publishing magazines for children that were designed to attract subscribers and to reinforce the need for regular contributions. Its first adult publication, *Night and Day*, was launched in 1877. It was followed by children's magazines including *The Children's Treasury*, *Our Darlings*, and *Bubbles* in the 1880s and 1890s, although these magazines were more focused on religious teachings than charity work. *Young Helpers' League Magazine* was launched in 1892 to encourage his young readers to engage with the charity and its aims. In the January 1896 issue of *Ups and Downs*, the Young Helpers' League is explained to readers.

32. Alfred B. Owen, 'Echoes of the Month', *Ups and Downs*, January 1895, 1.
33. Frank Vipond, 'At the Editor's Desk', *Ups and Downs*, January 1895, 4.
34. Owen, 'Echoes', 1.
35. Owen, 'Echoes', 1.
36. Corbett, *Nation Builders*, 56.
37. Vipond, 'With Our Friends', *Ups and Downs*, September 1895, 6.
38. Vipond, 'With Our Friends', 6.
39. 'Medal Winners', *Ups and Downs*, September 1895, 5.
40. 'Medal Winners', 5.
41. 'Medal Winners', 5.
42. 'Medal Winners', 5.
43. 'Medal Winners', 5.
44. 'Medal Winners', 5.
45. 'Medal Winners', 5.
46. 'Medal Winners', 5.
47. 'Medal Winners', 5.
48. 'Medal Winners', 6.
49. 'Here and There', *Ups and Downs*, February 1896, 2.
50. 'Here and There', *Ups and Downs*, November 1895, 7.
51. 'Here and There', 7.
52. 'With Our Friends', *Ups and Downs*, December 1895, 6.
53. 'With Our Friends', 6.
54. 'With Our Friends', 6.
55. 'With Our Friends', 6.
56. 'With Our Friends', 6.
57. 'With Our Friends', 6.
58. 'With Our Friends', 6.
59. 'Our Emigrants', *Ups and Downs*, January 1898, 83.
60. At certain times, the girls' receiving home Hazel Brae was closed owing to staffing issues and house upkeep. Wagner includes a description from Barnardo's diary about 'sealing up windows and every aperture' before setting fire to sulphur to fumigate the girls' dormitory for insects, remarking 'how infested the place has been, and how necessary a new regime was' (Wagner, *Barnardo*, 243).
61. Alfred Owen, 'Echoes of the Month', *Ups and Downs*, December 1895, 2.
62. Owen, 'Echoes of the Month', 2.
63. 'Our Girls', *Ups and Downs*, January 1896, 9.

164   Philanthropy in Children's Periodicals, 1840–1930

64. 'Our Girls', 9.
65. 'Our Girls', *Ups and Downs*, January 1896, 9.
66. 'Our Girls', *Ups and Downs*, January 1896, 10.
67. 'A Letter from a Former "Wild Thyme" Girl', *Ups and Downs*, January 1896, 10.
68. 'A Letter', *Ups and Downs*, 10.
69. 'A Letter', *Ups and Downs*, 10
70. 'Our Girls', *Ups and Downs*, January 1896, 11.
71. 'Our Girls', 10, 11.
72. 'With Our Friends', *Ups and Downs*, August 1895, 7.
73. 'Our Girls', *Ups and Downs*, January 1896, 10.
74. 'Our Girls', 10.
75. 'Opinions of Girls on "The Press"', *Ups and Downs*, February 1896, 11.
76. 'Opinions of Girls', 11.
77. 'Our Old Friends' Directory', *Ups and Downs*, October 1895, np.
78. 'Here and There', *Ups and Downs*, November 1895, 6.
79. 'Here and There', *Ups and Downs*, November 1895, 7.
80. 'Here and There', *Ups and Downs*, February 1896, 6.
81. 'Echoes of the Month', *Ups and Downs*, January 1896, 1.
82. 'Here and There', 6.
83. 'Here and There', 6.
84. 'Where Are the Nine?' *Ups and Downs*, February 1896, 3.
85. 'Where Are the Nine?', 3.
86. 'Waiting for More', *Ups and Downs*, March 1896, 3.
87. 'Here and There', *Ups and Downs*, February 1896, 5.
88. 'Here and There', 6.
89. 'Here and There', 6.
90. 'Story of the Girls' Donation Fund', *Ups and Downs*, March 1896, 9.
91. 'Story', 9. The girls first funded a Hazel Brae cot beginning in 1889.
92. 'Story', 9.
93. 'Story', 9.
94. 'Story', 9.
95. 'Story', 9. The hymn is 'While the Days Are Going By', with lyrics by George Cooper and music by Ira Sankey.
96. 'Girls' Donation Fund', *Ups and Downs*, April 1896, 9.
97. 'Girls' Donation Fund', 9.
98. 'Girls' Donation Fund', 9.
99. 'Girls' Donation Fund', *Ups and Downs*, July 1896, 11.

Charitable Subjectivity   165

100. 'Girls' Donation Fund', 11.
101. 'Girls' Donation Fund', *Ups and Downs*, August 1896, 10.
102. 'Girls' Donation Fund', 10.
103. 'Girls' Donation Fund', 10.
104. 'Girls' Donation Fund', 10.
105. 'Girls' Donation Fund', 10.
106. 'Girls' Donation Fund', 10.
107. 'Girls' Donation Fund', *Ups and Downs*, September 1896, 11. Emphasis in original.
108. 'Girls' Donation Fund', 11. Emphasis in original.
109. 'Girls' Donation Fund, *Ups and Downs*, April 1897, 9. Emphasis in original.
110. 'A Letter from Dr. Barnardo', *Ups and Downs*, July 1897, 11.
111. Barbara Code, 'The Duty of Contributing to the Home', *Ups and Downs*, October 1897, 38.
112. Code, 'The Duty', 38.

6

Transnational Charity

In June 1890, eight-year-old Gerald wrote to ask whether 'Dot', the editor of the *Otago Witness* children's column 'Our Little Folks', had heard about Barnardo's 'poor little children' and if she would consider asking other child readers of the column to send 'some pennies' to support them.[1] This letter highlights how knowledge about charitable institutions was circulating transnationally, as were ideas about children as transnational charitable donors. Studies of philanthropy have highlighted the ways in which ideas circulated within English-speaking countries, informed by similar developments in thinking about political economy, social science, and charity. Frank Christianson and Leslee Thorne-Murphy explain that, from the first half of the nineteenth century, 'a literature of philanthropy proliferated on both sides of the Atlantic, as increasing urbanization and industrialization created new demands on traditional social structures'.[2] Others have examined networks of reformers and activists to show how people were moving between places to share philanthropic ideas.[3] While most of this scholarship has focused on transatlantic connections, the ubiquity of similar philanthropic strategies in the British colonies alongside the United States and Great Britain indicates a transnational orientation for philanthropic activities.

This chapter argues that children's charitable activities can be placed within this transnational framework to better understand the extent to which philanthropic discourses were circulating throughout English-speaking countries. It draws on two children's columns, one in the *Otago Witness*, a regional newspaper covering the south-eastern region of New Zealand's South Island, and the other in the South Australian *Adelaide Observer*. These weekly

166

columns are both notable because of their presence in adult newspapers, which offered a different engagement with young readers than the dedicated monthly children's magazines discussed in other chapters. The publication of extensive correspondence sections in both columns offers a window into New Zealand and South Australian childhood and the ways that young people understood their charitable obligations. These columns contain different approaches to charitable work and the ways in which children were mobilised to attract readers and encourage their fundraising. In particular, it is argued that they reflect a transnational mode of charity that foregrounds the local but also extends beyond it.

In the sections that follow, transnational charity is first defined by considering the intercultural transfer of philanthropic ideas. This is followed by a discussion of the 'Our Little Folks' column in the *Otago Witness*, in which the child readers agitate for the establishment of a charitable fund for the Barnardo's charity. This is the launching point for a detailed exploration of how the transnationalism of Barnardo's is apparent in this column in the 1890s, how this outward-looking orientation is set alongside local need, and how this transnationalism again manifests in the form of support for the Belgian Relief Fund after the start of the First World War. In the second example, the 'Children's Column' of the *Adelaide Observer*, the organic approach to charity in the *Otago Witness* is contrasted with the focused strategy of the Sunbeam Society instantiated through the South Australia column. These child readers, it is argued, are enacting transnational charity through their participation in other charity groups with London origins and through their active engagement with other international charitable causes like the Ragged School in London, a mining disaster in New Zealand, and the Indian famine. However, local need is at times in tension with those international charities as competing demands are placed on limited funds. Together, these examples reflect not only the extent to which ideas about children's charity were circulating in British colonies like New Zealand and Australia, but also the degree to which these children were interested in and willing to raise funds for international causes.

Transnational charity

According to the *Oxford English Dictionary*, the term 'transnational' means 'extending or having interests extending beyond

168 Philanthropy in Children's Periodicals, 1840–1930

national boundaries or frontiers'.[4] Bill Ashcroft defines the 'trans-nation' as an 'endlessly mobile cultural phenomenon, a horizontal reality – distinct from the vertical, hierarchical authority of the state' in which culture 'exceed[s] the boundaries of the nation-state and operat[es] beyond its political structures through the medium of the local'.[5] In considering the idea of 'transnational charity', then, we need to consider how the idea of charity extends beyond national boundaries, especially as it pertains to young people. Paul Jay makes a related claim that transnationalism is a phenomenon characterised by 'complex back-and-forth flows of people and cultural forms'.[6] In Jay's discussion of transnational-ism, he reminds readers that the term is an adjective that modifies 'anything that can be thought of as having a transnational range, dimension, or character'.[7] Transnational charity is characterised by the movement of people, ideas, practices, and periodicals that defined what it meant to be charitable.

The rhetoric of charity that is deployed in the children's columns of New Zealand and Australian magazines is striking for its similarity to language appearing elsewhere in the British press. Tony Ballantyne explains how 'colonial intellectual life was energized by the movement of ideas and information' and how 'the proliferation of newspapers and popular journals, both in the metropole and in the colonies, also ensured the rapid circulation of a shared body of news and energized intellectual debate'.[8] In Clare Bradford's discussion of transnational children's literature, she asserts the 'colonial cultures of Australia, New Zealand, and Canada were much more attuned to each other than to the impe-rial centre'.[9] The examples discussed in this chapter simultane-ously confirm but also complicate this narrative of belonging. Bradford explains how this 'transnational consciousness' creates a 'dual identification' as British and colonial.[10] The examples of colonial children's charity reflect not only local concerns in which children raise funds for their local causes, but also their keen interest in British charitable causes and an awareness of their place in the world.

Ideas about charity were circulating transnationally along-side ideas about children and expectations of them. Moreover, the presence of these ideas in children's print culture also rein-forces the print medium and its seriality as essential to the ideal of transnational charity for children. Jude Piesse argues that the Victorian periodical can be understood as 'an inherently mobile, transnational form' in part because it can be characterised by 'its compulsion and capacity to circulate'.[11] Like the Victorian periodicals that were being distributed through the English-speaking world, their readers were also mobile, thereby enabling the circulation of charitable ideas throughout America and the British empire.

The problems caused by rapid industrialisation and urbanisation were widespread throughout the nineteenth century, and social reformers actively sought to develop new strategies and approaches to address problems ranging from prison reform, welfare, medicine, hygiene and sanitation, and temperance, among many others. Chris Leonards and Nico Randeraad make an argument for 'the transnational dimension of social policy from 1840 to 1880' while noting that 'the framework of the nation-state' has often been the origin of historical analysis.[12] They highlight transnational aspects of social reform, many of which informed the policies appearing in Australia and New Zealand, and explain how social reformers had a 'transnational outlook' and 'were eager to consult ideas and legislation in countries other than their own'.[13] British organisations clearly saw other parts of the English-speaking world as potential sources for their fundraising needs, using local branches, magazines, and news reports to celebrate achievements and encourage donations.

Thomas Adam makes a similar argument using the concept of 'intercultural transfer'. He focuses on philanthropy across several countries to argue that the 'cultural and social infrastructure of nineteenth-century cities' was a result of 'intensive contacts and transfers across geographic, linguistic, and later "imagined" national borders'.[14] This transfer, he explains, 'refers to the movement of material objects, people, and ideas between two separate and clearly defined cultures and societies'.[15] Despite the perception that Britain was 'home' among white settler colonists, the distinctness of their colonial locales was clear. Intercultural transfer occurred through the import and export of people and ideas, especially through print culture networks. While examining the transnational circulation of charity policies and strategies is beyond the scope of this chapter, considering children's charity as transnational offers an opportunity to explore how children in British colonies were inducted into habits of charitable behaviour and the extent to which those habits were themselves transnational in orientation.

170   Philanthropy in Children's Periodicals, 1840–1930

Barnardo's in the *Otago Witness*

The *Otago Witness* launched its inaugural children's column on 11 November 1876 by asking parents and elder siblings 'to aid us by directing the attention of the little ones to this column'.[16] With the aim of making the *Otago Witness* 'a more complete family paper', it added a column 'devoted to subjects interesting to the young'.[17] Located on the same page as 'The Ladies' Column', the 'Children's Column' appeared weekly until 1932.[18] Featuring poetry, short stories, essays, and puzzles, it initially occupied a column and a half. Relatively quickly, the young readers were invited to submit original contributions.[19] A follow-up notice containing more detail explains that '[i]t is our desire to make "The Children's Column" as interesting as possible, and with that view we invite the assistance of the children and those who possess the peculiar faculty for their entertainment . . . we wish to give all a chance'.[20] Although some essays and poems appeared intermittently, with the arrive of the editorial persona 'Dot' the column began to attain its vibrancy through interactions with young readers. Her first attributed column, 'Our Little Folks, by Dot', appeared on 16 July 1886, and in it she writes, 'Dot will be pleased to receive short letters from juvenile correspondents on any matters of interest to themselves – short stories of pet animals, descriptions of their favourite toys, their parties, amusements, &c.'[21] The following week, Ethel responds that '[a]s you ask for short letters I should like to write you one' and describes receiving *Chatterbox* from a kind friend while she was ill.[22] The children's correspondence continues in this vein, with letters describing pets, homes, and vacations, with Dot beginning to add brief responses to some letters in the following weeks.

Children's charitable knowledge appears in 'Our Little Folks', reflecting the transnational charitable orientation developed and reinforced in the column. When Gerald explains to Dot in 1890 that he sent 5s to Barnardo, he has evidently heard about Barnardo's charity somewhere, either from 'Our Little Folks' or from other activities occurring in the community.[23] Barnardo's 'Rescued for Life: The True Story of a Young Thief' was serialised in the column in 1883 and 'Kidnapped: A Narrative of Fact' in late 1885. News about his 'Babies Castle' appeared in 1884.[24] 'Our Little Folks' contained reports from Barnardo, including one that describes the 'immense amount of work being done by the conductors of the Homes' with support from New Zealand contributors at the Dunedin Garrison Hall Sunday School and two others from Canterbury.[25] That young people from the Sunday School are already sending contributions directly to Barnardo indicates the pervasive nature of charitable knowledge and demonstrates the children's transnational charity efforts. The report also describes Barnardo's plan to emigrate children to Canada, another form of transnationalism in which poor children themselves become transnational through their movement from England.[26] Thus children's interest in the Barnardo charity was reinforced through regular references in 'Our Little Folks'. At the same time, Barnardo also highlighted the interesting feature of overseas contributions in *Night and Day*, his monthly magazine for adult readers. His report on the 'numerous contributions and letters of sympathy good-will' from New Zealand with 'many children ... among the contributors' is reprinted in 'Our Little Folks'.[27]

Reports of children's fundraising for Barnardo's elsewhere in the *Otago Witness* reflect the extent to which charitable work was part of New Zealand settler culture. One report from Hokitika describes the 'great success' of a children's fancy dress bazaar in which '[c]hildren's dances in fancy costumes were greatly admired, and a substantial sum will accrue'.[28] The village of Portobello reports that Mr Barton 'has been giving a series of lectures in the various schools in the vicinity in aid of Dr Barnardo's homes for destitute children in London', and another article describes a plan among Oamaru pastoralists to send 100 frozen sheep to the Barnardo's Home in London.[29] In Puerua Hall, a soiree, concert, and dance resulted in £11 raised for the Home.[30] The children of the Women's Christian Association Sunday School were entertained by a lantern exhibition that included the stories of 'Jessica's First Prayer', a waif novel by Hesba Stretton, and 'a fine collection of pictures sent out by Dr. Barnardo, and illustrative of his work in the slums of London'.[31] These examples, which range across the southern part of the South Island, reflect Barnardo's effective advertising and the extent to which people were aware of his cause. One article explains how '[p]hilanthropy has many outlets for its exercise' with Barnardo's homes as one of the 'most praiseworthy'.[32] Barnardo's 'appeals for aid have been responded to from all parts of the globe, and New Zealand has afforded and continues to afford material help'.[33] The ubiquity of the charitable cause is such that regular events take place in and around Otago to raise awareness of the organisation and money for its support.

Gerald's interest in the Barnardo's charity is consequently unsurprising. In his letter to Dot, he explains how he saved his pennies 'in a little tin box' and after saving 4s 3d, his father gave him an additional 9d so that he was able to send 5s to Barnardo. Gerald wonders whether Dot has heard of these 'poor children' who have 'no homes' and 'no beds', whose clothes are 'only just rags' and who have 'no nice warm breakfast'.[34] His letter is an explicit call for readers of the column to raise funds for the Barnardo charity, and it signals not only the prevalence of the Barnardo name in colonial New Zealand, but also the extent to which children saw no impediments to raising money to help children overseas.

Dot's response supports and encourages Gerald's transnational charitable aims. She explains that she is familiar with the charity and that Barnardo and his fellow workers deserve 'very great credit, and assistance of all right-thinking people'.[35] She hopes that Gerald's example will be followed 'by many of the little folks'.[36] The idea that other readers might contribute is raised in the accompanying letter from Gerald's mother, who wonders what Dot would think of 'forming a juvenile club to raise subscriptions' since a word from Dot in support 'would be of great advantage, as your influence with the Little Folks is considerable'.[37] Dot is eager to hear from her readers, asking them to write and share their opinions on the proposal. She also publishes Barnardo's response to Gerald's contribution, in which he is 'greatly encouraged and cheered' by this 'helpful and opportune gift'.[38] He gestures toward the distance between London and New Zealand when he writes, 'I am delighted to think that my work here has such a warm corner – in the heart of your young son.'[39] The distance between the two countries is shortened through Barnardo's appreciation of the contribution and the sense of fellow-feeling that Gerald depicts in his letter. Together, people from all over can work to ameliorate the circumstances of the poor waifs in Barnardo's care.

The enthusiasm with which Dot's young readers responded indicates the transnational charitable ideal circulating in the nineteenth century. Bertie writes that he wishes to send money to Barnardo but feels it would be better to send it through the *Otago Witness*. He does not 'see any difficulty in starting a fund in connection with the Little Folks' column'.[40] The following month, a letter from F. Every refers to 2s that could be forwarded to Barnardo 'if the Little Folks would like to do as Gerald's mother suggests'.[41] Finally, on 11 September 1890, Dot agrees to the proposal, suggesting that the 'Little Folks might send a Christmas box to Dr. Barnardo'.[42] She lists the contributions received thus far and 'to test the feelings of the Little Folks in the matter, the list will by kept open till October 1' in order that money can be forwarded before Christmas.[43] This reference to the timing of the list reflects the distance between the fundraisers and where the money will be spent, further reinforcing the transnationality of this charitable work.

The Christmas Box was an invitation to some correspondents to write. Twelve-year-old Gertrude Provo writes, 'It is now a long time since I wrote to you, and you will possibly wonder who I am.'[44] Having seen the notice that Dot has started a collection, 'my sisters and myself made up our minds to send you all our savings . . . for the poor little children'.[45] The girls have sacrificed their savings for although '[w]e have not got much to send, we have sent you all that we have'.[46] One typical letter comes from M. Collie, who writes,

> I have got 1s, and I would like it sent to Dr. Barnardo's homes with the children's money. It is all my own. We have got one cow, and her name is Pet. She is so quiet that we can milk her anywhere. We have about half a mile to walk to school, and I hope I shall pass this examination.[47]

Young writers were happy to contribute to the charitable cause, yet charity is only one of their interests, as this reference to pets and school suggests. Young readers of the column raised £17 18s 5d, and Barnardo's acknowledgement was published in April 1891. He explains that '[t]he great delay in acknowledging your very kind and welcome gift has been chiefly owing to a serious accident which I sustained last month.'[48] Although he wishes to 'express my real gratitude to all your little folks individually . . . I trust that you will allow me, through your columns, to say "thank you" to one and all of those who have thus generously and self sacrificingly contributed.'[49] The newspaper that enables the collection of funds is also the venue by which Barnardo can share his appreciation for this transnational charity.

174   Philanthropy in Children's Periodicals, 1840–1930

Communication delays and multiple promotional strategies by Barnardo's meant that young people were regularly encouraged to make charitable donations. In early January 1891, and before the children's donation had been acknowledged, Dot writes of receiving a cable message on Christmas Eve reporting of Barnardo's urgent need for funds and asking 'Will Australia send a generous gift'.[50] Dot explains that the children's Christmas donation has arrived 'at a most opportune time' and will 'go some little way towards alleviating the sufferings of a few little homeless waifs, who otherwise could possibly not have been provided for'.[51] In light of Barnardo's appeal, Dot opened a second list and promised to acknowledge all subscriptions.

The transnationalism of the Barnardo charity is made explicit when a group of Barnardo boys come from London to New Zealand as part of a lecturing tour. The *Evening Post* reports that the boys are currently engaged in Australia and expect to be in New Zealand by the end of 1891.[52] In early 1892, reports begin to appear of their demonstrations and the monies raised. The boys play 'selections of music on bells, bagpipes, violin, cornet, etc., the whole going to make up an excellent and instructive entertainment'.[53] These boys are circulating as examples of transnational charity in which they have been 'rescued' from their impoverished circumstances in England and transformed into ideal charitable subjects who can travel through Australia and New Zealand to encourage people to contribute to the cause. They 'entertain' but are also the 'entertainment' as they demonstrate their cultural prowess through their musical accomplishments, much like the correspondence from Barnardo children in *Ups and Downs* enabled them to depict their multiple subjectivities.

Moreover, the readers of the 'Little Folks' column are responding to the transnational charitable ideal as they attend this entertainment. Lily, Jane, and Bridget write that they went to see the boys when they were visiting: 'It was very nice indeed, and we enjoyed ourselves very much.'[54] This ability to visit the boys replaces the collection organised by Dot as charitable activity is relocated from the pages of the newspaper to organised gatherings in the community. Dot explains in response to a query that she is 'not collecting anything for Dr. Barnardo just now, but a troop of rescued children will be in Otago soon, and you will then be able to contribute'.[55] The strategy of transnational appeals through the circulation of young people was evidently sufficiently

Transnational Charity   175

successful to warrant a further tour in 1909.[56] Unlike many other examples of children's print, in which fundraising is a perennial concern and represents a strong focus for the magazine, for 'Our Little Folks' it is one of many different concerns, reflecting the multifaceted interests of its child readers.

Transnational and local charities in 'Our Little Folks'

The establishment of the Young Helpers' League in 1892, discussed in Chapter 4, offered another venue through which New Zealand children could support the Barnardo charity. 'Our Little Folks' supported transnational charity by directing young readers to charitable organisations like the Young Helpers' League. As with the support for Barnardo's discussed in the previous section, readers raised the league as a possible charitable cause. Griffith Lewis writes that:

> Any boy or girl under 18 who sends six penny stamps to Miss Rachel Norton can become a member ... and a paper called the Young Helpers' League will be sent to them every quarter; it has pictures and nice little stories in it, and one story to be continued. They are mostly about poor little children. Any one who is a member of the Young Helpers' League must do all they can do to help the poor children who are crippled and sick, especially those under Dr. Barnardo's care, either by making things to sell at the bazaars or by collecting money among their friends, or sending money of their own.[57]

Griffith provides a useful overview about the Young Helpers' League and although he emphasises that the work is intended for Barnardo, helping other poor children is a possibility. Thirteen-year-old John Williamson writes in shortly thereafter noting that Norton's address has not been included. Griffith writes again with the address and offers to provide further details if anyone wants to 'know anything more about it'.[58]

The children's column enables the young people to correspond with each other about their charitable work. Two years after Griffith's letter is published, his eleven-year-old sister Dorothy wonders whether John Williamson ever joined the league. She hopes to encourage other readers to join so that she can earn a badge. She explains that 'I should like to get one very much; but still more I want to do all I can to help the poor little children.'[59]

176   Philanthropy in Children's Periodicals, 1840–1930

Dot does not know about John, but she hopes he will write to let everyone know. Dorothy's letter is followed by one from Ruth Lewis, also from Takaka and presumably sister of the other two correspondents. She wonders whether other children who write to the column have become members and invites those who might be interested to send one shilling in stamps to them and they 'will be pleased to get a post-office order' to send to the secretary.[60] In addition, she is keen to hear from other league members about 'how they are getting on, and if they know many belonging to the League where they live'.[61] Dot's response, encouraging her 'little Nelson Friends' to explain more about the Young Helpers' League, offers an opportunity for the young people to encourage others in charitable feeling and activity.[62] This strategy is more participatory than the one deployed in *Aunt Judy's Magazine*, in which Gatty picked the Great Ormond Street Hospital for Sick Children as the magazine's charitable cause, or that of the 'Sunbeam Society' in the *Adelaide Observer* discussed later in the chapter. In 'Our Little Folks', the children are often the ones who suggest ideas for charitable work instead of being guided by the editor.

In contrast to her benign support for the Young Helpers' League, Dot took a more active role to raise funds for the local Free Kindergarten in Dunedin. In a December 1894 letter to 'My Dear Little Folks', Dot describes a walk through the city to see those 'needing your help and sympathy'.[63] On a 'steep, ugly street' with 'dirty, dingy shops and warehouses', filled with 'dirty, wretched, squalid little houses' and 'rotten old tumble-down shanties', stand 'slouching men and untidy women' but no children.[64] The young people can be found in the Free Kindergarten, 'the gentle, kindly shelter that these little street waifs have grown to love' for 'instead of drunkenness, quarrelling blows, and evil sights and sounds, they are in an atmosphere of gentlest love and patience and kindness'.[65] Dot's letter is notable, given her more neutral stance about her readers' interest in raising funds for international charities like Barnardo's. Instead, she directly addresses her readers:

> You who have happy homes of your own on the wide, breezy plains, among the great solitary hills by the blue lake, or near the surf-broken shore, you who are far removed from want, sin, and misery, you who make my great army of friendly 'Little Folks', what will you do for these little waifs and strays? You children who so dearly love your pets and your gardens must, I know, be both tender and self-denying.

Where could you show it better than in an effort to help these little ones, children like yourselves?[66]

By working together on this common goal, Dot explains, Little Folks 'scattered all over New Zealand, strangers to each other and to me, might yet feel that you have a good work of sweet unselfishness of *your very own*, a band of brotherhood and sisterhood which would give you all a common interest and kindly sympathy'.[67] Dot imagines a charitable public among her New Zealand readers that draws on shared experiences in reasonably well-to-do homes located in distinctly New Zealand pastoral settings. These young people, she assumes, will be motivated to contribute funds for other children whose circumstances are considerably worse, but who are united through their national identity. The initial contributions of 1s 7d are reported two weeks later.[68] Dot laments the slow growth of the fund on 10 January 1895, writing that '[a]t the beginning of the week I was almost despairing of doing anything for the poor little folks of the kindergarten, but almost each day since then a letter with stamps has come to hand, till we really have made a very good start', with contributions totalling 2s 9d.[69]

Unlike the waifs of London, who are seemingly better known, the poor of New Zealand are less familiar to readers. Nelly writes that 'I did not think you had so many waifs in your fair city'.[70] Whether this lack of knowledge contributed to the general disinterest was unclear. Dot writes, 'I will confess that I have been a little disappointed that the interest among my little folks has not been wider'.[71] Nonetheless, by early March, one pound had been sent to the kindergarten from thirty-six contributors. However, Dot is concerned about a decline in the number of letters and reminds readers that they do not need to send stamps in with their letters: 'Please do not stop writing' if you have no stamps, 'for if our pleasant friendship and correspondence is to suffer because of the Kindergarten Fund, I must give up the fund altogether'.[72] The fund continued, nonetheless, with a second pound forwarded in May and a third pound in early June. Moreover, even though Dot's audience is predominantly local, as is the cause itself, the transnational aspect to this charity is apparent in the 'several' contributions she notes from Australia and one from New Mexico in the United States.[73] The fund picked up speed thereafter with a total of ten pounds raised by the end of 1895 and a further five pounds by the end of 1896.[74] Dot responded to a query from

178   Philanthropy in Children's Periodicals, 1840–1930

Ruby in May 1899 that the 'Little Folks have done very well for the Kindergarten Fund, and I do not expect any more stamps for it now'.[75] When Ice sends five pence for the Kindergarten Fund in 1905, Dot explains that it was closed 'years and years ago' and that 'I have frequently announced since that there was to be no more money or stamps collected on any account'.[76] Owing at least in part to more substantial editorial support, the fund was successful in attracting children to a local charitable cause in a more sustained way than some of the child-initiated efforts responding to the calls to action from London-based charities like Barnardo's.

The final transnational charitable activity appearing in the *Otago Witness* that I want to discuss is the Belgian Relief Fund. After Germany's invasion of Belgium at the start of the First World War in August 1914, the fund was designed to assist the Belgians and separate this fundraising from more general efforts. New Zealand children, like all those from settler colonial countries, made significant contributions on the home front, even when they were – like New Zealand children – far from the front. Charlotte Bennett writes that children far from the main wartime action were 'also affected by the conflict [since] educational activities in these regions were ... disturbed' as '[t]eachers left for military service, curricula were changed to include war lessons, and children were involved in school-directed war-effort activities'.[77] Jeanine Graham similarly explains how young people in New Zealand 'were active in both community and school-based fundraising ventures during the war'.[78] The Belgian cause in particular was a source of 'spontaneous' fundraising that 'gave many communities an early opportunity to involve both school children and adults in small and easily planned activities'.[79]

Correspondence in the children's column certainly indicates the ubiquitous nature of their transnational wartime charitable work, and the column promotes these behaviours by encouraging Belgian Relief Fund fundraising through its pages. The first mention in the children's column, titled 'Dot's Little Folk' (DLF), appears in October 1914, when Dot proposes that, while some children may have already been helping their parents with donations of money or clothing, others might be interested in contributing to a DLF branch if one were established: 'With this end in view, I am prepared to receive donations of clothing or money for the relief of those brave people, who, now more than ever, are in need of

Transnational Charity   179

assistance.'[80] She generates sympathy through emotive rhetoric about the terrible circumstances in Belgium:

> It is terrible to think of a quiet, peace-loving people suddenly, and practically without reason, attacked and driven from their homes, which were then given to the flames, while fathers, sons, and all males capable of bearing arms were ruthlessly slaughtered by an overwhelming force, because they dared to defend their country.[81]

The reader is expected to identify with the peaceful citizens who have been unjustly attacked and killed, leaving behind devastated families who are now homeless and without food. Unlike the slow progression of the Kindergarten Fund and minimal mention in the correspondence, the war and the Belgian Relief Fund appear in the children's correspondence soon after Dot's letter. Billy, of Hidden Bush, writes that '[a] concert will be held here on Friday night in aid of the Belgians, and I hope it will be a success ... The Belgians want something done for them, as they have lost their homes and their country is ruined.'[82] He specifically identifies the transnational aspect of this charitable work, wondering if the Belgians 'have any idea what the people on this side of the world are doing to help them'.[83] He concludes by noting he has included one shilling for the DLF Belgian Fund. In the same issue, Tabitha Mew sends half a crown in stamps for the fund, and Dot responds that '[t]he way my young people are responding ... shows they still uphold the old traditions'.[84] Although she seems to be implying that charity might be considered old-fashioned, she is grateful to find young readers willing to assist people badly affected by the war.

   Just as the correspondence about the Young Helpers' League indicated the multiple ways that children were engaging in transnational charity work, the correspondence discussing the war and the Belgian Relief Fund is likewise multifaceted. Cottage Girl explains that she often goes to the pictures on Saturday night and then asks, 'What do you think of the war, Dot? I am enclosing 2s 6d for the Belgian Relief Fund. I shall be glad when the war is over.'[85] Dot responds, 'If everyone realised the fearful suffering of these people they would sacrifice some little luxury to give them the necessaries of life.'[86] Cottage Girl's mention of the war and her donation is striking for its juxtaposition with the everyday activities in which she participates, such as attending

180   Philanthropy in Children's Periodicals, 1840–1930

the cinema, as well as the status of her garden, her job, and the animals she cares for on a farm. Dot's response reminds readers of the terrible circumstances overseas and of the need to sacrifice to help those less fortunate. Her comment reinforces the value and urgency of supporting the fund and reminds readers of the need to sacrifice.

Whether children were always happy about the sacrifices they were expected to make is unclear. Bennett has shown how New Zealand's 'overwhelming focus on the conflict resulted in numerous social and economic constraints that negatively impacted children'.[87] Even when the correspondents do not send money for the fund, they are still aware of the need to help the Belgians. Daisy Blackburn writes,

> Our examination is over, and my mate and I received a proficiency certificate. The war is all that most people think about just now. Are not the Belgians being treated cruelly? It is dreadful to think of the poor people being sent out of their homes, and then seeing them burnt to the ground. There is a concert in aid of the Belgian Relief Fund to be held at Hillend next Wednesday. Our school gave 15s to the Ambulance Fund. These are only 25 children, so they did not do so badly.[88]

The transnational charity enacted by Daisy is through her school, but then reported in the correspondence column, where she also sympathises with the Belgians' treatment. Lily of Cardona likewise writes, 'At present our school is busy sewing for the poor Belgians, and I am glad to be able to enclose 6d for the fund you have opened, and I also hope the Little Folk will be able to make your fund up to raise a nice little sum.'[89] The idea of charitable work for the Belgians was evident in multiple places in a young person's life, not just in the pages of their newspaper but also more obviously at home and at school.

These examples in the *Otago Witness* demonstrate children's transnational charitable ethos. They responded positively to both local and international demands for funds. They felt confident in proposing that other readers might be interested in raising funds for a particular cause, which indicates the ubiquity of charity work among young people and in the wider community. It also attests to the influence of the children's column in encouraging this charitable ideal.

The Sunbeam Society in the *Adelaide Observer*

The second half of this chapter turns to another colonial children's column that started later than the one appearing in the *Otago Witness* and ran for fifteen years, between 1894 and 1909. This weekly column was published in the *Adelaide Observer* and Saturday's issue of Adelaide's *Evening Journal* and was edited by David Bottrill, a philanthropist and journalist.[90] Its aim was to form a society among young readers of the paper 'with a view to obtaining and giving help in cases of distress amongst children, whether from accident, bereavement, or poverty'.[91] Like Dot, who wanted know whether children were interested in supporting the kindergarten, 'Uncle Harry' likewise wants to hear from readers about whether they are interested in this proposal before establishing the Sunbeam Society to spread light and warmth. This sunshine is explicitly situated in financial terms, as Uncle Harry remarks that 'I am sure that there are hundreds of children who would be able to save a penny or more to send in now and again whenever a distressful case is reported.'[92] Although he does not define a clear scope for these cases, evidence from the column reflects a transnational charitable outlook where children supported cots in the Adelaide children's hospital and also international causes in London, New Zealand, and India.

The transnationalism of children's charities is evident in some of Uncle Harry's letters. As he is establishing the column and laying out his plans in July 1894, he explains that he 'will be glad . . . to receive now and again short reports from the Secretaries of the various Societies or institutions for children', naming the Boys' Institute, Boys' Brigade, Boys' Field Club, Band of Hope, Ministering Children's League, Junior Christian Endeavour, Rechabite, and other lodges.[93] His listing of these institutions indicates not only the pervasive presence of charitable institutions in Adelaide in the 1890s, but also the expectation that readers will be interested in hearing about their work. Moreover, many of these organisations originated outside of Australia, indicating the transnationalism of much of Australian charitable fundraising.

The children who wrote to Uncle Harry eagerly supported the formation of the Sunbeam Society while also indicating that they were already active in other organisations. Seven-year-old Elsie May writes that 'I think your plan is a very good one, and I will try my best to help you and I will get all the children here to

182   Philanthropy in Children's Periodicals, 1840–1930

help you.'[94] Her support extends beyond simply joining the society to actively encouraging others to become members as well. Uncle Harry is '[g]lad to know that [Verma] belong[s] to the Ministering Children's League' already and invites her to tell him more about it when she writes next.[95] He is similarly pleased to learn that Ethel Wheeler belongs to a Band of Hope and Christian Endeavour Society.[96] This phrasing suggests a combined society in which children were performing both temperance and charitable work. Despite these other commitments, Ethel strongly supports the establishment of the Sunbeam Society. Elsie Watts concludes her letter by explaining that the competition Uncle Harry has established – in which the three best letters received in a given week will be published in full – 'will greatly encourage your little nephews and nieces to help you in your thoughtful endeavor to save many people much misery'.[97] Elsie's correlation between awarding prizes and charitable work reflects the success of the periodical press in encouraging reader engagement through these kinds of strategies.

Enthusiasm for the Sunbeam Society is readily apparent within a few weeks, with children beginning to send in subscriptions even before it officially launched on 1 September 1894. News of the society spread beyond the borders of the colony too. Uncle Harry remarks how delighted he is by the number of letters arriving from boys and girls 'all over the colony (aye, and out of the colony too)'.[98] He even extends the deadline for the second essay competition on 'How I Spend Saturday, Sunday, and Monday' as 'there seems to be a likelihood of some of your cousins in the other colonies competing'.[99] In the formal announcement of the founding of the society, Uncle Harry explains that children between the ages of five and fifteen may become members. Although subscription is 'quite voluntary', new members are 'invited to contribute when making application to join, and thereafter whenever and whatever they are able'.[100] Contributions will primarily be directed towards the 'Sunbeam Society's Cot' in the Children's Hospital of North Adelaide. However, in cases of 'exceptional distress or need arising amongst children, the aid of members and associates [over the age of fifteen] will be specially asked'.[101] The thirty pounds required annually for the cot 'is a large amount, no doubt, to be raised by children; but if we all try we shall not be so very long in doing it'.[102]

Alongside this fundraising goal, Uncle Harry also set out the organisational structure of circles to support the society.

Transnational Charity   183

Any neighbourhood with at least six members or associates are encouraged to 'form themselves into a "Sunbeam Circle"', the meetings of which 'may be simply for social intercourse, or to do work of a Dorcas Society nature, or for the purpose of study, or the pursuit of some hobby such as stamp or coin collecting'.[103] Despite the minimal obligations imposed on a circle, Uncle Harry confesses 'to a feeling of slight disappointment' that applications were not arriving very quickly.[104] Nonetheless, by the end of the first month, he is delighted to announce that another hundred members have joined, bringing the total to over two hundred, and that the first circle, called the 'Wordsworth Sunbeam Circle', has been formed. Enclosed with the circle's letter is 1s 6d in stamps and notification of their intention to send some wildflowers to the Children's Hospital. The second circle, named after writer Charles Kingsley, was announced on 6 October 1894, and two weeks later Uncle Harry announced 350 members and nearly six pounds for the cot.[105] Subsequent circle names include Pansy, Longfellow, and Florence Nightingale.[106] One notable cot name is the 'Barnardo Sunbeam Circle' named, Uncle Harry supposes, 'after the London doctor who has devoted his life to the rescue and restoration of the "waifs and strays" of London'.[107] These names undoubtedly reflect the transnational circulation of literary texts and charitable ideals as well as the popularity of certain writers.

Evidence of the transnational circulation of charitable ideas is explicit in the 'Children's Column' in multiple ways. One of the earliest is Uncle Harry's attempt to develop a connection with the Guild of Kindness operating in the 'Children's Column' of the Glasgow *Weekly Herald*. He explains in January 1895 how he has written to 'Aunt Maria' to inquire if she would be interested in a cross-publication opportunity whereby she would publish the Sunbeam Society's prize-winning essays on 'How I Spent Christmas Day' in her paper and he could print Scottish essays on the same topic. Thus 'the children of this colony would have a good opportunity of know just how their little Scottish cousins spent their Christmas Day, and *vice versa*'.[108] Uncle Harry seems to have been somewhat optimistic in his timeline. He wrote his letter in November, but Aunt Maria's response only appears in a March issue of the following year. She explains that the guild has been very busy making its 'first public effort [by] holding a bazaar and toy exhibition' and is encouraged by its success to continue with similar work.[109] While the timing may now be too

184   Philanthropy in Children's Periodicals, 1840–1930

late for a Christmas competition, she 'should only be too pleased if we could . . . join hands with your members over the sea. I think mutual benefit and interest would accrue.'[110] The charitable ideas being promoted in both periodicals can be shared and bolstered through this connection between young people in different corners of the world.

Uncle Harry's decision to contact the *Weekly Herald* is an interesting one. Frederick Milton has noted the pervasive presence of children's societies in the British provincial press, in which a 'conscious effort was made to not only provide original material for young readers, but also to engage with them by offering an open forum for their contributions in the form of a "society"'.[111] With the earliest society beginning in 1876 and the rapid increase in their formation in the 1890s, Uncle Harry would presumably have had a number of options with whom he might have initiated communication.[112] The connection with the Glasgow paper thus suggests a degree of transnational happenstance that may have been facilitated by Scottish-Australian networks enabled through emigration in the nineteenth century.[113] Uncle Harry presumably had access to the newspaper via local Australian newsagents, and indeed the *Observer* regularly reprinted chess puzzles from the *Weekly Herald* during this period.

The transnational connection established between the two papers was marked by lengthy gaps in the materials appearing in the column. Only in May 1895 do the prize-winning essays appear. Uncle Harry writes that with a membership of over 70,000 in the Guild of Kindness, the much more modest 1,500 Sunbeam Society members 'look small' in comparison.[114] Nonetheless, the power of the society is that is 'does not depend merely upon numbers'.[115] Instead, the secret of their success is that 'almost every member has done and is doing *something* to help it along'.[116] Aunt Maria's letter indicates the interest her readers have in the society and extends her congratulations on the Sunbeam Society's efforts for the Children's Hospital, as 'this success proves the healthy and lively interest there is in your Society, and speaks eloquently for the admirable manner in which you conduct its affairs'.[117] In Uncle Harry's response, he asks his readers, 'What do you say to that loving pat on the back from far away Glasgow? Let us, in return, offer "Aunt Maria" and her . . . members our heartiest congratulations on the splendid success of their first big bazaar.'[118] The mutual interest in charitable work is evidence of the transnational circulation of charitable ideals and of ideals about children and childhood. Neither editor has any doubt that their readers will be eager to learn about Christmas happenings on the other side of the world and that they are united in their interest in charitable work.

Transnational and local charities in the 'Children's Column'

The interest in London-based charitable work that is evident in the 'Children's Column' of the *Otago Witness* is also apparent in the *Adelaide Observer*. In October 1895, Uncle Harry writes of a letter he received from the secretary of the John Ruskin Sunbeam Circle suggesting that the society should help to provide 'a Christmas dinner for some of the poor little waifs and strays of London'.[119] Uncle Harry uses similar affective language that was discussed in Chapter 4 to emphasise the sad circumstances of London's poor as they crowd around a baker's shop or at a pie stall on the street hoping for something to eat. He is sure that the child readers are already well acquainted with these 'sad scenes' through their picture-books and magazines and hopes that members will each send in a penny for the 'Sunbeam Christmas Dinner Fund'.[120] Within a month, £27 4s 9d was raised, and John Kirk, the Secretary of the Ragged School Union and Shaftesbury Society, was asked to organise the dinner.[121]

The Sunbeam Society's charitable work often featured multiple campaigns operating at the same time. Alongside the ongoing contributions for the children's hospital cot were other demands for fundraising. Even as readers awaited reports on the success of the Sunbeam Christmas Dinner, for instance, they were participating in the second annual toy drive. Uncle Harry writes about how pleased he is by their generous toy donations. He 'hardly expected there would be as many as last year' because many of the circles were likely to distribute their gifts locally this year rather than sending them to him, yet he reports on 'nearly twice as many articles sent this time'.[122] In this letter, he also includes a brief announcement about 'the glorious news' that the Christmas Dinner Fund was 'the means of giving a good dinner to not less than SEVEN HUNDRED poor little waifs in London'.[123] Even as one campaign is wrapping up, another is getting started.

Multiple reports in the *Observer* about the Christmas dinner emphasise the significance of the children's contributions to the

186 Philanthropy in Children's Periodicals, 1840–1930

charitable landscape. One appears in a general news section and describes the children's excitement about the food and entertainment where Uncle Harry's letter was read aloud to the children. The value of this charitable work was emphasised through the description of the boys and girls as 'poverty-stricken' and how joyful they were at 'the prospect of a hearty meal'.[124] The newspaper's significance in this charitable activity also received mention. The correspondent explains that a number of British papers are discussing the event and giving credit to the 'Children's Sunbeam Society of South Australia connected with the *Register*, *Observer*, and *Evening Journal* of Adelaide'.[125] This transnational charity is enabled through the circulation of the weekly newspaper in South Australia and the development of a readership that is interested in and able to donate to a charity located a long distance away. This outward-looking focus is a significant element of the society that begins with local causes but extends to wherever children may be in need.

Moreover, the event is sufficiently successful to be shared, celebrated, and hopefully replicated in future years. Like the periodical, which appears regularly each week, so too can a charitable donation be offered each year. Uncle Harry includes a letter in the 'Children's Column' from Kirk, who thanks the members 'most heartily' and explains that 'we are not without the hope that the happy relationship and link thus established may be strengthened as the days go by'.[126] Another report of the event also appearing in the 'Children's Column' begins by explaining the novelty of this dinner funded by children in the colonies and similarly hopes to see it repeated, either by Sunbeam members or by other children within the British empire. The *Liverpool Mercury* describes it as 'a charming beginning of a new custom' in which the London children of the Ragged School sit down to a dinner provided by the children of South Australia.[127] This scheme is assumed to be just the beginning and will in future years 'spread to other colonies, and will undoubtedly grow and become a new and tender bond binding England and her Australian relatives in closer union'.[128] The correspondent also explains that the dinner has been mentioned in *Lloyd's Weekly Newspaper*, a paper with a global readership of at least four million, indicating that news of the event will be spread worldwide and highlighting the charitable ethos of the young people: 'The little folks . . . have just shown that they are not unmindful of the needs of London's poorest children.'[129] Uncle Harry's letter is to be reprinted in the Ragged School magazine, *In His Name*, there to be read in 'thousands of homes of Old England'.[130] The influence of South Australian children's charity work will be felt around the world as news of the event is shared through global print networks. Uncle Harry's concluding comment is that the children's charitable efforts are like an acorn that grows into a 'great oak tree, and having seen the enthusiasm caused in England by the little acorn you sent across the seas, we hope you will live to send us later on the sapling, and still later on the full-grown tree'.[131] The money raised for this initial transnational charitable effort can continue to grow into even more fundraising.

Given the charitable networks between Britain and the colonies discussed in this chapter and elsewhere, to a certain extent the Sunbeam Society's idea to support the Ragged School with a Christmas dinner is unsurprising. The charitable networks were clearly established and flourishing, yet they were not always exclusively operating between London and its colonies. The ways that children were encouraged to help others was based on need. Thus in Uncle Harry's 11 April 1896 letter, he references the generous response to the Christmas Dinner Fund even as he turns readers' attention to a 'widely different' case.[132] Children's knowledge about current events is assumed when he writes that '[m]ost of you, perhaps, know that there has recently been a terrible colliery explosion' in the New Zealand mining town of Brunnerton.[133] With the deaths of more than sixty men, 'a great number of women and children have been bereft of husband and father'.[134] Uncle Harry encourages readers to 'show how deeply we sympathize with those who are in such deep distress' by sending in a penny.[135] The competing demands of charity are evident as he acknowledges 'how carefully some of you are hoarding your pocket money so as to have something to spend at the various Circle Bazaars in aid of the Creche Building Fund', another fundraiser in support of a local child care facility. Nonetheless, he hopes to raise a penny from each of the now 4,000 Sunbeam Society members and plans to ask the Brunnerton mayor whether the money can be used 'entirely on behalf of the children'.[136] He concludes by alluding to the necessity of sacrifice since '[o]ne can hardly call it an act of generosity if some one else supplies the means'.[137] True sacrifice is necessary for charity work, and it allows Uncle Harry to request additional funds from children without assuming that adults will

188   Philanthropy in Children's Periodicals, 1840–1930

be the ones supplying the money. Within a week, the children's charitable ethos was evident in the ten pounds received. Their sympathy is 'as prompt as it was generous, and you have once again made your Uncle feel proud of you'.[138] His only disappointment is that only thirty-three of more than one hundred circles have made donations. By mid-May, however, the Sunbeam children had donated £15 5s 4d, which Uncle Harry duly forwarded to the mayor along with an extra £2 19s 3d to comprise one penny per member.[139]

The sacrifices necessary for fundraising were essential given Uncle Harry's hope that the Sunbeam Society could raise the sum of £300 in three months on behalf of the Creche Building Fund. Alongside his letter to the Sunbeams in the 'Children's Column' inviting them to contribute is a response to criticisms that he 'expects too much' from members.[140] He is unwavering in his belief that the young people are up to the challenge and reminds critics that the society has over 3,500 members and more than 120 circles have been formed. The average donation per circle from bazaars and concerts in the previous year was more than five pounds. Even if some circles are unable to participate, he forecasts that the receipts will likely compare favourably. Given that much of that money may well be coming from 'the pockets of the parents and relatives', he is confident that children's sacrifices will inspire similar actions from the adults.[141] Thus, the young people should be

> allowed as free a hand as possible in their efforts to raise this amount; give them all the assistance and encouragement you can; teach them to face whatever difficulties may arise, but do not add to these difficulties by one disparaging or disapproving word.[142]

Adults have a responsibility to enable and support young people in their charitable efforts. Uncle Harry's expectation is not that they will provide the money to the children directly, but that they will assist with efforts to enable the fundraising. The children were evidently successful in their charitable work, raising £600 of the £1,500 needed for the land and building.[143] The opening ceremony included a procession of 2,500 Sunbeam children organised by their circles to demonstrate their enthusiasm for the initiative to help poor children by providing them with care during the day while their mothers work.

Multiple campaigns appearing simultaneously in the 'Children's Column' added complexity to the charitable work being undertaken by young people. Yet while the adults may have found this challenging, as some of the criticisms indicated, child writers seemingly managed the competing priorities with ease. Gertie Humphreys, Secretary of 'The Acacias' Sunbeam Circle, writes that the circle has raised £10 7s from their bazaar. Acknowledging that they were 'greatly helped by the presence and support of the Lady and Sir Edwin Smith', she is pleased to send £5 for the Creche Building Fund and 12s as their contribution for the hospital cot. She reports that she has already sent 7s for the Brunner Relief Fund and the circle members plan to 'divide the rest amongst deserving institutions'.[144] Uncle Harry notes that since 'The Acacias' Circle had previously submitted four guineas, its members have contributed nearly ten pounds to the Creche Fund. The amounts allocated may indicate the relative priority placed by the members on different objectives, in which case local causes are seemingly receiving more of the children's time and attention. Alternatively, this may reflect the financial goals defined by Uncle Harry, who is therefore responsible for privileging local need. Nonetheless, Gertie is clear about the dispersal of the funds as the circle turns its attention to the next fundraising event, a bazaar to be held in June. Her acknowledgement of Lady and Sir Edwin Smith is presumably owing to good manners, but also reflects the extent to which patronage was an important facet of charitable institutions in the nineteenth century. Thorne-Murphy explains that '[s]ince charity bazaars were almost exclusively associated with women, these events created distinctly feminized sites of civil society' in which women 'were making a firm, public statement' in support of the charitable cause through their participation.[145] Sir Edwin is credited with covering the expenses associated with the bazaar, while Lady Smith's influence over the event's organisation and its success is less explicitly articulated.

The tension between local and international charitable demands recurs towards the end of 1896, when plans were well underway for a second Sunbeam Christmas Dinner for the Ragged School children. An unforeseen demand for funds to support distressed farmers arose in the final quarter of that year as a period of extreme drought hit South Australia, with many crops in the region failing.[146] In a letter to the editor, Uno writes that 'our own poor children in the North [of the state] are not likely to get a dinner this Christmas' and that it would be 'far better' to help them than to send the money overseas.[147] In Uncle Harry's response, he explains that the funds have already been promised but that all money donated in excess of the required amount for the dinner will be given to the Distressed Farmers' Fund. He agrees that 'it is our duty to first provide for those at hand' and that he would not have committed the Sunbeams to such a large amount for the Christmas Dinner (£41 13s 4d) if he had any idea of the local need that would arise.[148] In his instructions to child readers about the Christmas Dinner Fund, he also reminds them that no one is to collect funds. Instead, their donations are entirely voluntary. During a time of competing priorities, charitable donors must navigate how to meet their obligations while also responding to a sudden and urgent need. That these priorities are split between those local and international needs adds a new dimension to the question of how much money is reasonable for children to raise through sacrifice rather than collecting, especially when the precedent of supporting international causes has already been established and supported by the young people.

The final campaign of interest to the construction of a transnational charitable ideal appeared in the 'Children's Column' beginning in 1900. Uncle Harry once again assumes his readers have a degree of knowledge about the world, declaring that 'I believe there are many of my readers who could rapidly guess what I am going to write about.'[149] He goes on to explain that 'the burden that is lying heavily upon my heart ... is this awful INDIAN FAMINE. Oh, "Sunbeams", do you think we can even faintly realize how awful it is?'[150] The scope of the tragedy 'seems too dreadful to contemplate' given that the number of deaths exceeds the total population of the Australian colonies and New Zealand. Yet even beyond the 'appalling number of victims' is the terrible reality that they died a 'cruelly lingering death'.[151] Despite having just closed the 'In Memoriam Lifebuoy Fund' and the ongoing appeal for wounded soldiers in South Africa, Uncle Harry calls on his 'steadfast and loyal' Sunbeams to respond.[152] Two pennies will be sufficient to feed an Indian child for one day, and so he asks every one of his Sunbeams to give that amount.

Child readers readily supported this appeal and commented on the dire situation in India. Twelve-year-old Eileen Shannon reflects on the terrible famine and that such a small amount would be

Transnational Charity   191

sufficient to feed a child. She writes that 'I do not think there is a more deserving object than this one. It really does seem terrible to think of poor little children like ourselves starving, and the most we can do is to deny ourselves some little thing . . . and I sincerely hope your appeal will be liberally responded to.'[153] Eileen is able to empathise because other children like her are starving. While she can also see that the contribution is relatively small compared to the gravity of the situation, she is hopeful that these small amounts will come together to produce a more significant total through a liberal response.

Nine-year-old Elsie Mitchell situates her charitable activities within the wider framework of her stay at Mount Lofty for five weeks. She and her brother recently visited the local convalescent home: 'The Matron was very kind; she took us all over the building. The children look so happy and well cared for; we took them some toys and books. We are going to see them again.'[154] In addition to these visiting duties, she and her brother are raising money for the Sunbeam Society. She includes with her letter the ten shillings that she and her brother have saved for the cot fund, which they have earned 'since Christmas by doing little pieces of work for mother and keeping the garden tidy. Now we are going to see how much we can earn for the Indian Famine Fund.'[155] Her language signals a relatively simple shift from one charitable fund to another. She and her brother will continue to earn money to donate through their regular activities and will donate those funds to the relevant charity based on the timing of the donation. The two causes, for her, are equivalent, whether they are local, like the cots, or transnational, like the famine.

Uncle Harry plans a jumble sale in support of the Indian Famine Fund, to which the Sunbeams are asked to send items for sale. After a modest beginning, with few initial contributions, the young people realised £12 6s 6d from the jumble fair, for a total of £54.[156] Other correspondence elsewhere in the press also indicates the extent to which the Indian Famine Fund was a source of charitable work. Children in Perth were involved in a similar fundraising scheme for the Indian Famine Fund. 'Aunt Dorothy', running 'The Golden Rule Society' in the 'Children's Column' of Perth's *Daily News*, hosted a bazaar with proceeds benefiting different charitable institutions.[157] The objective of 'The Golden Rule Society' is 'To be helpful to children, and teach them to be helpful to one another', and its motto is 'We aim to help all those

192   Philanthropy in Children's Periodicals, 1840–1930

in need; to lighten sorrow, and to lessen pain'. Like the Sunbeam Society, children are encouraged to help others in need, especially children. The bazaar raised nearly £17 with £2 allocated to the Indian Famine Fund. Twelve-year-old Rose Wilson, writing to 'Cinderella's Letter Box' as part of the Melbourne *Leader*'s 'Children's Column', explains that '[t]he pupils of the school to which I go are having a "Fancy Fair" on Friday evening next . . . and the proceeds are going to our "Tennis Club", and the "Indian Famine Fund" and I hope it will be a success.'[158] These examples demonstrate the ubiquity of bazaar and jumble fairs across Australia in which children were participating.

Yet the jumble fair contributions were merely one part of a range of charity work undertaken by circle members with a variety of charitable causes in mind. A letter from Mrs Annie Foreman, the leader of the 'Wells and Jones' Circle, shows how members are kept busy with their circle activities:

> The meetings are held at my house every Wednesday evening from 7 to 9. We read 'Uncle Harry's Letter', receive the contributions, and appoint members for sick visiting. Four or more members take turns every Sunday to visit the sick, reading or singing to them and cheering them in any way they can. I am pleased to say they are always welcomed. Last quarter they paid twenty-one visits, taking flowers and, in some instances, soup, jelly, or such little comforts when the person is in poor circumstances. We have sent a parcel of 'medical comforts' for the sick and wounded soldiers, and two small parcels to the Jumble Fair. The members' contribution amounted to 12s; we sent 4s for lemons, 5s 6d for Indian Famine Fund, leaving us 2s 6d in hand. We are practising now for a concert, which we expect to have on Friday, July 6. We have thirty-two members on the roll, all of whom attend well – indeed, our average attendance in twenty-eight . . . I am very pleased to tell that the BOY members attend and work remarkably well.[159]

This description of the 'Wells and Jones' Circle reflects the vibrancy of the charitable work. In addition to accumulating monetary contributions at regular meetings, local institutions are supported through visits and bringing along small comforts for people who are unwell. This work sits alongside the collections for parcels for the wounded soldiers and items to be sold at the jumble sale. They also organise and run concerts and presumably other entertainments to encourage donations from other members of the local community, which are then allocated for various funds.

Conclusion

Children's charity work in both New Zealand and South Australia can be characterised by regular engagement with weekly children's columns that encouraged financial donations but also, equally importantly, engagement through correspondence. This readerly participation enabled the editors to disseminate information about the charitable causes and encourage children's sacrifices for both local and transnational institutions. Children's letters demonstrate their charitable ethos and their sympathy for others who were less fortunate. In these local columns, with smaller readerships and presumably less opportunity to attract new readers, children were encouraged to sacrifice rather than collect money from friends and family. Their willingness to contribute regularly to a range of local and transnational causes reflects a transnational charitable ideal in which all needs are deserving of money and support to relieve distress. Moreover, the extent to which child correspondents presented ideas of their own, explained how they were engaged in charity work elsewhere, or demonstrated their knowledge about other, often transnational, charitable institutions demonstrates the intracultural transfer of charitable ideas throughout the English-speaking world.

Notes

1. 'Letters from Little Folks', *Otago Witness*, 26 June 1890, 39.
2. Frank Q. Christianson and Leslee Thorne-Murphy, 'Introduction: Writing Philanthropy in the United States and Britain', in *Philanthropic Discourse in Anglo-American Literature, 1850–1920*, ed. Frank Christianson and Leslee Thorne-Murphy (Bloomington: Indiana University Press, 2017), 4.
3. See, for instance, Chris Leonards and Nico Randeraad, 'Building a Transnational Network of Social Reform in the Nineteenth Century', in *Shaping the Transnational Sphere: Experts, Networks and Issues from the 1840s to the 1930s*, ed. Davide Rodogno, Bernhard Struck, and Jakob Vogel (New York: Berghahn Books, 2015), 111–30; Thomas Adam, *Buying Respectability: Philanthropy and Urban Society in Transnational Perspective,*

194 Philanthropy in Children's Periodicals, 1840–1930

1840s to 1930s (Bloomington: Indiana University Press, 2009); Katharina Rietzler, 'From Peace Advocacy to International Relations Research: The Transformation of Transatlantic Philanthropic Networks, 1900–1930', in *Shaping the Transnational Sphere*, 173–93; Mark Lawrence Schrad, 'The Transnational Temperance Community', in *Transnational Communities: Shaping Global Economic Governance*, ed. Maria-Laure Djelic and Sigrid Quack (Cambridge: Cambridge University Press, 2010), 255–81.

4. *Oxford English Dictionary*, s.v. 'transnational, adj', July 2023. <https://doi.org/10.1093/OED/3337940338>

5. Bill Ashcroft, 'Beyond the Nation: Australian Literature as World Literature', in *Scenes of Reading: Is Australian Literature a World Literature?*, ed. Robert Dixon and Brigid Rooney (Melbourne: Australian Scholarly Publishing, 2013), 36.

6. Paul Jay, *Transnational Literature: The Basics* (London: Taylor & Francis, 2021), 3.

7. Jay, *Transnational Literature*, 9.

8. Tony Ballantyne, *Orientalism and Race: Aryanism in the British Empire* (Houndmills: Palgrave Macmillan, 2002), 12.

9. Clare Bradford, 'Children's Literature in a Global Age: Transnational and Local Identities', *Barnboken* 34:1 (2004): 21.

10. Bradford, 'Children's Literature', 21.

11. Jude Piesse, *British Settler Emigration in Print, 1832–1877* (Oxford: Oxford University Press, 2015), 21, 22.

12. Chris Leonards and Nico Randeraad, 'Building a Transnational Network', 111, 112.

13. Leonards and Randeraad, 'Building a Transnational Network', 113–14.

14. Adam, *Buying Respectability*, 3.

15. Adam, *Buying Respectability*, 3.

16. 'Children's Column', *Otago Witness*, 11 November 1876, 19.

17. 'Children's Column', 19.

18. After the *Otago Witness* ceased publication in June 1932, the column moved to the *Otago Daily Mail*.

19. 'Children's Column', *Otago Witness*, 2 December 1876, 19.

20. 'Children's Column', *Otago Witness*, 30 December 1876, 19.

21. 'Our Little Folks', *Otago Witness*, 16 July 1886, 35. Louisa Baker, a collaborator of editor William Fenwick, was the original 'Dot' between 1886 and 1893 (Sherry Olsen and Peter Holland, 'Conversation in Print Among Children and Adolescents in the South Island of New Zealand, 1886–1909', *Journal of the History*

Transnational Charity 195

of Children and Youth 12, no. 2 [Spring 2019]: 222). The column title was changed to 'Dot's Little Folk' beginning on 15 March 1900.

22. 'Our Little Folks', *Otago Witness*, 23 July 1886, 35.
23. 'Letters from Little Folks', *Otago Witness*, 26 June 1890, 39.
24. 'Rescued from Life' was serialised between 17 February and 3 March 1883. 'Kidnapped' appeared in October 1883.
25. The report on the Babies' Castle first appeared in *Night and Day* and was reprinted in the children's column on 15 March 1884. 'Dr Barnardo's Good Work', *Otago Witness*, 30 August 1884, 27.
26. See Michelle J. Smith and Kristine Moruzi, 'Transnational Children's Periodicals', in *Handbook of Transnational Periodical Research*, ed. Marianne Van Remoortel and Fionnuala Dillane (Leiden: Brill, forthcoming).
27. 'Dr Barnardo's Homes', *Otago Witness*, 23 January 1886, 28.
28. 'Telegraphic', *Otago* Witness, 22 April 1887, 21.
29. 'The Country', *Otago Witness*, 26 August 1887, 17. 'Local and General', *Otago Witness*, 25 January 1889, 10.
30. 'Country Items', *Otago Witness*, 21 March 1889, 13.
31. 'Local and General', *Otago Witness*, 8 August 1889, 1.
32. 'Local and General', *Otago Witness Supplement*, 24 October 1889, 1.
33. 'Local and General', 1.
34. 'Letters from Little Folks', *Otago Witness*, 26 June 1890, 39.
35. 'Letters from Little Folks', 39.
36. 'Letters from Little Folks', 39.
37. 'Letters from Little Folks', 39.
38. 'Letters from Little Folks', 39.
39. 'Letters from Little Folks', 39.
40. 'Letters from Little Folks', *Otago Witness*, 24 July 1890, 39.
41. 'Letters from Little Folks', *Otago Witness*, 28 August 1890, 39.
42. 'Letters from Little Folks', *Otago Witness*, 11 September 1890, 39.
43. 'Letters from Little Folks', 39.
44. 'Letters from Little Folks', *Otago Witness*, 2 October 1890, 35.
45. 'Letters from Little Folks', 35.
46. 'Letters from Little Folks', 35.
47. 'Letters from Little Folks', 35.
48. 'Letters from Little Folks', *Otago Witness*, 20 April 1891, 35.
49. 'Letters', 35.
50. Barnardo's cable message was reprinted in numerous other periodicals in Australia and New Zealand, including the *Christchurch*

Star (24 December 1890), *Southland Times* (26 October 1890), Brisbane's *Telegraph* (24 December 1890), Melbourne's *Age* (25 December 1890), *Brisbane Courier* (25 December 1890), *Hobart Mercury* (25 December 1890), and Melbourne's *Leader* (27 December 1890), among others. For details about how London news was distributed to newspapers in Australia and New Zealand, see Ross Harvey ('Bringing the News to New Zealand: The Supply and Control of Overseas News in the Nineteenth Century', *Media History*, 8, no. 1 [2002]: 21–34) and Simon J. Potter (*News and the British World: The Emergence of an Imperial Press System, 1876–1922* [Oxford: Oxford University Press, 2003]. The New Zealand reprintings quoting the cable message directly ('Will Australia send a generous gift') suggest it was seen as applicable for New Zealand audiences as well.

51. 'Letters from Little Folks', *Otago Witness*, 1 January 1891, 35.
52. *Evening Post*, 22 October 1891, 22.
53. 'Dr. Barnardo's Boys', *Auckland Star*, 13 January 1892, 5.
54. 'Our Little Folks', *Otago Witness*, 17 March 1892, 41.
55. 'Our Little Folks', *Otago Witness*, 7 January 1892, 41.
56. Two readers of the 'Dot's Little Folk' column, Burns and Johnson, write of another tour in 1909: 'Dr. Barnardo's Boys paid a visit to this district and were well worth the patronage' ('Dot's Little Folk', *Otago Witness*, 10 March 1909, 83).
57. 'Our Little Folks', *Otago Witness*, 12 May 1892, 40.
58. 'Our Little Folks', *Otago Witness*, 30 June 1892, 40.
59. 'Letters from Little Folks', *Otago Witness*, 20 September 1894, 45.
60. 'Letters from Little Folks', 45.
61. 'Letters from Little Folks', 45.
62. 'Letters from Little Folks', 45.
63. 'Letters from Little Folks', *Otago Witness*, 13 December 1894, 45.
64. 'Letters from Little Folks', 45.
65. 'Letters from Little Folks', 45.
66. 'Letters from Little Folks', 45.
67. 'Letters from Little Folks', 45. Emphasis in original.
68. 'Letters from Little Folks', *Otago Witness*, 27 December 1894, 45.
69. 'Letters from Little Folks', *Otago Witness*, 10 January 1895, 45.
70. 'Letters from Little Folks', 45.
71. 'Letters from Little Folks', *Otago Witness*, 21 February 1895, 45.
72. 'Letters from Little Folks', *Otago Witness*, 8 March 1895, 45.
73. 'Letters from Little Folks', *Otago Witness*, 6 June 1895, 45.

74. 'Otago Witness Little Folks' Kindergarten Fund', *Otago Witness*, 19 December 1895, 30; 'Kindergarten Fund', *Otago Witness*, 17 December 1896, 19.
75. 'Letters from Little Folks', *Otago Witness*, 11 May 1899, 57.
76. 'Dot's Little Folk', *Otago Witness*, 3 May 1905, 73.
77. Charlotte Bennett, '"Now the war is over, we have something else to worry us": New Zealand Responses to Crises, 1914–1918', *Journal of the History of Childhood and Youth* 7, no. 1 (Winter 2014): 20.
78. Jeanine Graham, 'Young New Zealanders, and the Great War: Exploring the Impact and Legacy of the First World War, 1914–2014', *Paedagogica Historica* 44, no. 4 (2008): 431.
79. Graham, 'Young New Zealanders', 432.
80. 'Dot's Little Folk', *Otago Witness*, 14 October 1914, 79. Ethel Fraser assumed editorship of the page in 1913 (Bennett, 'Now', 21).
81. 'Dot's Little Folk', 79.
82. 'Dot's Little Folk', *Otago Witness*, 11 November 1914, 71.
83. 'Dot's Little Folk', 71.
84. 'Dot's Little Folk', 71.
85. 'Dot's Little Folk', *Otago Witness*, 4 November 1914, 75.
86. 'Dot's Little Folk', 75.
87. Bennett, 'Now', 23.
88. 'Dot's Little Folk', *Otago Witness*, 11 November 1914, 71.
89. 'Dot's Little Folk', *Otago Witness*, 18 November 1914, 74.
90. Bottrill became a full-time journalist at the *Register* to manage the society. In 1909, he left to publish his own children's paper, the *Sunbeam*, but it was financially unsuccessful and closed in 1911 (Margaret Barbalet, 'Bottrill, David Hughes [1866–1941]', *Australian Dictionary of Biography*, National Centre of Biography, Australian National University, adb.anu.edu.au/biography/bottrill-david-hughes–5301, published first in hardcopy 1979, accessed 27 September 2023).
91. 'Children's Column', *Adelaide Observer*, 14 July 1894, 35.
92. 'Children's Column', 35.
93. 'Children's Column', *Adelaide Observer*, 21 July 1894, 35. The Boys' Brigade started in Australia around 1885 after being formed in Glasgow in 1883 (M. E. Hoare, *Boys, Urchins, Men: A History of The Boys' Brigade in Australia and Papua-New Guinea 1882–1976* [Sydney: Reed, 1980], 23, 25). The Boys' Field Club was founded in 1887 by Catton Grasby, a South Australian educationalist, and by the 1890s 'involved about

198   Philanthropy in Children's Periodicals, 1840–1930

1500 boys in its excursions and camps', encouraging the practical study of natural science and healthful recreation (Drew Hutton and Libby Connors, *History of the Australian Environmental Movement* [Cambridge: Cambridge University Press, 1999], 44; and John Ramsland, 'Grasby, William Catton [1859–1903]', *Australian Dictionary of National Biography*, Australian National University, https://adb.anu.edu.au/biography/grasby-william-colton-6459/text11059, 1983, accessed 19 September 2023). The Ministering Children's League was founded in London by the Countess of Meath in 1885 (E. S. Curry, 'The Charities of Children', *Quiver* 61 [January 1904], 144); The Christian Endeavour was founded by the Reverend Francis E. Clark in Maine in 1881. Soon after it began, a junior society was developed for younger youth (Brian C. Hull, *A Brief Overview of the Christian Endeavor Society* [Wilmore: First Fruits Press, 2019], 14).

94. 'Children's Column', *Adelaide Observer*, 28 July 1894, 5.
95. 'Children's Column', 5.
96. 'Children's Column', 5.
97. 'Children's Column', 5.
98. 'Children's Column', *Adelaide Observer*, 11 August 1894, 35.
99. 'Children's Column', 35.
100. 'Children's Column', *Adelaide Observer*, 1 September 1894, 35.
101. 'Children's Column', 35.
102. 'Children's Column', 35.
103. 'Children's Column', 35. 'Dorcas Society' refers to a women's group making clothing for the poor.
104. 'Children's Column', *Adelaide Observer*, 15 September 1894, 35.
105. 'Children's Column', *Adelaide Observer*, 20 October 1894, 35.
106. 'Children's Column', *Adelaide Observer*, 3 November 1894, 35.
107. 'Children's Column', *Adelaide Observer*, 17 November 1894, 35.
108. 'Children's Column', *Adelaide Observer*, 5 January 1895, 35.
109. 'Children's Column', *Adelaide* Observer, 2 March 1895, 35. *The Nursing Record and Hospital World* reported in January 1896 of a Glasgow-based 'Guild of Kindness' that organised a scheme for Christmas toys to be collected and then distributed among the various children's institutions and hospitals. Evidently, the first year of the bazaar was successful enough to bear repeating ('Reflections from a Board Room Mirror', *The Nursing Record and Hospital World*, 4 January 1896: 14).
110. 'Children's Column', 35.

111. Frederick Milton, 'Uncle Toby's Legacy: Children's Columns in the Provincial Newspaper Press, 1873–1914', *International Journal of Regional and Local Studies* 5, no. 1 (2009): 105.

112. Milton, 'Uncle Toby's Legacy', 105.

113. Peter Gibson traces the emigration patterns of Scots between 1788 and 1939, identifying Australia as a destination for a 'significant number' of emigrants ('Scottish Emigration to Australia, 1788–1939', *Descent* 30, no. 2 [June 2000]: 81). Graham Jaunay traces the difficulties of identifying the number of Scottish emigrants to South Australia specifically ('Nineteenth Century Emigration from Scotland to South Australia', *The South Australian Genealogist* 50, no. 1 [February 2023]: 12–22). See also Eric Richards, 'Varieties of Scottish Emigration in the Nineteenth Century', *Historical Studies* 21, no. 85 (1985): 473–94 and Malcolm Prentis, *The Scots in Australia* (Sydney: UNSW Press, 2008).

114. 'Children's Column', *Adelaide Observer*, 18 May 1895, 35.

115. 'Children's Column', 35.

116. 'Children's Column', 35.

117. 'Children's Column', 35.

118. 'Children's Column', 35.

119. 'Children's Column', *Adelaide Observer*, 19 October 1895, 34.

120. 'Children's Column', 34.

121. 'Children's Column', *Adelaide Observer*, 23 November 1895, 35.

122. 'Children's Column', *Adelaide Observer*, 4 January 1896, 40.

123. 'Children's Column', 40.

124. 'The Sunbeam Society Dinner to the Ragged School Children', *Adelaide Observer*, 8 February 1896, 15.

125. 'The Sunbeam Society Dinner', 15.

126. 'Children's Column', *Adelaide Observer*, 8 February 1896, 35.

127. Qtd in 'Children's Column', 35.

128. 'Children's Column', 35.

129. 'Children's Column', 35.

130. 'Children's Column', 35.

131. 'Children's Column', 35.

132. 'Children's Column', *Adelaide Observer*, 11 April 1896, 35.

133. 'Children's Column', 35.

134. 'Children's Column', 35.

135. 'Children's Column', 35.

136. 'Children's Column', 35.

137. 'Children's Column', 35.

200 Philanthropy in Children's Periodicals, 1840–1930

138. 'Children's Column', *Adelaide Observer*, 25 April 1896, 35.
139. 'Children's Column', *Adelaide Observer*, 16 May 1896, 30.
140. 'Children's Column', *Adelaide Observer*, 22 February 1896, 35.
141. 'Children's Column', 35.
142. 'Children's Column', 35.
143. 'The New Adelaide Creche Opening Ceremony', *Adelaide Observer*, 15 August 1896, 41.
144. 'Children's Column', *Adelaide Observer*, 9 May 1896, 35.
145. Leslee Thorne-Murphy, *Bazaar Literature: Charity, Advocacy, and Parody in Victorian Social Reform Fiction* (Oxford: Oxford University Press, 2022), 3.
146. Karen Downing, Rebecca Jones, and Blake Singley, 'Handout or Hand-up: Ongoing Tension in the Long History of Government Response to Drought in Australia', *Australian Journal of Politics and History* 62 (2016): 186–202.
147. 'Children's Column', *Adelaide Observer*, 7 November 1896, 35.
148. 'Children's Column', 35.
149. 'Children's Column', *Adelaide Observer*, 7 April 1900, 41.
150. 'Children's Column', 41.
151. 'Children's Column', 41.
152. 'Children's Column', 41. The 'In Memoriam Lifebuoy Fund' was launched on 3 February 1900 after the drowning deaths of Sunbeam niece associate Sissie Martin and her friend Maud Saunders. The fund was to support the purchase of a lifebuoy to be placed on the beach and required five pounds in donations ('"Sunbeam" In Memoriam Lifebuoy Fund', *Adelaide Observer*, 3 February 1900, 35). On 24 February 1900, in response to news of injured soldiers in South Africa fighting the Second Boer War, 'Aunt Sophie' asks each circle to send 'a parcel of things suitable for invalids and convalescents' that she describes as 'medical comforts', including cocoa, extract of beef, jelly powers, jams, and preserves. She particularly asks for lemons and requests that those unable to send the fruit should contribute a penny per member for their purchase ('Children's Column', *Adelaide Observer*, 24 February 1900, 35).
153. 'Children's Column', *Adelaide Observer*, 5 May 1900, 37.
154. 'Children's Column', 37.
155. 'Children's Column', 37.
156. 'Children's Column', *Adelaide Observer*, 16 June 1900, 36.
157. 'Children's Column', *The Daily News*, 2 June 1900, 7.
158. 'The Children's Column', *The Leader*, 30 June 1900, 42.
159. 'Children's Column', *Adelaide Observer*, 23 June 1900, 36.

7

Charitable Habits

The previous chapter demonstrated how transnational charitable practices were operating in the weekly children's columns published in colonial newspapers. This chapter turns to the Junior Red Cross, an organisation that explicitly established transnational practices through the sharing of ideas, materials such as Junior Red Cross magazines, and child-authored content.[1] Yet the focus here is not on the organisation's transnationality, but instead on how charitable habits were established and promoted through the Junior Red Cross magazines published in Canada, New South Wales, and the United States. In its comparison of three different magazines published beginning at the end of the First World War, this chapter marks a significant temporal step into the twentieth century and a charitable shift that consciously expands beyond the fundraising that characterised much nineteenth-century charity work.[2]

Pierre Bourdieu's idea of *habitus* provides a framework for understanding how charitable habits are created among young people through the pages of their magazines. The preceding chapters have demonstrated how magazine editors were deeply interested in motivating charitable behaviours among child readers not only for their fundraising and their ability to inspire donations among adults, but also for their future potentiality as adult contributors. This chapter examines the strategies deployed in the magazines to create habits of charity for young people. It examines three of the earliest Junior Red Cross organisations to explore how they produced habits of charity incorporating service, health, and international friendliness. Each organisation had a different timeline for its beginning, as well as the publication

202   Philanthropy in Children's Periodicals, 1840–1930

of its Junior Red Cross magazine, with the New South Wales *Junior Red Cross Record* and the American *Junior Red Cross News* both launching in 1919 and the *Canadian Red Cross Junior* in 1922.[3] These publications emerged out of a shared understanding of how children had already been assisting with the war effort and how, in peace time, they could turn their attention to other worthwhile objectives. While all three reflect the same broad objectives of the Junior Red Cross, each magazine also demonstrates its own unique implementation. The Canadian magazine was more concerned with children's health than either of the other magazines, while also focusing on habits of service and international friendliness. In contrast, the New South Wales publication was primarily interested in discussing young people's habits of service through nursing for soldiers injured in the war and fundraising for them and their families. The American magazine highlights the importance of international friendliness in its charitable framework. Despite these differences, the magazines demonstrate how charitable habits coalesce into a new definition of children's charitable work, in which more is expected of Junior Red Cross members than simply raising awareness and funds for a particular charitable cause. Instead, young people are expected to transform themselves physically and ideologically as well as raising funds for specific charities. These charitable habits are practised through individual and collective action that is repeated over time to enable this transformation.

Although children actively contributed to a variety of fundraising and other charitable activities during the First World War, many of which were organised by or for the national Red Cross organisations, the Junior Red Cross was not formally established until 1922, with adoption of the Resolution by the General Council of the League of Red Cross Societies '[t]hat every National Red Cross Society should endeavour to organize the enrolment of schoolchildren as Junior Members'.[4] At that time, Junior Red Cross organisations had already been established in twenty-one countries, up from the three at the conclusion of the war.[5] Melanie Oppenheimer describes how the Junior Red Cross 'tapped into a new and prescribed role that children and youth could play within Red Cross into the future' in which young people could 'improve international relations through the establishment of a global children's network'.[6] The newly established League of Red Cross Societies created a Bureau of Junior

Membership that 'would play a leading role' in building Junior Red Cross memberships across national societies to promote international friendliness and good will.[7]

Theorising habits

The *Oxford English Dictionary* defines a habit as 'a settled disposition or tendency to act in a certain way, especially one acquired by a frequent repetition of the same act until it becomes almost or quite involuntary'.[8] In principle, the charity magazine in the nineteenth century often inspired a 'tendency' to donate funds, undoubtedly in the hope that it would become a habit that continued into the future and eventually into adulthood. The three-pronged objectives of the Junior Red Cross demand a more expansive understanding of the behaviours requested of its young members and how they are framed. According to Bourdieu, *habitus* is a set of 'individual and collective practices' that are produced by and emerge from 'a system of dispositions'.[9] The patterns of charitable behaviour that are so apparent in the nineteenth and early twentieth centuries, then, are comprised of individual actions set within a collective ideology that encourages people to support worthy charitable causes. Karl Maton explains that *habitus* creates a connection between the individual and the collective because, although the individual circumstances of one's life 'maybe unique in their particular *contents*', they are 'shared in terms of their *structure* with others of the same social class, gender, ethnicity, sexuality, occupation, nationality, region and so forth'.[10] In addition, as Smiljka Tomanović asserts, age is a significant social category that informs young people's circumstances as a 'class of conditions of existence'.[11] The family forms one of the main structures for the 'everyday practice of childhood', and the educational system is another important venue through which children's behaviours and practices are established.[12]

Moreover, *habitus* is a 'product of history' that 'produces individual and collective practices . . . in accordance with the schemes generated by history'.[13] The similarities between the charitable attitudes discussed in earlier chapters are a result of the historical trajectory of *habitus*, which has 'an infinite capacity for generating . . . thoughts, perceptions, expressions and actions', within limits set by 'the historically and socially situated conditions of its production'.[14] These limits help to explain many of

204 Philanthropy in Children's Periodicals, 1840–1930

the similar attitudes towards charitable service embodied in the Junior Red Cross, but also the potential for historical change or rupture to produce new opportunities within the charitable *habitus*. The Junior Red Cross focus on health and citizenship is a response to the radical change of the First World War since, as Diane Reay explains, 'Habituses are permeable and responsive to what is going on around them. Current circumstances are not just there to be acted upon, but are internalized and become yet another layer to add to those from earlier socializations.'[15] Yet even this expansion of the charitable field is enabled by the *habitus* of the post-war period. Bourdieu explains how the 'corrections and adjustments the agents themselves consciously carry out presuppose mastery of a common code' and 'cannot succeed without a minimum of concordance between the *habitus* of the mobilizing agents'.[16] The development of the Junior Red Cross ideal of childhood as service-oriented, healthy, and outward-looking owes its success to a shared understanding among adult charity workers of the need for change in the post-war period, while also maintaining its connection of the charitable ideals of the past.

Habitus is an embodied experience and thus is 'not composed solely of mental attitudes and perceptions'.[17] Instead, the charitable *habitus* articulated in and through Junior Red Cross magazines is embodied through 'standing, speaking, walking, and thereby feeling and thinking'.[18] As Claire Edwards and Rob Imrie explain, 'Habitus, then, seeks to focus on the corporeal, embodied experiences of everyday life and to understand systems of interaction between individual social beings and broader social structures'.[19] The *habitus* of charity is produced by a set of practices that are 'inscribed on bodies', and Junior Red Cross magazines attempt to enact the *habitus* of children's charity through the organisation's three main activities of service, health, and citizenship.[20]

Canadian Red Cross Junior

Like children around the world during the First World War, Canadian children actively contributed to a variety of fundraising and other charitable activities to support the war effort, many of which were organised by or for the Canadian Red Cross. In Saskatchewan, groups of children began working for the Red Cross as early as 1914, although the Junior Red Cross was not formally established in Canada until 1920.[21] For instance, the

Junior Red Cross branch based at the File Hills boarding school in Saskatchewan is congratulated in an early issue of *Canadian Red Cross Junior* for their hard work which began in 1916. This branch, comprised of seventy 'Indian' children and located on a reserve, had earned 'about three hundred dollars' and 'now that they know the service the Junior Red Cross is giving to crippled children they are going to work with renewed energy' and plan to make their branch 'one of the best in the province'.[22] Children across the country were encouraged to join to

> acquire habits of healthy living, become actively interested in their own health and that of others, find opportunities for the exercise of their natural altruism and develop a friendly interest in their contemporaries in all the civilized countries of the world.[23]

Within this description, the main objectives of the Junior Red Cross became apparent: health, service, and international friendliness. James Robertson, Chairman of the Canadian Red Cross Society Council, explained that the primary purpose of the Junior Red Cross was to interest boys and girls 'in learning and doing voluntarily those things which promote health knowledge and health habits, linking up a knowledge of hygiene with habits of living so that the child may have them for all time'.[24] The Canadian Junior Red Cross was seen as a 'peacemaking tool' through which public health work became a 'nation-building endeavour' as well as 'a way to transmit the spirit of giving'.[25] The similarities between Junior Red Cross and broader educational objectives helps to explain the alliance between the Junior Red Cross and schools. The incorporation of Junior Red Cross materials into classroom curricula undoubtedly contributed to its success, with 157,155 children by 1928 and 425,000 in 1939.[26] As 'one of the very few ... organizations that has had access to the classrooms in all provinces in Canada', its 'emphasis on health, citizenship and international understanding closely approximated the changing curricular interests' after the First World War.[27]

Canadian Red Cross Junior was launched in 1922 under the editorship of Jean Browne, the National Director of the Junior Red Cross. This monthly magazine contains stories, plays, informational articles, poems, games, and music alongside articles about Junior Red Cross activities in Canada and abroad. It incorporates a variety of content that encouraged members to embody the

206   Philanthropy in Children's Periodicals, 1840–1930

values of the organisation, which include becoming healthy, but also focuses on charitable activities that would help others to become healthy and learning more about young people around the world. The magazine formulated a healthful *habitus* by simultaneously asserting the idea of the healthy child as innately natural and inherently good while also instructing children about how to be healthy and how to help others to be healthy.

In Canada, the Junior Red Cross was particularly interested in improving children's health. The *habitus* of healthy children in the magazine includes a definition predicated on the able-bodied child who is 'crucial to the smooth operation of traditional theories of democracy, citizenship, subjectivity, beauty, and capital'.[28] The healthy child's body meets norms pertaining to weight, activity, and its physical movement through space, but is also subject to regulatory practices related to cleanliness and emotion. Children are asked to regulate their own behaviours to meet this normative ideal, but the organisation rarely discussed the possibility that children might not be able to satisfy the requirements of the *habitus*. The Junior Red Cross school health campaign operated alongside the increasing intervention of school health doctors and nurses into children's lives through regular inspections. A formal school medical programme 'detected contagious disease, discovered physical defects in pupils . . . inculcated hygienic habits in young people, provided for their physical training, and improved the methods and materials of health instruction'.[29] Thus the school medical programme simultaneously examined children's bodies for physical imperfections when measured against a normative standard as well as inspecting them for communicable diseases. This medical examination of children's bodies was accompanied by a concurrent campaign to instruct children in proper habits of health, hygiene, and physical development.

Canadian Red Cross Junior was an obvious method by which the Junior Red Cross shared health, hygiene, and physical development objectives with its members. The publication was intended to 'attract and interest children and young people, and to be of service to teachers and organizers of Junior work'.[30] One of the main methods for encouraging children to learn about and embody health was through the establishment of 'The Health Game', which introduced twelve health rules in the magazine to encourage proper eating habits, hygiene practices, and regular exercise. The rules included regular baths; frequent brushing of teeth; drinking milk and eating plenty of fresh fruit and vegetables; using a handkerchief when coughing or sneezing; daily outdoor activities; and sleeping at least ten hours each night. These rules presumed access to healthy food that was predicated on a standard of living in which such food was regularly available. The model of the health game was intended to be entertaining for children while also providing a clear set of rules to be followed.

While Bourdieu argues that the field ('the pitch or board on which it is played, the rules, the outcome at stake, etc.') of the game is clearly understood as 'an arbitrary social construct', the stakes of the health game are clearly articulated in the magazine.[31] The consequences of failure are both moral and physical, with children who fail to abide by the rules seen as spiritually weak and physically inferior. Yet the rationale for the rules, and the context which made the introduction of these rules necessary, is elided. Canadian children were merely told that they should follow these rules for the betterment of themselves, their friends and family, and their nation. Healthy children were the product of this *habitus*, and the normativity associated with the idea of 'health' remained unquestioned.

Prize competitions were a common way that *Canadian Red Cross Junior* supported the *habitus* of child health as they encouraged children to learn and remember these healthy habits. A health poster competition was one such example. Readers under the age of fifteen were asked to illustrate one or more of the health rules. The winning poster by fourteen-year-old Gladys L. Cook of Hamilton, Ontario is reproduced in the magazine, with a smiling and healthy Gladys pictured below. Entitled 'HEALTH RULES FOR YOU', the poster directs readers to see the rules as relevant and applicable to them since they are rules 'for you' as the reader.[32] Cook has illustrated six rules with simple drawings of children performing these good behaviours. Readers are encouraged to see themselves following the health rules and consequently becoming both healthy and happy. The poster competition functions like a game, much as the 'Health Game' does, containing rules, winners and losers, and a field of play. The *habitus* of health enacted in and through the magazine means that competitors are presumably sufficiently in agreement with the magazine's principles to submit to the competition, thereby encouraging reader identification with the magazine and its ideals. The participatory culture of the magazine is encouraged through these types of competitions.

208   Philanthropy in Children's Periodicals, 1840–1930

Readers want to 'play' the game by submitting their visualisation of the rules and contributing to the magazine's culture of health. Through the inclusion of Cook's photo, she becomes – or at least appears to be – an example of the model of healthy childhood that the magazine encourages. She embodies the health rules while also contributing to the magazine's construction of the *habitus* of health through her participation in the competition.

A 1923 *Canadian Red Cross Junior* health story competition likewise encourages child readers to provide examples of how health could be embodied and how challenges to health could be overcome. In the winning story, 'The Runt and the Red Cross Rules', author W. Owen Conquest of Calgary, Alberta demonstrates how healthy children could help unhealthy ones by encouraging them to become healthy. This competition was aimed at members aged fourteen and over, with submissions of less than 600 words and dealing with a health topic. Three prizes were to be awarded, with ten dollars for first prize, eight dollars for second, and five dollars for third.[33] The *habitus* of health dominates the story. New student Billy Hooley is quickly nicknamed the 'Runt' and described as a poor, unhealthy child who neither knows about nor follows the health rules. His weak body is a consequence of ignorance, poverty, and the lack of maternal care. The tellingly named teacher, Miss I. M. Kind, approaches Junior Red Cross members to see if they would be interested in helping the Runt become 'a healthy normal child'.[34] Soon they have organised a benefit concert to raise money, with which they anonymously provide Billy the food he needs to become healthy and instructions about proper health habits. By following the rules of the health game, a weak, underdeveloped body can be transformed into a specimen of health and vigour. In addition to regular good food and fresh air, Billy is instructed in hygiene practices before receiving a complete list of the 'Rules of the Health Game'. The successful potential of the health game is demonstrated when he gradually gains his strength and wins a running race. From a child who, because of his ill health, could contribute only minimally to Canadian society, he has been transformed into an athlete. Sporting achievement has long been connected to nationalism, and Billy models Canada's success in producing healthy children when he wins his race.[35] In this story, the healthy Junior Red Cross members help other, less fortunate, children to embody the ideal of health, and unhealthy children are encouraged to pursue the health habits to become contributing members of society. The implied child reader of the magazine thus has a dual obligation as a member of the Junior Red Cross. Not only must she be healthy, but she must also help others to be healthy as well. As the editor explains: 'The JRC member takes upon himself the obligation of *actually putting into practice* the facts he has been taught about health.'[36] The child reader must do more than simply consider the health habits; he or she must also help others to become healthy.

To become a good Canadian citizen, the Junior Red Cross encouraged habits of health, but also expanded upon the wartime necessity of helping others through charitable giving. The fundraising in *Canadian Red Cross Junior* is oriented towards health, as readers are reminded in June 1922:

> [T]here are many unfortunate children in the world who, through no fault of their own, cannot enjoy good health, because of some physical defect. We all know of such cases that are not receiving the necessary treatment because their parents are unable to pay for it. It is the work of Junior Red Cross branches to raise money to make possible the treatment of such children.[37]

The healthy child readers of the magazine are expected to help other children who require medical attention – and possibly surgical intervention – to be healthy. In 'A Letter from the Editor' in September 1922, the editor reminds child readers to '[p]ractice all the good health habits that you already know' so that there will not be 'so much sickness and suffering in the world'.[38] She also hopes that members 'will give even more thought . . . towards helping less fortunate children'.[39] The health habits are intended to produce healthy bodies, but they will ideally be accompanied by charitable behaviours that enable others to become healthy as well. In 'A Junior Red Cross Patient in Saskatchewan', for example, readers are introduced to Gladys, a 'happy-looking little lady' who was born with deformed feet and who would 'always be a cripple' without a 'very difficult and expensive operation'.[40] With the help of the Junior Red Cross, she undergoes a successful operation. Her feet are now 'like those of other children', and when she grows up, she may have forgotten that she has 'suffered a great affliction'.[41] Child readers are shown how their fundraising has helped to transform an unhealthy child, reinforcing the charitable rhetoric in the magazine and the value of their work.

210   Philanthropy in Children's Periodicals, 1840–1930

Ill health is explicitly made into a spectacle encouraging healthy and charitable disciplinary practices in the pair of photographs appearing directly under the article about Gladys. As discussed in Chapter 4, these types of contrasting photographs are designed to produce an emotional impact and inspire charitable giving. The two photos are of Stanley B, who lives in Nova Scotia and was also born with deformed feet. Unlike Gladys's feet, which are hidden under the bedcovers, Stanley is depicted in before and after photos. In the left-hand photo, Stanley is being helped to stand as he balances on feet that point inward. In the right-hand, post-operative photo, Stanley stands alone, dressed for the outdoors. His feet, now straightened, are encased in boots. Unlike the first photo, which emphasises his dependence on others, the latter photo depicts a child ready and able to play outdoors. The caption explains that, with the help of the Junior Red Cross, Stanley can now 'walk and run about and is a happy little boy'.[42] The photos are clear evidence of the original disability and Stanley's transformation into healthy able-bodiedness. Stanley is now a healthy child who – consciously or not – follows the rules of the health game by eating 'lots of bread and butter' and drinking 'plenty of milk'.[43] The *habitus* of health has produced a new, productive member of Canadian childhood.

The Canadian magazine's nationalism is apparent, with each of the early issues featuring an image of Canadian childhood, including a blond-haired child, a 'Sarcee Indian Girl', 'A Little Eskimo Girl', and 'A Sturdy Young Canadian' (see Fig. 7.1).[44] Each magazine issue promoted a national understanding of children's activities within the Junior Red Cross. Even in New South Wales, as I discuss below, the magazine focused on its Australianness, despite being intended specifically for state members. Juxtaposed to this national focus is an explicit interest in international friendliness and citizenship, which is the third main pillar of the Junior Red Cross. This pillar was an obvious response to the destructiveness of the First World War and a desire to create a *habitus* of international friendliness and humanitarian sympathy 'that would structure young people's identities and everyday practices not only during their time as [Junior Red Cross] members, but also during adulthood'.[45] Like the habits of regular financial contributions that many nineteenth-century charitable organisations hoped

Charitable Habits 211

Fig. 7.1 Cover of *The Red Cross Junior*, September 1922.

would continue into adulthood, the Junior Red Cross hoped to inculcate habits of international friendliness and cooperation in young people.

In the magazine's pages are regular positive reports about other Junior Red Cross Societies from around the world that highlight the importance of Junior Red Cross work and the similarities among the experiences of childhood. One such example that stresses the importance of the Junior Red Cross is 'American Juniors' Work

212 Philanthropy in Children's Periodicals, 1840–1930

in Europe'. In this May 1922 article, the author explains how American children's fundraising, 'amounting to over a million dollars, is being used entirely to help the European children to become healthier, happier and more useful citizens'.[46] The funds were used to introduce Austrian children to the 'Health Game', establish summer camps in Czecho-Slovakia, and build playgrounds in Albania, Belgium, and elsewhere. This record of what children's funds are able to accomplish is 'greatly to be admired' and is implicitly established as a model for what Canadian children could also accomplish if they wished.[47]

Cultural, geographic, and historical knowledge is essential to the development of an international outlook. A report about the Junior Red Cross work in Hungary, appearing in November 1922, suggests that young readers may not be familiar with European geography. It draws in the reader with an opening question: 'First of all, where is Hungary?'[48] This echoes a suggestion appearing at the top of an article about two young European boys who reunited with their families with the help of the Red Cross. The editor recommends in bold that '[b]efore commencing to read the following interesting article . . . get your maps of Europe and North America, so that you can follow the trips made by the two little chaps'.[49] Both articles indicate not only that Canadian children may be unfamiliar with geography, but also that they should take action to educate themselves by finding maps and learning where different countries are located.

A report in the Canadian magazine from the Junior Red Cross Society of Hungary reinforces the impact of the war and asserts the magazine's focus on internationalism. Despite 'sorrow and poverty and great discouragement', the Junior Red Cross movement is 'bringing back courage to the young people' and 'showing them that, though seemingly very poor, they are not beggars', since 'nobody is a beggar who has a generous soul and a will to help his fellow-beings'.[50] This fellow-feeling is evident through establishment of eighty-two Hungarian branches and a membership of 22,000. Over the past year, girls have made about a thousand garments alongside knitted and crochet work. Boys have also made pottery, bound books, and produced a variety of metal and leather products to be sold, with the proceeds going to the Junior Red Cross. In addition to these fundraising efforts, members have arranged meals for poor neighbourhood children, and school classes have taken poor families under their protection.

They have also started a magazine, with junior members contributing to its content.

A report on the Red Cross Juniors of Czecho-Slovakia by W. S. Gard reinforces the organisation's mission and incorporates cultural knowledge through the inclusion of photographs. Gard observes that '[t]hroughout the world there is a great and growing interest in the Junior Red Cross', with twenty-seven countries now having organisations.[51] Gard explains that '[w]herever school children are enrolled as Juniors they at once begin to gain an understanding of the value of citizenship and to learn the many ways in which they can serve their communities'.[52] Service and citizenship operate alongside one another, as the young people clean a park and some classrooms. Gard's concluding comment reinforces the value of these actions since '[i]n these, and in many other ways, not only the Czecho children but Juniors everywhere are learning through their activities the meaning of good citizenship.'[53] The accompanying photos depicted four children dressed in their national costumes and making toys to be shipped to Italy and Belgium, presumably in response to the war. One toy sits prominently on the tabletop, a doll dressed in a national costume. International friendliness is apparent in multiple ways, as the children make dolls to be shared with children in other countries but dress them in costumes that are distinct to the region. The inclusion of this report about the Czecho-Slovakian Junior Red Cross in a Canadian magazine encourages young Canadians to understand how service and citizenship are shared objectives among young people from different parts of the globe.

The link between service and international friendliness is explicitly identified after an earthquake in September 1923 seriously damaged Tokyo and Yokohama, causing massive casualties. The Juniors of Canada are informed in the October issue that they 'have now the great opportunity of showing their friendliness for the children of Japan'.[54] The author of the article on the disaster, likely Browne, explains that 'I am confident that the same enthusiasm for real service which the Canadian Juniors have shown in raising money to treat needy children in their own country, will now be demonstrated in their efforts to lend a hand to the helpless and homeless children of Japan.'[55] The evidence of the charitable habitus enabled through the pages of the magazine is evident in a report the following month describing the successful fundraising efforts across the country, including $4,000 from Junior members

214   Philanthropy in Children's Periodicals, 1840–1930

in British Columbia, $4,000 from Toronto, $180.74 from New Brunswick, and $163.13 from Prince Edward Island.[56] That the amounts are listed at the provincial level indicates the importance of separating out the contributions, especially from provinces with much smaller memberships. On the same page is a message from the director of the Junior Red Cross of Japan, General Yenji Ino-ue, who writes to thank the 'Children of Canada' for 'your deep and practical sympathy and your generous gifts to our children ... I will convey a message of your kindness to our children in Japan. I know their hearts will be touched by your friendliness.'[57] Despite the provincial breakdown identified in the internal reporting of the funds, the money is a gift from Canadian children as a whole and conducted in the spirit of friendliness that Ino-ue observes.[58]

The international friendliness that typifies the Junior Red Cross is not exclusively or even predominantly monetary, despite the example of the Japanese Relief Fund. Instead, friendliness is promoted through knowledge shared via reports of other Junior Red Cross organisations, and correspondence and scrapbooks shared internationally between branches. In article in October 1922, Browne encourages Canadian Juniors to develop scrapbooks to be shared with the international branches with whom they are already corresponding. She has had an opportunity to examine what she calls a 'booklet' created by the Junior Red Cross Branch in Presque Isle, Maine to share with Junior members in Holland and reports that it offers an opportunity to share information about their community. She describes the headings in the Presque Isle booklet (history, contribution to the war, geographical location, natural industries, general description, school activities, and conclusion) and thinks it would be a 'splendid idea' if some of the Canadian Junior Red Cross branches were to create 'such a booklet about your own community'.[59]

The written materials appearing in the booklets are rarely published in *Canadian Red Cross Junior*, although a letter from the High River, Alberta branch to Wellington, New Zealand Juniors is likely indicative of the tenor of such materials. Sarah Glassford argues that the magazine and the scrapbook-style portfolios created by members to be sent overseas promote 'a version of transnational-national citizenship that embedded a sense of shared global humanity within a framework of white, anglophone, British Canadian identity'.[60] This identity is clearly apparent in the letter, which begins by explaining that the Canadian girls and boys in grades six and seven 'thought it would be interesting for you to hear about our Province . . . and for us to hear about you'.[61] The children describe the geography of the region and summarise the 'important business places are five banks and five [grain] elevators'.[62] The town of about fifteen hundred people has five churches, a town hall, a high school, a public school, and a movie theatre. The latest addition is the aerodrome, containing five hangars which will hold ten aeroplanes for fire rangers to locate forest fires. The whiteness of the community is evident in the children's description of the province's history:

> Before white men came to this country, there were only Indians and great herds of wild buffalo roaming about the prairies. After it was inhabited by white men it rapidly developed into a ranching country and now the only buffalo we have are kept by the Government in the National Park.[63]

The dispossession of the Indigenous people from the land is not mentioned, although the young writers discuss the local animals (gophers, coyotes, badgers, porcupines, sparrows, and meadow larks) and flowers (violets, buttercups, buffalo beans, bluebells, and wild roses). They conclude with their hope that 'we have made our letter interesting to you and we would also enjoy receiving an interesting letter from you telling about your country and people'.[64] This letter signals the young people's interest in learning about the lives of others living far away. While obviously constrained by the need to speak a common language (Browne comments that the Dutch children to whom the Presque Isle booklet has been sent are in high school and 'can write their letters in English'[65]), this type of correspondence both produces and reflects the *habitus* of international friendliness that the organisation was trying to create.

Canadian Red Cross Junior's multi-pronged focus on health, service, and international friendliness reflects the objectives of the international Junior Red Cross, which is why it is the first to be discussed in this chapter. The British magazine (published quarterly beginning in 1924) and the New Zealand one (launched in 1925) are both similar to the Canadian one insofar as they reflect the overarching objectives of the organisation, and while each has some unique elements related to the historical origins of the Junior Red Cross and the impacts of war work, their contents

216   Philanthropy in Children's Periodicals, 1840–1930

are spread across all three areas of interest. In contrast, and as is demonstrated in the following two sections, the New South Wales and American magazines show how the specificities of the Junior organisations impacted the *habitus* produced in their pages.

New South Wales *Junior Red Cross Record*

The Australian Branch of the British Red Cross Society launched its publication, *New South Wales Red Cross Record*, as a record of its activities in 1914. As Oppenheimer explains, by the end of the war, the Australian Red Cross was 'firmly established as a major wartime voluntary organisation' and a formal arrangement between schools and the Junior Red Cross was inaugurated in July 1918.[66] Like the children in Canada, Australian children were also actively involved in contributing to the home front during the war and, in February 1916, the *Record* began including some content for younger readers such as an announcement of a competition for the best letter written by a boy or girl under the age of sixteen.[67] These letters are intended for the 'boys who are fighting for us' and must be accompanied by the coupon appearing below the competition announcement, thereby encouraging potential entrants to purchase a copy of the magazine.[68] The wartime focus on service is explicit in this initial invitation, in which children could provide entertainment and news of home to the soldiers at the front, and remained a significant feature of *Junior Red Cross Record for New South Wales* after its establishment in 1919.[69] While the magazine would eventually become more aligned with the overarching objectives of the Junior Red Cross to include international friendliness and citizenship, the *habitus* of service was its main focus, and it initially included little content on children's health.[70]

In 1914, the objectives of the New South Wales Junior Red Cross Society incorporated gendered aspects of wartime service. Its aims were to 'teach girls from the age of 14 years:- First Aid, St. John Ambulance Course, Signalling, Life Saving, water and otherwise, Camp Cooking with improvised utensils'.[71] The Patroness of the Society, Lady Edeline Strickland, writes that 'I have much pleasure in expressing my approval of the work of the Junior Red Cross Society. It gives a grand field for national work to all young women, and they have my warm sympathy.'[72] The specific areas in which they might provide assistance include helping blinded soldiers, growing food for hospitals, and establishing and supporting convalescent homes. This kind of assistance was perhaps more suitable for girls over the age of fourteen and indicates some slippage between older girls joining Voluntary Aid Detachments and younger children joining the Junior Red Cross. As the letter-writing competition indicates, the age range of child contributors could be quite broad.

'The Children's Pages', first appearing as part of the adult publication in March 1916 and conducted by writer Ella McFadyen, encourage children's engagement with the magazine and especially its content for young readers.[73] McFadyen comments on the 'wonderful response' to the letter-writing competition, remarking that '[o]ne thing I am sure that the boys liked to hear about, and that was the Red Cross news that so many put into their letters, while all accounts of patriotic work tend to show how faithfully we remember them'.[74] She included poetry and fiction in the children's column and encouraged children to submit to the regular competitions. In May 1916, she announced one on knitted socks and mittens and another on cooking a 'Victoria Sandwich', a sponge cake with jam and cream.[75] This issue also includes a poem by McFadyen, 'Mother Goose to Date', that relates the sacrifices made by various fairy tale and nursery rhyme characters. Cinderella, for instance, has 'foresworn the dance / And raffled her crystal shoes' while Little Miss Muffet 'hands out pies / To batches of new recruits'.[76] A story, 'The Sunbeam Boy', presumably by McFadyen, was published serially between July and November. This content is markedly different from that appearing in the *Canadian Red Cross Junior* but is evocative of more general children's pages in newspapers in that it features a variety of forms and genres to attract readers.

Expanding the organisational structure of the Junior Red Cross enabled it to adapt to new roles in the future. After the Junior Red Cross inaugural meeting was held in July 1918, 'The Children's Pages' were replaced by content specifically aimed at Junior Red Cross circles. Although the circles had been permitted to use school buildings for their activities, the Minister for Education supported a more formal alliance between the Australian Red Cross Society through the formation of circles in each school. Like the Canadian example, this enabled the 'extension and continuation of the [Junior Red Cross] Society into the post-war period'.[77]

218   Philanthropy in Children's Periodicals, 1840–1930

With the launch of *Junior Red Cross Record for New South Wales* in February 1919, the *habitus* of service is more consistent in the magazine. No longer a small part of the adult publication, *Junior Red Cross Record* offered young members a publication of their own.[78] However, unlike the Canadian magazine, with its target audience apparent from its cover images of young Canadians, the Australian publication features an injured soldier in hospital, with a nurse offering him a drink, while another soldier carries a stretcher in the background (see Fig. 7.2). Although ostensibly aimed at Junior members, the magazine's intended and actual audience was not initially clear. By 1921, however, the image was replaced with a wagtail and its nest, and a subtitle emphasises that the magazine is intended 'For Young Australians'.[79] In the foreword to the March 1919 issue, Honorary Secretary Mrs C. J. Royle notes that a copy of the magazine has been 'sent to many schools which do not possess a Circle' and she asks 'all these schools not only to subscribe to the paper for the school library, but also to join up with us by forming a Circle'.[80] She explains that it does not matter how few children join. Everyone should have an opportunity to become part of the organisation since 'it induces a feeling of friendship for all those who are concerned in the work. Although the war is over, the Red Cross activities will continue to be urgently wanted, and the Junior Society will be specially needed.'[81] The focus on service is implicit here, in which the feeling of friendship is based on the service work rather than the international friendliness that eventually appears in the magazine.

The importance of Junior Red Cross service work is evident in the advertisement, 'Why You Should Take THE JUNIOR RED CROSS RECORD'. By subscribing, 'you are helping to build up a great junior organisation which must be a help to our national life'.[82] In a direct address, readers are reminded that this is 'a bright and amusing paper run wholly in the interests of the children of New South Wales'.[83] Claiming to feature more competitions than any other Australian paper, it has 30,000 readers and hopes to double that readership by the end of the year. Reading the magazine is part of the service *habitus* to which children can and should contribute. The guidelines for this service work are laid out in 'For Busy Workers', which describes the 'very real and practical manner' in which the Junior Red Cross can help 'those who have fought for us'.[84] Its orientation towards returning soldiers is explicit, as is the clear requirement that children are not

Charitable Habits 219

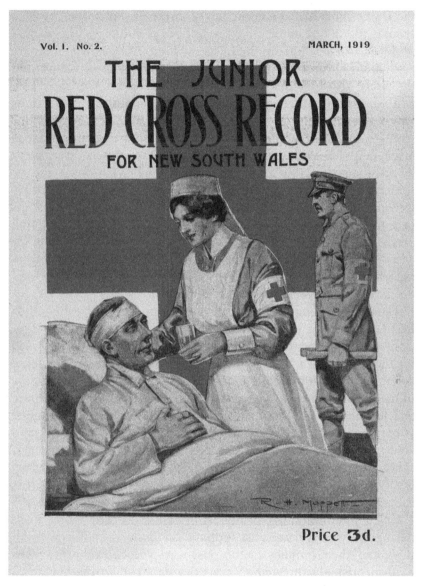

Fig. 7.2 Cover of *The Junior Red Cross Record for New South Wales*, March 1919.

'to spend your money or your parents' money'.[85] Instead, learning to make useful garments out of old or outgrown clothes would be 'splendid training' for young workers. The organisation's origins as a service organisation for teenage girls is evident, yet a report of

220 Philanthropy in Children's Periodicals, 1840–1930

the Dawes and Miller's Point Junior circle explains that they are sending along one guinea, the proceeds of a children's bazaar held by Jessie Hansen, aged nine, Eileen Walters (six), Norman Hoare (six), and Laurie Hoare (four).[86] The children are quite young, and the circle also includes two young boys, who are evidently able and willing to contribute to these charitable efforts. The 'Junior Circle Reports' on the following pages describe a variety of different activities. The Buxton Circle, with nineteen members, 'has given help in several directions' in which members 'sent away books, magazines, purple packets for Jack's Day, and toys for the soldiers' children at Christmas. They made caps and housewifes [sewing kits for soldiers], sent away eggs and sixty-two waratahs [a native plant] for Dependents' Day, and have made a beginning on their spinning.'[87] The circle had been busy gathering items for donation and had chosen to direct those items to a number of war-related causes that were being heavily promoted in the press, and presumably elsewhere, in the last months of 1918.

The military focus of the service work undertaken by the Junior Red Cross circles is evident throughout the magazine, but especially each April with replica of the 'Remembrance Card' designed for the children. In a magazine that typically featured fairly dense columns of print, the double-page spread appearing in the middle of the sixteen-page magazine was striking for its use of white space and for how it was designed to be hung elsewhere. It reminded young readers of the sacrifices made on behalf of king, home, and country, and how they were expected to feel love and gratitude to 'Those Gallant Men Who laid down Their Lives'.[88] The devastating losses at Gallipoli in 1916 were memorialised each April across the country and appeared annually in the magazine for decades.[89]

Given Junior Red Cross interest in assisting on the home front during the war years and its support for disabled and invalid soldiers and their families in the post-war period, its health focus is unsurprisingly directed to related areas. Unlike the Canadian organisation's focus on children's health from the first issues of the Junior magazine, the initial years of the New South Wales magazine aimed at returning soldiers to health, as the cover image suggests, and developing first aid skills. In February 1921, for instance, an article on first aid for Juniors describes how several patrons have suggested 'that we should give our Juniors a simple – very simple – course of lectures in First Aid', a proposal which resulted in several articles being published over the following months.[90]

Juniors who passed the examination paper set at the end of the course were granted a certificate. The articles for 'Our First Aid Notes' over the following months discuss burns and scalds, germs, the need for fresh air, treatment of cuts, poisonous foods, and drowning. Directly below the first of these articles is an image of a soldier in a wheelchair with a uniformed nurse standing beside him. The photo was taken at Graythwaite, the Red Cross Home at North Sydney for permanently disabled men that was supported by Junior members of the Red Cross, with many circles sending gifts. The ideas of health are intertwined on this page as the requirement that young people obtain first aid knowledge is set alongside the longer-term care requirements of disabled soldiers who should be supported through financial and material donations. In the following month, this expectation that children will support disabled men is made explicit with a call for donations to enable the purchase of a wheelchair for a soldier living at Graythwaite who is ineligible for repatriation assistance. On the following page, an article on 'Invalid Cookery' offers information about the 'very necessary and most-used foods given to the sick and convalescents'.[91] This content is markedly different from the health-related content that appeared in the Canadian magazine, since it almost exclusively focuses on helping injured soldiers return to health.

Nonetheless, *Junior Red Cross Record* does include some material on children's health, although it is not embedded into the monthly magazine content to the same extent as in the Canadian magazine. 'The Way to Health', for example, is a heavily didactic article drawing on religious doctrine to explain that God created man to be 'healthy and strong in mind and body; and that it is owing to the follies of men and women, or to the surroundings in which they are brought up, that diseases and suffering form a part of human existence'.[92] Young readers are told to do everything they can to 'improve the good points of your health and lessen the bad points . . . so that your children may be better and healthier than your self'.[93] This call to better health will help future generations of children to be healthier, which echoes sentiments about girls' health in the nineteenth century.[94] The author explains how '[g]irls often think they are more interesting if they are dragging out a complaint about their health' but urges them to 'clear this from their minds' since a 'healthy happy girl or boy' is admired by everyone and will cheer up 'everyone with whom they come in contact'.[95] The first steps along the way to health are fresh

222   Philanthropy in Children's Periodicals, 1840–1930

air, cleanliness, and clean and wholesome food; by keeping 'your hearts full of pity for those who cannot attain the same fulness of health', you will 'not go far wrong'.[96] The *habitus* of health is beginning to be instilled in young people, who are encouraged to follow these guidelines to enable their own health and to feel pity for those who are unable to enjoy the benefits of a healthy body.

The absence of more material specifically on children's health is perhaps surprising given that the influenza pandemic of 1919 had a significant impact on children's ability to attend school and significantly disrupted the state. However, the directions around fresh air, cleanliness, and clean food likely emerged from this disaster. Although the mortality rate for children was relatively low, more than about 15,000 Australians died, with about a third of those deaths from people between the ages of twenty-five and thirty-four.[97] Evelyn McKinnon reports in August 1919 that the New South Wales education department has asked the Junior Red Cross 'to refrain from asking the children to make any special effort during the next six months' since their scholarly work has been 'greatly interrupted' owing to the 'influenza scourge' and it will be difficult for them to recover their lost ground.[98]

The idea that health could be a game is introduced in December 1921. An article entitled 'The Health Game' reinforces the idea that good habits instilled in children will continue into adulthood. Teaching the health rules to young people is the 'simplest and best way for a nation to acquire good health habits'.[99] The nine rules introduced in this article include daily baths, fresh air, a nourishing breakfast, handwashing, eating moderately and regularly, drinking plenty of fresh water, wearing appropriate clothing, brushing your teeth, and sleeping at least seven hours near an open window. The article concludes by explaining that the prize for following these health rules is good health and '[e]veryone must judge for himself whether it is worth the effort'.[100] Although children are ostensibly given a choice about whether developing a *habitus* of health is worthwhile, the message is clear that this is an important objective for all Australians, who can help the nation to be healthier.

Moreover, the importance of health for the Junior Red Cross is emphasised through articles about children's health in other countries. An article entitled 'Health in Hawaii' begins by explaining, 'As you know, the Junior Red Cross in other lands does a great deal in the teaching of health and hygiene among the young people.'[101] The *habitus* of health is embedded into the Junior Red Cross, as this article indicates, although its implementation varied. Hawaiian Juniors pledge that

> [b]ecause I want to be strong, healthy and happy, I promise to obey the Junior Red Cross health rules, as well as I can. I will be cheerful; I will eat wholesome food; I will sleep long hours in fresh air; I will keep myself clean; and I will try to prevent accidents.[102]

The similarity between the Hawaiian, Canadian, and Australian health rules reflects the centralisation of these ideas through the League of Red Cross Societies and the ways that they are taken up relatively consistently across the countries.[103] The Hawaii Junior Red Cross also have a 'Health Creed' that reminds the children that 'I will learn the rules of healthful living and will practise them at all times: I will help others to be well also; and I will try to make the world happier through right living and thinking.'[104] The importance of sharing the health rules is embedded in this creed. Although the New South Wales magazine does not discuss this specifically, its focus on aiding soldiers in their return to health is the manifestation of this ideal. Indeed, the article concludes that the exercises and games that the Hawaiian children play to improve their health are already done 'for our boys and girls in the schools' and they are 'already well started along the road to health and happiness and have more time to give to helping children not so fortunate'.[105]

This focus on improving health for other young people in Australia becomes increasingly evident with the establishment of a convalescent children's home. A March 1924 article about 'Our First Junior Red Cross Home: The Story of "Shuna"' describes how a convalescent home for ex-soldiers was given to the Junior Red Cross for the purpose of housing twelve 'delicate' children who would benefit from time spent in the fresh air of the Blue Mountains.[106] Readers are informed that 'it is hoped that our Juniors will make it their special care' for '[n]othing could be better than for them to devote their energies to helping sick and delicate children back to sturdy health and the joy of living'.[107] While many Juniors are already 'doing great work' supporting cots in children's hospitals and homes, other circles with no special cause could turn their attention to raising funds for Shuna.[108] The young people responded to this call to action by visiting the home as well as collecting and forwarding gifts. As an example, the Blackheath

224   Philanthropy in Children's Periodicals, 1840–1930

Public School Circle sent a box of vegetables, potatoes, fruit, and nuts.[109] The young people at the nearby public school willingly supported the convalescing children, who are benefitting from the opportunity to stay at the home. They are 'having the happiest of times. Every child admitted was not only in need of change but came from a home where there was sickness and trouble caused through war service.'[110] By demonstrating how healthy and happy the children are becoming, the article emphasises the value of this charitable work and the *habitus* of health enabled through this charitable activity.

In addition to the focus on service and health that is evident in *Junior Red Cross Record*, the charitable *habitus* is also defined by international friendliness, although not to the same extent as the Canadians. The circle reports are primarily focused on local charity work and rarely make mention of international connections. Nonetheless, the magazine makes an effort to situate the Junior Red Cross within an international environment of shared interest in Junior Red Cross work. One of the typical examples is found in the 'All the World Over' series, which begins in March 1921. Each article, usually occupying a full page, discusses the activities undertaken by Junior Red Cross members around the world. In the June 1924 issue, for instance, readers learn that Austrian Juniors have enabled 450 'delicate children' from Austria, Hungary, Germany, and Switzerland to attend a six-week summer camp in Graz, Austria. This camp achieved positive outcomes, since 'not only was there a great improvement in their physical condition, but the happy result was achieved of bringing together children of different nations and creating bolds of friendship between them'.[111] This article reports on Czecho-Slovakian Juniors who raised funds for the children of Japan through the staging of a play on the subject of vaccination. They raised 1,200 Czech crowns to 'help the children who suffered through the earthquake'.[112] Like the Canadians, the Czecho-Slovakian children were evidently encouraged to assist Japanese children affected by the earthquake. In New South Wales, however, the awareness of the Japanese disaster did not translate into fundraising efforts.

The Junior magazines often featured content that was collected from other Junior Red Cross magazines to build its international community. The league translated selected material to be shared with members, such as the Czecho-Slovakian and Austrian Junior news discussed above, and editors could easily reprint material

Charitable Habits 225

from other English-language Junior Red Cross magazines. One such example is 'Going to School in Other Lands', which is reprinted from the American *Junior Red Cross News*. This article draws in readers with an imagined future, wondering

> How would you like to receive radio telephone message[s] from boys and girls all over the world telling you about their schools? This is probable in the future: then it will be much easier to get acquainted with young neighbors of other countries. All schools of the world may be linked with wireless telephones, and Junior Red Cross ideals and methods will be communicated in globe-circling flashes.[113]

This article establishes an imagined future based on the shared childhood experience of education in which news and information is quickly and easily shared via 'flashes' that enable the world to be linked. Until such time as this future is available, the article includes 'bits of news of schools of many lands which may make new friends for all'.[114]

The content in *Junior Red Cross Record* demonstrates the focus placed by the New South Wales organisation on service, first for soldiers returning from the war and then on their families, eventually settling on a range of activities designed to assist poor and ill Australian children. While the magazine eventually expanded its interest to include the other two pillars of children's health and international friendliness, the local service work remained the most significant component of the magazine until the late 1920s. In contrast to the American periodical discussed in the next section, connections with other Junior Red Cross organisations were rarely an important focus.

American *Junior Red Cross News*

American engagement with the First World War is quite distinct from that of the Canadians and the Australians given their neutrality until 1917. As Branden Little argues, given the American Red Cross's inability to successfully initiate relief campaigns prior to their entry into the war, 'it is all the more remarkable that the ARC transformed into the United States' leading relief society during the brief period of American belligerency, 1917–18'.[115] In President Woodrow Wilson's letter 'To the School Children of the United States', appearing in the first issue of *Junior Red Cross*

226   Philanthropy in Children's Periodicals, 1840–1930

News in September 1919, he observes that the American children who joined the Junior Red Cross in wartime 'worked hard and what you did is warmly appreciated by the whole country'.[116] In his direct address, he writes that 'I am sure that you wish to continue to be useful to your country and to children less fortunate than yourselves'.[117] The Junior Red Cross is planning 'larger and more systematic' work during peace time and will

> instruct you in ideals and habits of service, will show you how to be useful to your school, how to aid the older people in your community in their efforts to promote the health and comfort of the people among whom you live, and how to help children who are still suffering from the effects of the great war in foreign lands invaded by the enemy.[118]

In this letter, the mission of the American Junior Red Cross is evident. Service and international friendliness are the dominant concerns in its charitable *habitus*. According to Wilson, they can be brought together to create 'a world in which nations shall unite for purposes of peace and good will' so that 'you will come to understand [the children of other nations] better and they will understand and appreciate you more'.[119] This *habitus* of international friendliness is striking for its difference from the New South Wales publication, which was primarily interested in assisting Australian soldiers and their families, and the Canadian publication, which highlighted the importance of children's health. Instead, the *Junior Red Cross News* offered an ethos of international humanitarianism reflecting its wartime charitable efforts that was gradually transformed into international friendliness through local service.

The American Junior Red Cross had been actively participating in war efforts since the United States entered the First World War in 1917. Children were encouraged through school-based Junior Red Cross programmes to understand their wartime obligations, messaging that was consistent with Wilson's rationale for entering the war. Like the Canadian initiative, the American Junior Red Cross operated exclusively through schools, achieving its peak membership of 11 million schoolchildren in 1918.[120] Membership dropped in the 1920s, but never fell below 4 million in the inter-war years.[121] While some Junior wartime activities were focused on assisting American troops, most were designed to assist with relief measures for Allied civilians.[122] The first issue of *Junior Red Cross News*, the 'French Number', highlights the importance of assisting with the reconstruction of Europe after the devastation of the war, a theme that continues throughout the magazine's early years. 'A Victory Yet to be Won', published in October 1919, explains how '[w]ar is not over for children of Europe'.[123] The author acknowledges that '[w]ords have long since been exhausted in the effort to tell what war did to the children of Europe' in terms of their physical and mental development. While each nation is now in the process of rebuilding, 'American boys and girls of the Junior Red Cross are throwing the weight of their active sympathy and help' to develop a 'mutual understanding and friendliness which will not be blown aside in national disagreements'.[124] The initial efforts by Juniors were guided towards sympathy and assistance for young people badly impacted by the war, which would enable an international friendliness based on mutual understanding in the future.

Unlike the examples in Canada and Australia, which were both primarily concerned with helping people at home, American children contributed actively to European civilian relief efforts. In 'Flying Aboard the "Friendship"', Carlyle T. Williams begins by exclaiming, '[b]ut of course there's no question, now that we're Juniors. It is to Europe that we have been sending our gifts and our letters and our money.'[125] A map of Europe included with the article indicates that Juniors are 'doing something at each of the forty-three places' marked, including providing meals for Belgian schoolchildren and supporting children at a convalescent home near Rheims, on a ship in Venice, and at a day nursery in Florence. These efforts are essential, as the editorial letter from Austin Cunningham explains, in 'promoting happy childhood the world over through the inculcation of ideals and habits of service'.[126] Childhood around the world can be made happy through the efforts of young American Junior Red Cross members.

These wartime relief efforts were encouraged through magazine content expressing the gratitude. The first issue includes a letter written by Lucienne Plateau, who writes to 'Dear American Friends' of her wartime experiences attending school with 'the roar of the cannon, which often made the windowpanes in the school rattle', and her fear for her papa fighting in the trenches.[127] 'The hardest thing' that happened during the war, she explains, was when she was forced to flee her village with her mother and two younger siblings: 'We slept where we could in a barn or a stable. Everything we ate was black with dust. We were very thirsty.

228   Philanthropy in Children's Periodicals, 1840–1930

I assure you it was not a happy time.'[128] She thanks 'our friends the Americans', who enabled the family to return home almost three months later.[129] This letter describes the wartime privations experienced by children and families and thereby reinforces the idea of assisting those in need. It also situates Lucienne as a worthy recipient of such charity. Like the readers of *Junior Red Cross News*, she is a child who attends school and worries about her family. The impact of the war is much more personal for her, which helps to encourage American readers to participate in the *habitus* of charity.

The charitable *habitus* is underpinned by positioning readers as future adults with clear responsibilities. Young readers are reminded 'that as the future citizens of America and the world you are to carry forward all that is best in our civilization and not merely to carry it but to guard and preserve it'.[130] Already, Cunningham reminds his readers, 'you are sowing the seeds of international good-will' through relief projects and, he hopes, 'these examples of what you are doing today will cause some grown people . . . to wake up and shoulder a fairer proportion of the world's burdens, and do it with the same spirit of co-operation that you manifest'.[131] Children's efforts are designed to inspire adult engagement with the charitable cause in the form of this international goodwill that promotes peace and prosperity into the future. At the same time, children are able to accomplish objectives that their parents cannot. In 'The Letter of Greeting', John W. Studebaker, director of Junior memberships, explains,

> The children of America and the children of other countries are facing a world of new possibilities. Together you will be able to go further than your fathers and mothers could go in banishing selfishness and ignorance, disease and uncleanness from the earth. It will be your sacred mission in years to come to insure justice and preserve peace within and between the nations.[132]

The message of peace and justice is unsurprising after the casualties of war and its longer-term impacts, but this letter is sincere in its hope that the next generation might be able to prevent this kind of violence from recurring. It also signals the shift in American Junior Red Cross policy from war relief to international education as a method of promoting international friendliness. As Julia Irwin explains, if the Junior Red Cross 'wanted to force better

Charitable Habits   229

international relations and preserve world peace', it needed to 'devise activities that taught friendship rather than philanthropy, mutual respect rather than paternalism'.[133]

Service is always important to the *habitus* of charity promoted in *Junior Red Cross News*. An article published in October 1919 reinforces that 'local service' should be selected on the basis of its educational values, including 'the presence of social purposes, strong enough to attract and hold children together, and definite enough to give shape and point to their efforts'.[134] These local efforts can then supplement the 'wider, humanitarian aims' of the Junior Red Cross as an organisation that is both local and national.[135] The somewhat abstract language here is articulated more concretely through the metaphor of the candle in a later article, published in 1925. In this article, readers are invited to

> imagine that an American Junior, a Hungarian Junior, and ever so many other Juniors from various countries, all speaking different languages, are standing near each other, each one holding an unlighted candle in his hand. Suppose one of these Juniors should say in his own language, 'Let's light our candles'. Of course, the others would not understand. But suppose, instead of that, he took his own candle, which was already lighted, and went to one of the other Juniors and lighted his candle for him, and then the other Junior passed his light on to still another – that would be a language which all would understand.[136]

The local service activities are the lighted candles that, through sharing news of their efforts, can inspire other candles to be lighted as well. The practical manifestations of this metaphor come from the local service activities performed by children, but they had worldwide implications as their light was spread through different war-torn countries.

One of the service activities that aligned nicely with its educational objectives was the development of a school portfolio, which also enabled the international friendliness that the Junior Red Cross organisation aimed to achieve. In October 1921, a fictionalised letter to the 'Dear Juniors of America' from 'Your friends in England, France, Italy, Holland, Switzerland, Czecho-Slovakia, Roumania, Spain, Belgium, Albania, and Canada' explains that '[w]e have just learned that the Junior Red Cross of America is ready and willing to help us get acquainted'.[137] These fictional schoolchildren are eager to receive information, stamps, pictures, and postcards from an American class about America and the class's home city or town, school life, sports and games, and parks and monuments. In exchange, children from one of these other countries will write back. The article includes a photo of some of the pages from an American portfolio to be sent to a foreign school, and children are encouraged to think of how 'splendid' it would be to 'have real friends *all around* the world'.[138] Like the portfolios being created by the Canadians, the contents are rarely published in the magazine itself. However, one brief article mentions that the Canadian Juniors are 'very much interested in international school correspondence' and reprints an excerpt from *Red Cross Junior* that an 'interesting' portfolio on birds and plants was received from Juniors in Knoxville, Tennessee, with 'a very attractive cover decorated with sweet peas' and contents that were 'beautifully illustrated with colored illustrations of plant and animal life'.[139]

The distribution of the portfolios was evidently complex and signals the efforts of the Junior Red Cross to facilitate its *habitus* of international friendliness. The article inviting American Juniors to create a portfolio to be shared internationally also informs them to write to obtain 'Pamphlet A.R.C. 610, revised' and an information card. The pamphlet presumably included the details about the portfolio; the information card is to be filled out in triplicate; and sufficient postage must be included so that the material can be forwarded to the Paris office for distribution.[140] In a later article, readers are told that '[s]chool correspondence portfolios are great travelers and must pass through many hands before they reach their destination'.[141] A portfolio prepared in California for a school in Czechoslovakia, for instance, is sent to San Francisco before being forwarded to national headquarters, then on to Prague to be translated, before being sent to the school. The reply from the receiving school makes a similar journey on its return. In contrast, portfolios destined for English-speaking countries have a simpler journey, since translation is not required.

Both the report on the Knoxville portfolio and the informational article explaining how the portfolios travel and are translated suggest that children were interested in their circulation through the international community. However, as Little observes, the extent of children's voluntary participation in these activities is difficult to determine. Opting out of participating in Junior Red

Charitable Habits   231

Cross activities 'would have been a difficult task for a student who preferred not to do the work personally or whose family discouraged their participation'.[142] The alignment between the American Junior Red Cross and the school system meant that it would have been challenging for a young person to withdraw from activities. Nonetheless, the high number of schoolchildren participating during the interwar period suggests an ongoing willingness among young people to contribute to the *habitus* of service and international friendliness embodied through the American Junior Red Cross.

Conclusion

This chapter has drawn on three Junior Red Cross magazines developed as part of an international organisation to show how charitable habits were conveyed and reinforced through the pages of individual publications. These magazines – and the Junior Red Cross organisations they represent – emerge out of distinct national origins and, initially at least, reflect how each organisation chose to prioritise those elements most relevant for their members in view of changing educational and charitable priorities in the post-war period. Children in Canada, Australia, and the United States were all active in fundraising for the war, and those charitable habits were repurposed as part of the Junior Red Cross focus on service, health, and international friendliness. The Junior Red Cross hoped these habits would continue into the future as the children became adults who retained their interest in peace, justice, and health on an international scale.

Notes

1. See Annemarie Valdes, '"*I, being a member of the Junior Red Cross, gladly offered my services*": Transnational Practices of Citizenship by the International Junior Red Cross Youth', *Transnational Social Review* 5, no. 3 (2015): 161–75, for her discussion of how the Junior Red Cross school correspondence programme was transnational.
2. Portions of this chapter were first published by Kristine Moruzi, 'Embodying the Healthy, Charitable Child in the Junior Red Cross', in *The Embodied Child: Readings in Children's Literature and Culture*, edited by Roxanne Harde and Lydia Kokkola. © 2018,

232 Philanthropy in Children's Periodicals, 1840–1930

Taylor & Francis. Reproduced with permission of The Licensor through PLSclear.

3. Alongside these earlier publications, the British *Junior Red Cross Journal* began in 1924, and the New Zealand *Junior Red Cross Journal* in 1925.

4. José Gomez Ruiz, 'How the Junior Red Cross Was Born', *International Review of the Red Cross (1961–1997)*, 4, no. 36 (1964): 148.

5. Ruiz, 'How the Junior Red Cross', 149.

6. Melanie Oppenheimer, 'Realignment in the Aftermath of War: The League of Red Cross Societies, the Australian Red Cross and Its Junior Red Cross in the 1920s', in *The Red Cross Movement: Myths, Practices and Turning Points*, ed. Neville Wylie, Melanie Oppenheimer, and James Crossland (Manchester: Manchester University Press, 2020), 130.

7. Oppenheimer, 'Realignment', 130.

8. Oxford English Dictionary, s.v. 'habit, n., sense III.9.a', September 2023. (https://doi.org/10.1093/OED/3105659060)

9. Pierre Bourdieu, *The Logic of Practice*, trans. Richard Nice (Cambridge: Polity Press, 1990), 54.

10. Karl Maton, 'Habitus', in *Pierre Bourdieu: Key Concepts*, ed. Michael James Grenfell (Durham: Taylor & Francis, 2014), 52. Emphasis in original.

11. Bourdieu, *Logic*, 58.

12. Smiljka Tomanović, 'Family Habitus as the Cultural Content for Childhood', *Childhood* 11, no. 3 (August 2004): 343.

13. Bourdieu, *Logic*, 54.

14. Bourdieu, *Logic*, 55.

15. Diane Reay, '"It's all becoming a habitus": Beyond the Habitual Use of Habitus in Educational Research', *British Journal of Sociology of Education* 25, no. 4 (2004): 434.

16. Bourdieu, *Logic*, 59.

17. Reay, 'It's all becoming a habitus', 432.

18. Bourdieu, *Logic*, 70.

19. Claire Edwards and Rob Imrie, 'Disability and Bodies as Bearers of Value', *Sociology* 37, no. 2 (2003): 241.

20. Bourdieu, *Logic*, 59.

21. Sarah Glassford, '"International Friendliness" and Canadian Identities: Transnational Tensions in Canadian Junior Red Cross Texts, 1919–1939', *Jeunesse: Young People, Texts, Cultures* 10, no. 2 (2018): 53.

22. I use the term 'Indian' here because that usage is common during this period, but I recognise that the term is rooted in colonialism and racism. 'File Hills Indian Junior Red Cross', *Canadian Red Cross Junior* (May 1922): 2.

23. 'The Canadian Red Cross Society', *British Empire Red Cross Conference* (London: British Red Cross Society, 1930), 93.

24. James W. Robertson, 'Peace-Time Policy and Health Progress of the Red Cross in Canada', *The Canadian Medical Association Journal* 19, no. 1 (July 1928): 92.

25. Sarah Glassford, *Mobilizing Mercy: A History of the Canadian Red Cross* (Montreal & Kingston: McGill-Queen's University Press, 2017), 146.

26. Nancy M. Sheehan, 'Junior Red Cross in the Schools: An International Movement, a Voluntary Agency, and Curriculum Change', *Curriculum Inquiry* 17, no 3. (1987), 250; Glassford, *Mobilizing Mercy*, 151. Sheehan also reports 1,482,729 members across 43,020 branches in 1961.

27. Sheehan, 'Junior Red Cross', 247.

28. Carole A. Breckenridge and Candace Vogler, 'The Critical Limits of Embodiment: Disability's Criticism', *Public Culture* 13, no. 3 (2001): 350.

29. Sutherland, *Children in English-Canadian Society*, 49.

30. Canadian Red Cross Society. *Annual Report* 1919: 17. By 1930, it had a paid circulation of approximately 30,000 ('Canadian Red Cross Society' 93).

31. Bourdieu, *Logic*, 67.

32. 'Reproduction of the First Prize Poster in the Children's Prize Poster Competition', *Canadian Red Cross Junior* (January 1923): 14.

33. 'February Prize Competition for Health Stories', *Canadian Red Cross Junior* (February 1923): 3.

34. W. Owen Conquest, 'The Runt and the Red Cross Rules', *Canadian Red Cross Junior* (September 1923): 10.

35. See Chris Shilling, *The Boy in Culture, Technology and Society* (London: Sage Publications, 1995).

36. 'Junior Red Cross', *Canadian Red Cross Junior* (December 1923): 9. Emphasis added.

37. 'What Is the Junior Red Cross?', *Canadian Red Cross Junior* (June 1922): 3.

38. Browne, Jane. 'A Letter from the Editor', *Canadian Red Cross Junior* (September 1922): 16.

39. Browne, 'A Letter', 16.
40. 'A Junior Red Cross Patient in Saskatchewan', *Canadian Red Cross Junior* (June 1922): 11.
41. 'A Junior Red Cross Patient', 11.
42. 'A Junior Red Cross Patient', 11.
43. 'A Junior Red Cross Patient', 11.
44. The cover images from the April, May, June, and September 1922 issues respectively.
45. Glassford, '"International Friendliness"', 56.
46. 'American Juniors' Work in Europe', *Canadian Red Cross Junior* (May 1922): 11.
47. 'American Juniors' Work in Europe', 11.
48. 'The Junior Red Cross Society of Hungary', *Canadian Junior Red Cross* (November 1922): 7.
49. 'A Boy from the Ukraine', *Canadian Junior Red Cross* (May 1922): 4.
50. 'The Junior Red Cross Society of Hungary', 7.
51. W. S. Gard, 'Red Cross Junior of Czecho-Slovakia', *Canadian Junior Red Cross* (January 1923): 6.
52. Gard, 'Red Cross Junior of Czecho-Slovakia', 6.
53. Gard, 'Red Cross Junior of Czecho-Slovakia', 6.
54. 'Junior Japanese Relief Fund', *Canadian Red Cross Junior* (October 1923): 3.
55. 'Junior Japanese Relief Fund', 3.
56. 'The Japanese Relief Fund', *Canadian Red Cross Junior* (November 1923): 13.
57. Yenji Ino-ue, 'A Message to Canada's Juniors from the Director of the Junior Red Cross of Japan', *Canadian Red Cross Junior* (November 1923): 13.
58. Decisions to raise money for international causes like the Japanese Relief Fund were evidently made at the national level. The Australian *Junior Red Cross Record* makes no mention of this cause in the final months of 1923.
59. Jean E. Browne, 'The Presque Isle Booklet', *Canadian Red Cross Junior* (October 1922): 3.
60. Glassford, '"International Friendliness"', 53.
61. 'Junior Red Cross Correspondence With New Zealand, *Canadian Red Cross Junior* (September 1923): 3.
62. 'Junior Red Cross Correspondence', 3.
63. 'Junior Red Cross Correspondence', 3.
64. 'Junior Red Cross Correspondence', 3.

65. Browne, 'The Presque Isle Booklet', 3.
66. Oppenheimer, 'Realignment', 131, 137.
67. See Rosalie Triolo's *Our Schools and the War*, especially Chapter 3 on 'Doing good for others', for a discussion of Australian schools' efforts during the First World War (Melbourne: Australian Scholarly, 2012).
68. 'Children's Competition', *New South Wales Red Cross Record* (February 1916): 46.
69. South Australia began publishing its own magazine, *South Australian Junior Red Cross Courier*, in 1929, with three issues in the first year, and then quarterly beginning in 1930.
70. For a history of beginnings of the Junior Red Cross in New South Wales, see Annie Campbell, '". . . thousands of tiny fingers moving": The Beginning of the Junior Red Cross Movement in New South Wales, 1914–1925', *Journal of the Royal Australian Historical Society* 90, no. 2 (2004): 184–200.
71. 'Junior Red Cross Society', *New South Wales Red Cross Record* (March 1916): 9.
72. 'Junior Red Cross Society', 9.
73. After the war, McFadyen edited the children's page of the *Sydney Mail* for eighteen years and published a number of popular books for children (Emily Gallagher, 'Ella May McFadyen [1887–1976]', People Australia, National Centre of biography, Australian National University, https://peopleaustralia.anu.edu.au/biography/mcfadyen-ella-may–27619/text3664, accessed 13 October 2023).
74. Ella McFadyen, 'Competition Results', *New South Wales Red Cross Record* (April 1916): 58; 'Letters to Soldiers', *New South Wales Red Cross Record* (April 1916): 58.
75. 'Children's Competitions', *New South Wales Red Cross Record* (May 1916): 50.
76. Ella McFadyen, 'Mother Goose to Date', *New South Wales Red Cross Record* (May 1916): 50.
77. Campbell, '". . . thousands of tiny fingers moving"', 190.
78. The adult and junior magazines were merged in 1924. In 1930, *Junior Red Cross Record* was again on its own, with the motto 'The Child for the Child' appearing on the cover along with an illustration of a brightly dressed child wearing a Junior Red Cross badge visiting a sick child.
79. Cover, *Junior Red Cross Record* (January 1921): np.
80. C. J. Royle, 'Foreword', *Junior Red Cross Record* (March 1919): 3.
81. Royle, 'Foreword', 3.

236   Philanthropy in Children's Periodicals, 1840–1930

82. 'Why You Should Take THE JUNIOR RED CROSS RECORD', *Junior Red Cross Record* (January 1921): 19.

83. 'Why You Should Take', 19.

84. 'For Busy Workers', *Junior Red Cross Record* (March 1919): 4.

85. 'For Busy Workers', 4.

86. 'For Busy Workers', 4.

87. 'Junior Circle Reports', *Junior Red Cross Record* (March 1919): 5. Jack's Day was a fundraising event for Australian Navy sailors and the merchant marine. Purple packets were available at stalls as a form of 'lucky dip' organised by Ethel Turner to support 'Homes' Day', to fund building materials for cottages for disabled soldiers and sailors, and for widows and orphans. Soldiers' Dependents' Day was intended to raise funds to support women until their male family members returned from war.

88. 'Remembrance Card', *Junior Red Cross Record* (April 1919): 8–9.

89. The image appeared in the April issue of magazine until at least 1939.

90. 'First Aid Course for Our Juniors', *Junior Red Cross Record* (February 1921): 12.

91. R. E. Piper, 'Invalid Cookery', *Junior Red Cross Record* (March 1921): 10.

92. 'The Way to Health', *Junior Red Cross Record* (October 1921): 9.

93. 'The Way to Health', 9.

94. See Chapter 4 on girls' health in Kristine Moruzi's *Constructing Girlhood Through the Periodical Press, 1850–1914* (Aldershot: Ashgate, 2012).

95. 'The Way to Health', 9.

96. 'The Way to Health', 9.

97. Peter Curson and Kevin McCracken, 'An Australian Perspective of the 1918–1919 Influenza Pandemic', *NSW Public Health Bulletin* 17, no. 7–8 (August 2007): 103, 105.

98. Evelyn MacKinnon, 'The Junior Red Cross', *Junior Red Cross Record* (August 1919): 12.

99. 'The Health Game', *Junior Red Cross Record* (December 1921): 4.

100. 'The Health Game', 4.

101. 'Health in Hawaii', *Junior Red Cross Record* (February 1923): 14.

102. 'Health in Hawaii', 14.

103. See Oppenheimer, 'Realignment'.

104. 'Health in Hawaii', 14.

105. 'Health in Hawaii', 14.

Charitable Habits   237

106. 'Our First Junior Red Cross Home: The Story of "Shuna"', *Junior Red Cross Record* (March 1924): 44. Shuna was one of three 'pre-ventoria' homes for children of ex-servicemen who were thought to be at risk of contracting tuberculosis (Melanie Oppenheimer, *The Power of Humanity: 100 Years of Australian Red Cross 1914–2014* [Sydney: HarperCollins, 2014], 73).

107. 'Our First Junior Red Cross Home', 44.

108. 'Our First Junior Red Cross Home', 44.

109. 'News from the J. R. C. Mountain Home', *Red Cross Record* (May 1924): 35.

110. 'News', 35.

111. 'All the World Over', *Red Cross Record* (June 1924): 47.

112. 'All the World Over', 47.

113. 'Going to School in Other Lands', *Junior Red Cross Record* (March 1923): 14.

114. 'Going to School', 14.

115. Branden Little, 'Failure to Launch: The American Red Cross in an Era of Contested Neutrality, 1914–17', in *The Red Cross Movement: Myths, Practices and Turning Points*, ed. Neville Wylie, Melanie Oppenheimer and James Crossland (Manchester: Manchester University Press, 2020), 97.

116. Woodrow Wilson, 'To the School Children of the United States', *Junior Red Cross News* (September 1919): 1.

117. Wilson, 'To the School Children', 1.

118. Wilson, 'To the School Children', 1.

119. Wilson, 'To the School Children', 1.

120. Julia F. Irwin, 'Teaching "Americanism with a World Perspective": The Junior Red Cross in the U.S. Schools from 1917 to the 1920s', *History of Education Quarterly* 53, no. 3 (August 2013): 258.

121. Irwin, 'Teaching', 258.

122. Irwin, 'Teaching', 261.

123. Lyman Bryson, 'A Victory Yet to be Won', *Junior Red Cross News* (October 1919): 6.

124. Bryson, 'A Victory', 7.

125. Carlyle T. Williams, 'Flying Aboard the "Friendship"', *Junior Red Cross News* (May 1920): 3.

126. Austin Cunningham, 'The Editor's Letter to You!', *Junior Red Cross News* (May 1920): 16.

127. Lucienne Plateau, 'From a Little French Girl', *Junior Red Cross News* (September 1919): 21.

128. Plateau, 'From a Little French Girl', 21.

238   Philanthropy in Children's Periodicals, 1840–1930

129. Plateau, 'From a Little French Girl', 21.
130. Cunningham, 'The Editor's Letter', 16.
131. Cunningham, 'The Editor's Letter', 16.
132. John W. Studebaker, 'A Letter of Greeting', *Junior Red Cross News* (September 1919): 2.
133. Irwin, 'Teaching', 269. Irwin also explains why the 'new international education program ... faced significantly more resistance' (276) as 'educators questioned both the content of the JRC's lessons and whether it still had a legitimate place in the school' (256).
134. 'The Educational Aspect of a Junior Red Cross Program of Local Service', *Junior Red Cross News* (October 1919): 2.
135. 'The Educational Aspect', 2.
136. 'The Universal Language of Service', *Junior Red Cross News* (January 1925): 74.
137. Dorothea Campbell, 'Corresponding With Many Lands', *Junior Red Cross News* (October 1921): 19.
138. Campbell, 'Corresponding', 19.
139. 'What the Canadian Juniors Think of Our Portfolios', *Junior Red Cross News* (November 1924): 45.
140. Campbell, 'Corresponding', 19.
141. 'The Journey of the Portfolios', *Junior Red Cross News* (November 1924): 45.
142. Branden Little, 'A Child's Army of Millions: The American Junior Red Cross', in *Children's Literature and Culture of the First World War*, ed. Lissa Paul, Rosemary Ross Johnston, and Emma Short (London: Routledge, 2015), 290.

8

Conclusion: Charitable Children, Real and Imagined

Philanthropy in Children's Periodicals, 1840–1930: The Charitable Child has made visible the myriad ways that children were involved in charity in the nineteenth and early twentieth centuries. It has attempted to answer a series of questions related to how magazines situated children's charity, the degree of charitable agency that can be attributed to young people, how children were motivated to undertake charitable giving, and how habits of charity were created and reinforced. It examines the magazine as the form through which ideas about charity, and especially children's charity, were circulated and embodied through evidence of young people's activities. The tension at the heart of this project is informed by what Jacqueline Rose calls the 'impossibility of children's fiction' in which writing for children is intended 'to secure the child who is outside the book, the one who does not come so easily within its grasp'.[1] Children's periodicals operate differently to the fiction that Rose describes, yet in their charitable ethos they are equally interested in securing child readers and motivating them to undertake charity work. The discussion in this book oscillates between the childhood models of charity – embodied in fiction, editorials, informational articles, and illustrations – and the real children who discuss, debate, and enact charitable habits. The evidence of these latter children is apparent in their financial contributions, their correspondence, the reports of their hospital visits, and their photographs. Real children undertaking charitable work are evident in these magazines, and this evidence reflects their engagement with the charitable ideal promoted in their pages.

The 'charitable child' is deployed in two distinct ways in children's magazines and columns. First, this child is the object of

239

240   Philanthropy in Children's Periodicals, 1840–1930

charity: a figure mobilised through image and text to motivate young readers into taking action to relieve suffering. Second, and even more saliently, this child is understood through the lens of benevolence as someone who could help others, who acknowledged that responsibility, and who responded to the call to action. The ubiquity of this charitable work is evident from the wide range of causes to which children contributed, the diversity of which deserves further examination. Young people in the nineteenth century were encouraged to help the poor, the sick, and the injured. They were also invited to support animal welfare, vegetarianism, temperance, missions at home and abroad, child rescue, emigration, girls' friendly societies, industrial schools, orphanages, and much more. As the century progressed, charitable organisations came to see young people as a vital source of financial and moral support for their causes.

The examples in this book underscore the interconnected ideas about charity that were circulating in the nineteenth century and how they manifested in children's periodicals and children's columns. The success of a charitable cause in a magazine was dependent on the establishment of a charitable public in its pages that shared an understanding of the importance of this work and how it should be prioritised. While some of the earliest charitable publics were clearly and obviously based on a Christian framework, that explicit religious ethos declined over time, though it undoubtedly underpinned charitable efforts into the twentieth century. The motivations for children's charitable work can be difficult to assess because of their opaqueness in magazine pages and because children were aware of the adult gatekeepers who determined appropriate charitable commentary. Yet young people were unquestionably acting as charitable agents as they agreed to raise money for a cause identified in a magazine. Their fundraising efforts might include sacrifice, in which they agreed to forego treats or donate their own money. They might also make articles to be sold, perform entertainments, organise charity bazaars, or take on additional chores to earn money. In addition, support for a cause was not always financial, with children also taking on responsibilities to visit patients in hospital, for instance.

The charity magazine edited and published by charitable organisations was able to mobilise print to support its organisational structure. By operating in cooperation with the organisation, as we saw with *Band of Hope Review*, *Young Helpers' League Magazine*,

Ups and Downs, and the Junior Red Cross magazines, the print publication encouraged young readers to engage with the cause through the magazine. This deft strategy deployed print culture to reinforce the charitable ideal of the period and to develop a distinct charitable public. It thus both defined and reinforced charity as a key concept to be embodied by young people through their charitable activities. Similarly, the juvenile missionary magazines developed in the 1840s tied together missionary objectives and clear fundraising goals in which the organisational structure of Sunday Schools enabled monetary collections that enabled further missionary activities.

In a related, albeit different fashion, magazines and children's columns that were not dedicated to a specific charity had more flexibility in how they discussed their charitable cause, but they also had wider readerships that may not have been specifically attracted by the charitable content. This meant that they had to include a broader range of content that extended beyond the limits of the charitable cause. *Aunt Judy's Magazine* and children's columns like the one found in the *Otago Witness* demonstrate this variety, while the *Adelaide Observer*'s 'Children's Column' established a column dedicated to children's charitable work.

The First World War disrupted charitable patterns through the reduced availability of print, owing to paper restrictions and high prices. As a form of charity, wartime giving was obviously a significant part of children's charitable work, yet this work is less apparent in print form. Instead, most of this activity was supported through schools and at home. The emergence of the Junior Red Cross out of wartime activities reflected the importance of transforming young people's efforts to focus on health, service, and international friendliness. This organisation offers a distinctly modern understanding of children's charitable work defined by more than simply fundraising and instead incorporating additional ideologies into young people's charitable habits. The idea that children's charity might be expanded beyond monetary objectives to include changes to one's physical health and the development of an ongoing ideal of service and internationalism signals a shift in the charitable ideal of childhood in the twentieth century.

While different magazines at times highlight individual accomplishments, the collective nature of children's charity is paramount. Multiple magazines and columns emphasise how small contributions from a large number of young people can aggregate into substantial amounts to support a particular charity. Children's individual contributions were sometimes listed, but a more common strategy was to identify the totality of the work undertaken by young people in the form of financial targets to support beds in hospitals or other charitable objectives. When supported through charitable infrastructures such as circles, habitations, branches, public schools, and Sunday Schools, children contributed as much as they could or made non-monetary donations to support the cause. Any one child's contribution might be quite small, but collectively they came together to make a significant contribution.

Children were thus actors in the charitable field, demonstrating their motivation and agency through the activities in which they participated. Evidence of this agency is apparent across all the examples, with children writing to express satisfaction with their collective efforts or to encourage others to do more. They also felt confident enough as readers to propose additional charitable work, indicating the prevalence of charity in everyday life in England and throughout the English-speaking world. In this sense, charitable ideas were circulating throughout America and the British empire as part of a transnational charitable ideal that was informed by shared expectations of who should be helping others.

The charitable ideal in children's periodicals was predominantly defined for white, middle-class children with the time and the money to be able to support a charitable cause. In certain contexts, however, this ideal explicitly included working-class and poor children. Missionary work in particular was an area to which all children would contribute regardless of their financial standing since missions would still benefit from children's prayers even if they did not have the resources to contribute financially. Moreover, as the temperance campaigns demonstrate, children could be important messengers who influenced adults to change their behaviours. The child as a signifier of innocence was important in this charitable field as it not only mobilised adults to contribute to the cause, but also raised awareness that not all children were equally cared for and that they would benefit from charitable interventions to improve their circumstances.

The transnational circulation of charitable ideals alongside specific charities is a significant finding of this book. That charitable ideals circulated through the periodical press and especially in children's magazines is perhaps unsurprising given the print networks operating between England, America, and the British colonies. Children in all these countries were encouraged to see themselves as people who had a responsibility to help others. Similarly, given how ideas about charity were circulating, it is perhaps also unsurprising that the charities themselves were also interested in establishing local offices to attract funds or directing readerly attention to British organisations seeking funds. British poverty owing to industrialisation and inadequate social infrastructure was juxtaposed with the bucolic ideal of the colonies and a presumed interest among colonials in supporting England. Barnardo's was one such charity, with a robust marketing strategy that was transnational in scope and distribution. This British need sometimes came into conflict with local demand placed on a small population of young people with relatively limited funds. Yet young people demonstrated their generosity by contributing to a range of local and international charitable causes, reflecting their genuine willingness to assist those in need.

While the language of charity deployed in the magazines tended to reify the binary between charitable donor and charitable recipient, this book demonstrates the rhetorical subjectivity that was at times adopted by young people to allow them to navigate between identity categories. Multiple examples show how children who were the objects of charity also positioned themselves as charitable donors through direct financial contributions or indirect activities. In their correspondence to the magazines, these young people display their rhetorical sophistication by showing gratitude while also demonstrating their capacity and willingness to be charitable. This indicates the pervasive nature of charity, in which all children regardless of class, circumstance, or even country understood their obligations to care for others.

The prevalence of the charitable ideal was important in raising future adults who also understood the need to help others. The futurity of the child was an integral aspect of many charitable organisations' desires to recruit young people and contributed to wide-ranging attempts to recruit across classes. Temperance and child rescue organisations in the nineteenth century and the Junior Red Cross in the early twentieth century were all keen to introduce children to their organisation so that they could not only support the cause as young people but would also continue to support it as they became adults. For the Junior Red Cross, in particular, this support extended beyond financial contributions and into ideological world views that encouraged international friendliness, peace, and justice. In other cases, children's engagement with a particular charitable cause was less important for its longevity, yet their induction into more general patterns of philanthropy was understood to have long-lasting implications as they grew into adulthood.

The periodical as a form was essential to the development of these charitable practices. Its seriality and repetition enabled the development and reinforcement of a charitable ideal among young readers. While much of the messaging around children and charitable expectations remained remarkably consistent throughout the period, the strategies defined in the periodical press were adapted to respond to changing technologies and expectations. Towards the end of the nineteenth century, the emergence of photography enabled young readers to see themselves in the magazine's pages when they achieved fundraising goals or contributed to collective charitable activities. At around the same time, editors increasingly sought children's written submissions to fill their columns and to enable them to interact with young people. The participatory nature of correspondence columns and competitions enabled young people to actively engage with the magazine.

Moreover, the seriality of the periodical was pivotal to charitable achievement. The ability to regularly report on funds raised, activities being performed, and the success of the charity enabled the editor to keep the cause at the forefront of readers' attention. Indeed, the relative priority of a given cause is evident from the column inches dedicated to it, and editors frequently mobilised affective language to remind readers of their responsibilities and motivate their charitable behaviour. The consistent use of affective language to raise awareness indicates that adults felt such language would persuade young people to act. The magazine's ability to convince readers of the value of its cause and the urgency of the need in a regular, repeating fashion was one of its defining features. All children's magazines faced the perennial concern of an ageing readership, which was an issue even if they were not trying to recruit readers for adult publications or to become members of adult organisations. Children's periodicals were always trying to attract and retain readers who were defined by age, and this meant they needed to reflect contemporary tastes and adapt to changes in the market. In the longer-running publications, strategic shifts in content and editorial attitudes reflected these attempts to adapt, especially through the adoption of new technologies and participatory practices that encouraged young readers to engage with the magazine. By the turn of the twentieth century, a variety of strategies were operating in children's magazines to engage young people with the charitable cause and with the affordances of the print form.

This book has demonstrated the centrality of print for young people to the charitable culture that permeated the English-speaking world in the nineteenth and early twentieth centuries. By the end of the twentieth century and into the twenty-first century, print magazines are no longer a medium by which children are actively encouraged to support a charitable cause through fundraising and other charitable activities. One key change likely involved ideas about children, in which they were no longer understood as vital contributors to charitable culture and were instead increasingly removed from actively participating in it. At the same time as the position of young people was changing, shifts in children's periodical culture meant that the magazine was no longer an appropriate place for identifying charitable causes that required support. Expanding this research into twentieth-century children's periodicals would offer an opportunity to explore how and why this development occurred.

Note

1. Jacqueline Rose, *The Case of Peter Pan; or the Impossibility of Children's Fiction* (London: Macmillan, 1984), 2.

Bibliography

49th Annual Report of Dr. Barnardo's Homes. London: np, 1914.

Aberdeen, Ishbel. 'The Girl's Own Home'. *Girl's Own Paper*, October 1882.

'Activities of Circles'. *New Zealand Junior Red Cross Journal*, February 1928.

Adam, Thomas. *Buying Respectability: Philanthropy and Urban Society in Transnational Perspective, 1840s to 1930s*. Bloomington: Indiana University Press, 2009.

Address. London: Bell & Daldy, 1871.

Alexander, Kristine. 'Agency and Emotion Work'. *Jeunesse* 7, no. 2 (2015): 120–8.

'All the World Over'. *Red Cross Record*, June 1924.

Altick, Richard D. *The English Common Reader: A Social History of the Mass Reading Public, 1800–1900*. Columbus: Ohio State University Press, 1957.

'American Children's Periodicals, 1841–1850'. https://www.merrycoz. org/bib/1850.xhtml#06.1842.04, accessed 15 January 2021.

'American Juniors' Work in Europe'. *Canadian Red Cross Junior*, May 1922.

Anderson, Benedict. *Imagine Communities: Reflections on the Origin and Spread of Nationalism*. London: Verso, 1991.

Ash, Susan. *Funding Philanthropy: Dr. Barnardo's Metaphors, Narratives and Spectacles*. Liverpool: Liverpool University Press, 2016.

Ashcroft, Bill. 'Beyond the Nation: Australian Literature as World Literature'. In *Scenes of Reading: Is Australian Literature a World Literature?*, edited by Robert Dixon and Brigid Rooney, 34–46. Melbourne: Australian Scholarly Publishing, 2013.

'At the Editor's Desk'. *Ups and Downs*, September 1895.

Bibliography 247

'The Atalanta Letter-Bag'. *Atalanta*, December 1891.

'Aunt Judy's Correspondence'. *Aunt Judy's Magazine*, February 1868.

'Aunt Judy's Correspondence'. *Aunt Judy's Magazine*, January 1869.

'Aunt Judy's Correspondence'. *Aunt Judy's Magazine*, March 1869.

Avery, Gillian. *Childhood's Pattern: A Study of Heroes and Heroines of Children's Fiction, 1770–1950*. London: Hodder and Stoughton, 1975.

Bagnell, Kenneth. *The Little Immigrants: The Orphans Who Came to Canada*. Toronto: Macmillan, 1980.

Ballantyne, Tony. *Orientalism and Race: Aryanism in the British Empire*. Houndmills: Palgrave Macmillan, 2002.

The Band of Hope Manual: The Formation and Management of Bands of Hope (Junior and Senior). London: United Kingdom Band of Hope Union, nd.

Banham, Christopher Mark. 'Boys of England'. In *Dictionary of Nineteenth-Century Journalism in Great Britain and Ireland*, edited by Laurel Brake and Marysa Demoor, 69. London: Academia Press and The British Library, 2009.

Barbalet, Margaret. 'Bottrill, David Hughes [1866–1941]'. *Australian Dictionary of Biography*, adb.anu.edu.au/biography/bottrill-david-hughes–5301, published first in hardcopy 1979, accessed 27 September 2023.

'Barnardo's Boys'. *Evening News*, 22 November 1895.

Barnardo, Thomas. '"My First Arab", or How I Began My Life's Work'. *Young Helpers' League Magazine*, January 1892–December 1894.

— 'Preface'. *Young Helpers' League Magazine*, January 1892–December 1894.

— 'Waif and His Friends', *Young Helpers' League Magazine*, January 1892–December 1894.

Batson, C. Daniel. *The Altruism Question: Toward a Social-Psychological Answer*. New York: Psychology Press, 1991.

Beetham, Margaret. 'Open and Closed: The Periodical as a Publishing Genre'. *Victorian Periodicals Review* 22, no. 3 (1989): 96–100.

Bennett, Charlotte. '"Now the war is over, we have something else to worry us": New Zealand Responses to Crises, 1914–1918'. *Journal of the History of Childhood and Youth* 7, no. 1 (Winter 2014): 19–41.

Berlant, Lauren. *The Female Complaint: The Unfinished Business of Sentimentality in American Culture*. Durham: Duke University Press, 2008.

Berridge, Victoria. *Demons: Our Changing Attitudes to Alcohol, Tobacco, and Drugs*. Oxford: Oxford University Press, 2014.

248   Philanthropy in Children's Periodicals, 1840–1930

Blackman, Lisa, John Cromby, Derek Hook, Dimitris Papadopoulos, and Valerie Walkerdine, 'Creating Subjectivities'. *Subjectivity* 22 (2008): 1–27.

Blake, Joseph. *The Day of Small Things, Or A Plain Guide to the Formation of Juvenile Home and Foreign Missionary Associations in Sunday and Day Schools and Private Families*. Sheffield: W. Townsend & Son, 1868.

Boucher, Ellen. *Empire's Children: Emigration, Welfare, and the Decline of the British World, 1869–1967*. Cambridge: Cambridge University Press, 2014.

Bourdieu, Pierre. *The Logic of Practice*. Translated by Richard Nice. Cambridge: Polity Press, 1990.

'A Boy from the Ukraine'. *Canadian Junior Red Cross*, May 1922.

Bradford, Clare. 'Children's Literature in a Global Age: Transnational and Local Identities'. *Barnboken* 34, no. 1 (2004): 20–34.

Breckenridge, Carole A. and Candace Vogler. 'The Critical Limits of Embodiment: Disability's Criticism'. *Public Culture* 13, no. 3 (2001): 349–57.

Bremner, Robert H. *Giving: Charity and Philanthropy in History*. New Brunswick: Transaction Publishers, 2000.

Browne, Jean E. 'A Letter from the Editor'. *Canadian Red Cross Junior*, September 1922.

— 'The Presque Isle Booklet'. *Canadian Red Cross Junior*, October 1922.

Bryson, Lyman. 'A Victory Yet to be Won'. *Junior Red Cross News*, October 1919.

Bullen, Elizabeth, Kristine Moruzi and Michelle J. Smith. 'Children's Literature and the Affective Turn: Affect, Emotion, Empathy'. In *Affect, Emotion, and Children's Literature: Representation and Socialisation in Texts for Children and Young Adults*, edited by Kristine Moruzi, Michelle J. Smith and Elizabeth Bullen, 1–16. New York: Routledge, 2017.

Bunge, Marcia. 'The Child, Religion, and the Academy: Developing Robust Theological and Religious Understands of Children and Childhood'. *Journal of Religion* 86, no. 4 (2006): 549–79.

Burke, Lois. 'The *Young Woman* and Scotland: The Late-Victorian Writings of Ethel Forster Heddle and Isabella Fyvie Mayor in Girls' Print Culture'. *Scottish Literary Review* 14, no. 1 (Spring/Summer 2022): 43–64.

Campbell, Annie. '". . . thousands of tiny fingers moving": The Beginning of the Junior Red Cross Movement in New South Wales, 1914–1925'.

Bibliography   249

Journal of the Royal Australian Historical Society 90, no. 2 (2004): 184–200.

Campbell, Dorothea. 'Corresponding With Many Lands'. *Junior Red Cross News*, October 1921.

'Canada'. *The Globe*, 27 December 1875.

'The Canadian Red Cross Society'. In *British Empire Red Cross Conference*, 91–7. London: British Red Cross Society, 1930.

Canadian Red Cross Society. *Annual Report*, 1919.

Carissima. 'Lena's Lesson'. *Young Helpers' League Magazine*, January 1901–December 1902.

Chappell, Jennie. 'Cyril's Sacrifice'. *Band of Hope Review*, 1889.

'Children's Column'. *Otago Witness*, 11 November 1876.

'Children's Column'. *Otago Witness*, 2 December 1876.

'Children's Column'. *Otago Witness*, 30 December 1876.

'Children's Column'. *Adelaide Observer*, 14 July 1894.

'Children's Column'. *Adelaide Observer*, 21 July 1894.

'Children's Column'. *Adelaide Observer*, 28 July 1894.

'Children's Column'. *Adelaide Observer*, 11 August 1894.

'Children's Column'. *Adelaide Observer*, 1 September 1894.

'Children's Column'. *Adelaide Observer*, 15 September 1894.

'Children's Column'. *Adelaide Observer*, 20 October 1894.

'Children's Column'. *Adelaide Observer*, 3 November 1894.

'Children's Column'. *Adelaide Observer*, 5 January 1895.

'Children's Column'. *Adelaide Observer*, 2 March 1895.

'Children's Column'. *Adelaide Observer*, 18 May 1895.

'Children's Column'. *Adelaide Observer*, 19 October 1895.

'Children's Column'. *Adelaide Observer*, 23 November 1895.

'Children's Column'. *Adelaide Observer*, 4 January 1896.

'Children's Column'. *Adelaide Observer*, 8 February 1896.

'Children's Column'. *Adelaide Observer*, 22 February 1896.

'Children's Column'. *Adelaide Observer*, 11 April 1896.

'Children's Column'. *Adelaide Observer*, 25 April 1896.

'Children's Column'. *Adelaide Observer*, 9 May 1896.

'Children's Column'. *Adelaide Observer*, 16 May 1896.

'Children's Column'. *Adelaide Observer*, 7 November 1896.

'Children's Column'. *Adelaide Observer*, 24 February 1900.

'Children's Column'. *Adelaide Observer*, 7 April 1900.

'Children's Column'. *Adelaide Observer*, 5 May 1900.

'Children's Column'. *Adelaide Observer*, 16 June 1900.

'Children's Column'. *Adelaide Observer*, 23 June 1900.

'Children's Column'. *The Daily News*, 2 June 1900.

250   Philanthropy in Children's Periodicals, 1840–1930

'The Children's Column'. *The Leader*, 30 June 1900.

'Children's Competition'. *New South Wales Red Cross Record*, February 1916.

'Children's Competitions'. *New South Wales Red Cross Record*, May 1916.

'Christmas and New Year's Juvenile Offering'. *Wesleyan Juvenile Offering*, 1846.

Christianson, Frank. *Philanthropy in British and American Fiction: Dickens, Hawthorne, Eliot, and Howells*. Edinburgh: Edinburgh University Press, 2007.

Christianson, Frank Q. and Leslee Thorne-Murphy. 'Introduction: Writing Philanthropy in the United States and Britain'. In *Philanthropic Discourse in Anglo-American Literature, 1850–1920*, edited by Frank Christianson and Leslee Thorne-Murphy, 1–12. Bloomington: Indiana University Press, 2017.

'Circular. To the Wesleyan Ministers, the Local Missionary Officers, Committees and Collectors, and other Friends of the Wesleyan Missions'. *Wesleyan Missionary Notices*, February 1844.

Clarissa. 'Giving and Receiving'. *Young Helpers' League Magazine*, January 1901–December 1902.

— 'How Alice Helped'. *Young Helpers' League Magazine*, January 1901–December 1902.

Clarke, H. F. *How to Avoid Leakage Between the Band of Hope and the Adult Society*. London: Church of England Temperance Society, 1894.

Code, Barbara. 'The Duty of Contributing to the Home'. *Ups and Downs*, October 1897.

Conquest, W. Owen. 'The Runt and the Red Cross Rules'. *Canadian Red Cross Junior*, September 1923.

'Contributions Wanted!' *Young Helpers' League Magazine*, January 1899–December 1900.

Cooper, George and Ira Sankey. 'Where the Days Are Going By'. https://digital.lib.niu.edu/islandora/object/niu-gildedage%3A23865, accessed 26 May 2023.

Corbett, Gail. *Nation Builders: Barnardo Children in Canada*. Toronto: Dundurn Press, 2002.

Corsaro, William A. 'Collective Action and Agency in Young Children's Peer Cultures'. In *Studies in Modern Childhood: Society, Agency, Culture*, edited by Jens Qvortrup, 231–47. Houndmills: Palgrave Macmillan 2005.

'Cot Chronicle'. *Young Helpers' League Magazine*, January 1901–December 1902.

'The Country'. *Otago Witness*, 26 August 1887.

'Country Items'. *Otago Witness*, 21 March 1889.

Cover, *Junior Red Cross Record*, January 1921.

Cruikshank, Barbara. *The Will to Empower: Democratic Citizens and Other Subjects*. Ithaca: Cornell University Press, 1999.

'The Cumberland Street Children's Hospital'. *The Monthly Packet of Evening Readings for Younger Members of the English Church*, January 1871.

Cunningham, Austin. 'The Editor's Letter to You!' *Junior Red Cross News*, May 1920.

Cunningham, Hugh. *Children and Childhood in Western Society Since 1500*. London: Taylor & Francis, 2020.

— *Children of the Poor: Representations of Childhood since the Seventeenth Century*. Oxford: Blackwell, 1991.

'Current Literature'. *The Spectator*, 1 February 1879.

Curry, E. S. 'The Charities of Children'. *Quiver* 61, January 1904.

Curson, Peter and Kevin McCracken. 'An Australian Perspective of the 1918–1919 Influenza Pandemic'. *NSW Public Health Bulletin* 17, no. 7–8 (August 2007): 103–8.

Davin, Anna. 'Waif Stories in Late Nineteenth-Century England'. *History Workshop Journal* 52 (2001): 67–98.

Dixon, Diana. 'Children and the Press, 1866–1914'. In *The Press in English Society from the Seventeens to Nineteenth Centuries*, edited by Michael Harris and Alan Lee, 133–48. London: Associated University Presses, 1986.

'Dot's Little Folk'. *Otago Witness*, 3 May 1905.

'Dot's Little Folk'. *Otago Witness*, 10 March 1909.

'Dot's Little Folk'. *Otago Witness*, 14 October 1914.

'Dot's Little Folk'. *Otago Witness*, 11 November 1914.

'Dot's Little Folk'. *Otago Witness*, 18 November 1914.

Downing, Karen, Rebecca Jones, and Blake Singley. 'Handout or Hand-up: Ongoing Tension in the Long History of Government Response to Drought in Australia'. *Australian Journal of Politics and History* 62 (2016): 186–202.

'Dr Barnardo's Boys'. *Auckland Star*, 13 January 1892.

'Dr Barnardo's Good Work'. *Otago Witness*, 30 August 1884.

'Dr Barnardo's Homes'. *Otago Witness*, 23 January 1886.

Dr Barnardo's Homes for Orphan and Destitute Children: Annual Report for 1891. London: np, 1891.

Dr Barnardo's Homes for Orphan and Destitute Children of the Waif Class Annual Report. London: np, 1893.

Draper, Susan. 'A Letter from a Friend in Melbourne to the Children in England'. *Wesleyan Juvenile Offering*, January 1849.

'Drinking Fountain Fund'. *Boy's Own Magazine*, July 1868.

Drotner, Kirsten. *English Children and Their Magazines, 1751–1945*. New Haven: Yale University Press, 1988.

Dyhouse, Carol. *Girls Growing Up in Late Victorian and Edwardian England*. London: Routledge, 1981.

'Echoes of the Month'. *Ups and Downs*, January 1896.

'Editor's Chat'. *Young Helpers' League Magazine*, January 1892–December 1894.

'The Editor's Salam, Or Introductory Address'. *Juvenile Missionary Magazine*, June 1844.

'The Educational Aspect of a Junior Red Cross Program of Local Service'. *Junior Red Cross News*, October 1919.

Edwards, Claire and Rob Imrie. 'Disability and Bodies as Bearers of Value'. *Sociology* 37, no. 2 (2003): 239–56.

Elleray, Michelle. 'Little Builders: Coral Insects, Missionary Culture, and the Victorian Child'. *Victorian Literature and Culture* 39, no.1 (2011): 223–38.

— *Victorian Coral Islands of Empire, Mission, and the Boys' Adventure Novel*. Milton: Taylor & Francis Group, 2019.

Elliot, Dorice Williams. *The Angel Out of the House: Philanthropy and Gender in Nineteenth-Century England*. Charlotteville: University Press of Virginia, 2002.

E. M. L. 'Little Annie's Christmas'. *Aunt Judy's Magazine*, November 1871.

Endpaper. *Young Helpers' League Magazine*, January 1892–December 1894.

Evening Post, 22 October 1891.

'The Famine-Stricken Children in India'. *Good Words for the Young*, December 1877.

'February Prize Competition for Health Stories', *Canadian Red Cross Junior*, February 1923.

'File Hills Indian Junior Red Cross', *Canadian Red Cross Junior*, May 1922.

'First Aid Course for Our Juniors'. *Junior Red Cross Record*, February 1921.

Flegel, Monica. 'Changing Faces: The NSPCC and the Use of Photography in the Construction of Cruelty to Children'. *Victorian Periodicals Review* 39, no. 1 (Spring 2006): 1–20.

'For Busy Workers'. *Junior Red Cross Record*, March 1919.

Bibliography   253

Frank, Robert. 'Motivation, Cognition and Charitable Giving'. In *Giving: Western Ideas of Philanthropy*, edited by J. B. Schneewind, 130–52. Bloomington: Indiana University Press, 1996.

'A Friend'. 'Letter of a Missionary's Wife, in New Zealand, to the readers of the "Juvenile Offering"'. *Wesleyan Juvenile Offering*, January 1849.

Gallagher, Emily. 'Ella May McFadyen (1887–1976)', People Australia, National Centre of biography, Australian National University, https://peopleaustralia.anu.edu.au/biography/mcfadyen-ella-may-27619/text3664, accessed 13 October 2023.

Gard, W. S. 'Red Cross Junior of Czecho-Slovakia'. *Canadian Junior Red Cross*, January 1923.

Gibson, Peter. 'Scottish Emigration to Australia, 1788–1939'. *Descent* 30, no. 2 (June 2000): 81–8.

Giffen, Allison and Robin L. Cadwallader. 'Introduction'. In *Saving the World: Girlhood and Evangelicism in Nineteenth-Century Literature*, edited by Allison Giffen and Robin L. Cadwallader, 1–15. London: Routledge, 2018.

Gilderdale, Anna. 'Where "Taniwah" Met "Colonial Girl": The Social Uses of the *Non de Plume* in New Zealand Youth Correspondence Pages, 1880–1920'. In *Children's Voices from the Past: New Historical and Interdisciplinary Perspectives*, edited by Kristine Moruzi, Nell Musgrove, and Carla Pascoe Leahy, 53–84. Cham: Palgrave Macmillan, 2019.

Ginsberg, Lesley. 'Minority/Majority: Childhood Studies and Antebellum American Literature'. In *The Children's Table: Childhood Studies and the Humanities*, edited by Anna Mae Duane, 105–23. Athens: University of Georgia Press, 2013.

'Girls' Donation Fund'. *Ups and Downs*, April 1896.

'Girls' Donation Fund'. *Ups and Downs*, April 1897.

'Girls' Donation Fund'. *Ups and Downs*, August 1896.

'Girls' Donation Fund'. *Ups and Downs*, July 1896.

'Girls' Donation Fund'. *Ups and Downs*, September 1896.

Glassford, Sarah. '"International Friendliness" and Canadian Identities: Transnational Tensions in Canadian Junior Red Cross Texts, 1919–1939', *Jeunesse: Young People, Texts, Cultures* 10, no. 2 (2018): 52–72.

— *Mobilizing Mercy: A History of the Canadian Red Cross*. Montreal & Kingston: McGill-Queen's University Press, 2017.

Gleason, Mona. 'Avoiding the Agency Trap'. *History of Education* 45, no. 4 (2016): 446–59.

The Globe, 14 November 1895.

'Going to School in Other Lands'. *Junior Red Cross Record*, March 1923.

Gorsky, Martin. *Patterns of Philanthropy: Charity and Society in Nineteenth-Century Bristol*. Woodbridge: The Royal Historical Society and The Boydell Press, 1999.

Graham, Jeanine. 'Young New Zealanders, and the Great War: Exploring the Impact and Legacy of the First World War, 1914–2014'. *Paedagogica Historica* 44, no. 4 (2008): 429–44.

Gubar, Marah. *Artful Dodgers: Reconceiving the Golden Age of Children's Literature*. Oxford: Oxford University Press, 2009.

Gwynfryn. 'The Hospital for Sick Children'. *Aunt Judy's Magazine*, January 1868.

'Habitations Formed'. *Young Helpers' League Magazine*, January 1892–December 1894.

Hall, Stuart. 'The Question of Cultural Identity'. In *Modernity and Its Futures*, edited by Stuart Hall, David Held, and Tony McGrew, 273–326. Cambridge: Polity Press, 1992.

Harrison, Brian. *Drink and the Victorians: The Temperance Question in England, 1815–1872*. 2nd edition. Staffordshire: Keele University Press, 1994.

Harvey, Ross. 'Bringing the News to New Zealand: The Supply and Control of Overseas News in the Nineteenth Century'. *Media History*, 8, no. 1 (2002): 21–34.

'The Health Game'. *Junior Red Cross Record*, December 1921.

'Health in Hawaii'. *Junior Red Cross Record*, February 1923.

Heller, Michael. 'Company Magazines 1880–1940: An Overview'. *Management & Organizational History* 3, no. 3–4 (2008): 179–96.

'Here and There'. *Ups and Downs*, February 1896.

'Here and There'. *Ups and Downs*, November 1895.

Higginbotham, Peter. *Children's Homes: A History of Institutional Care for Britain's Young*. Barnsley: Pen & Sword Books, 2017.

Hillel, Margot. '"Give us all missionary eyes and missionary hearts": Triumphalism and Missionising in Late-Victorian Children's Literature'. *Mousaion* 29, no. 3 (2011): 179–92.

— '"Nearly all are supported by children": Charitable Childhoods in Late-Nineteenth- and Early-Twentieth-Century Literature for Children in the British World'. In *Creating Religious Childhoods in Anglo-World and British Colonial Contexts, 1800–1940*, edited by Hugh Morrison and Mary Clare Martin, 163–80. London: Routledge, 2017.

Himmelfarb, Gertrude. *Poverty and Compassion: The Moral Imagination of the Late Victorians*. New York: Vintage, 1991.

Bibliography   255

Hoare, M. E. *Boys, Urchins, Men: A History of The Boys' Brigade in Australia and Papua-New Guinea 1882–1976*. Sydney: Reed, 1980.

Hodson, Thomas. 'Bangalore'. *Wesleyan Juvenile Offering*, July 1859.

Hoff-Clausen, Elisabeth. 'Rhetorical Agency: What Enables and Restrains the Power of Speech?' In *The Handbook of Organizational Rhetoric and Communication*, edited by Øyvind Ihlen and Robert L. Heath, 287–301. Hoboken: John Wiley & Sons, 2018.

Hogan, Patrick Colm. *What Literature Teaches Us About Emotion*. Cambridge: Cambridge University Press, 2011.

Hordle, William. 'Launching of the New Ship'. *Juvenile Missionary Magazine*, June 1844.

'Houseless and Homeless'. *Young Helpers' League Magazine*, January 1901–December 1902.

'How I Managed to get Some Extra Money for Missions During My Holidays'. *At Home and Abroad*, 1903.

'How the Little Children in America Get Money for the Missions'. *Wesleyan Juvenile Offering*, July 1857.

Hughes, Linda K. and Michael Lund. 'Textual/Sexual Pleasure and Serial Production'. In *Literature in the Marketplace: Nineteenth-Century British Publishing and Reading Practices*, edited by John O. Jordan and Robert L. Patten, 133–48. Cambridge: Cambridge University Press, 1995.

Hull, Brian C. *A Brief Overview of the Christian Endeavor Society*. Wilmore: First Fruits Press, 2019.

Hutton, Drew and Libby Connors. *History of the Australian Environmental Movement*. Cambridge: Cambridge University Press, 1999.

'Importation of Waifs'. *The Globe*, 27 September 1881.

'In the Gordon Ward, Her Majesty's Hospital'. *Young Helpers' League Magazine*, January 1901–December 1902.

'Income of the Wesleyan Missionary Society for 1858'. *Wesleyan Juvenile Offering*, May 1859.

Ino-ue, Yenji. 'A Message to Canada's Juniors from the Director of the Junior Red Cross of Japan'. *Canadian Red Cross Junior*, November 1923.

Irwin, Julia F. 'Teaching "Americanism with a World Perspective": The Junior Red Cross in the U.S. Schools from 1917 to the 1920s'. *History of Education Quarterly* 53, no. 3 (August 2013): 255–79.

James, Herbert T. *Industrial Bands of Hope*. London: Church of England Temperance Publication Depot, 1891.

'The Japanese Relief Fund'. *Canadian Red Cross Junior*, November 1923.

Jaunay, Graham. 'Nineteenth Century Emigration from Scotland to South Australia'. *The South Australian Genealogist* 50, no. 1 (February 2023): 12–22.

Jay, Paul. *Transnational Literature: The Basics*. London: Taylor & Francis, 2021.

'J. M. C. D. S. O. First List'. *At Home and Abroad*, 1904.

'The "John Wesley" Missionary Ship'. *Wesleyan Juvenile Offering*, November 1847.

'The "John Wesley" Missionary Ship'. *Wesleyan Juvenile Offering*, September 1846.

'The "John Williams"'. *Juvenile Missionary Magazine*, November 1844.

'The "John Williams" in the West India Dock'. *Juvenile Missionary Magazine*, June 1844.

Johnston, Anna. *Missionary Writing and Empire, 1800–1860*. Cambridge: Cambridge University Press, 2003.

Jordan, W. K. *Philanthropy in England, 1480–1660: A Study of the Changing Pattern of English Social Aspirations*. London and New York: Routledge, 2006.

'The Journey of the Portfolios'. *Junior Red Cross News*, November 1924.

'Junior Circle Reports'. *Junior Red Cross Record*, March 1919.

'Junior Japanese Relief Fund'. *Canadian Red Cross Junior*, October 1923.

'Junior Red Cross', *Canadian Red Cross Junior*, December 1923.

'The Junior Red Cross'. *New Zealand Junior Red Cross Journal*, June 1927.

'A Junior Red Cross Patient in Saskatchewan', *Canadian Red Cross Junior*, June 1922.

'Junior Red Cross Society'. *New South Wales Red Cross Record*, March 1916.

'The Junior Red Cross Society of Hungary'. *Canadian Junior Red Cross*, November 1922.

'Juvenile Christmas Offerings for 1858'. *Wesleyan Juvenile Offering*, May 1856.

'Juvenile Immigration'. *The Globe*, 2 October 1875.

'Juvenile Missionary Offerings for the Year 1843, made at Christmas, or in early January, 1844'. *Wesleyan Juvenile Offering*, 1844.

Keen, Suzanne. 'A Theory of Narrative Empathy'. *Narrative* 14, no. 3 (2006): 208–36.

Kidd, Alan J. 'Philanthropy and the 'Social History Paradigm'. *Social History* 21, no. 2 (May 1996): 180–92.

Bibliography 257

'Kindergarten Fund'. *Otago Witness*, 17 December 1896.

Kohli, Marjorie. *The Golden Bridge: Young Immigrants to Canada, 1833–1939*. Toronto: Natural Heritage Books, 2003.

Koven, Seth. *Slumming: Sexual and Social Politics in Victorian London*. Princeton: Princeton University Press, 2004.

Lancy, David F. 'Unmasking Children's Agency'. *AnthropoChildren* 2 (2012): 1–20.

'Launch of the "John Welsey"'. *Wesleyan Juvenile Offering*, February 1847.

Law, Graham. 'Quiver'. In *Dictionary of Nineteenth-Century Journalism in Great Britain and Ireland*, edited by Laurel Brake and Marysa Demoor, 524–5. Gent: Academia Press and the British Library, 2009.

Lazarus, Richard S. *Emotion and Adaptation*. New York and Oxford: Oxford University Press, 1991.

Leonards, Chris and Nico Randeraad. 'Building a Transnational Network of Social Reform in the Nineteenth Century'. In *Shaping the Transnational Sphere: Experts, Networks and Issues from the 1840s to the 1930s*, edited by Davide Rodogno, Bernhard Struck, and Jakob Vogel, 111–30. New York: Berghahn Books, 2015.

'A Letter from a Former "Wild Thyme" Girl'. *Ups and Downs*, January 1896.

'Letter from an Old Missionary'. *Wesleyan Juvenile Offering*, February 1844.

'A Letter from Dr. Barnardo'. *Ups and Downs*, July 1897.

'Letters from Little Folks'. *Otago Witness*, 26 June 1890.

'Letters from Little Folks'. *Otago Witness*, 24 July 1890.

'Letters from Little Folks'. *Otago Witness*, 28 August 1890.

'Letters from Little Folks'. *Otago Witness*, 11 September 1890.

'Letters from Little Folks'. *Otago* Witness, 2 October 1890.

'Letters from Little Folks'. *Otago Witness*, 1 January 1891.

'Letters from Little Folks'. *Otago Witness*, 20 April 1891.

'Letters from Little Folks'. *Otago Witness*, 20 September 1894.

'Letters from Little Folks'. *Otago Witness*, 13 December 1894.

'Letters from Little Folks'. *Otago Witness*, 27 December 1894.

'Letters from Little Folks'. *Otago Witness*, 10 January 1895.

'Letters from Little Folks'. *Otago Witness*, 21 February 1895.

'Letters from Little Folks'. *Otago Witness*, 8 March 1895.

'Letters from Little Folks'. *Otago Witness*, 6 June 1895.

'Letters from Little Folks'. *Otago Witness*, 11 May 1899.

'Letters to Soldiers'. *New South Wales Red Cross Record*, April 1916.

258   Philanthropy in Children's Periodicals, 1840–1930

Little, Branden. 'A Child's Army of Millions: The American Junior Red Cross'. In *Children's Literature and Culture of the First World War*, edited by Lissa Paul, Rosemary Ross Johnston, and Emma Short, 283–300. London: Routledge, 2015.

— 'Failure to Launch: The American Red Cross in an Era of Contested Neutrality, 1914–17', In *The Red Cross Movement: Myths, Practices and Turning Points*, edited by Neville Wylie, Melanie Oppenheimer, and James Crossland, 97–112. Manchester: Manchester University Press, 2020.

'Local and General'. *Otago Witness*, 25 January 1889.

'Local and General'. *Otago Witness*, 8 August 1889.

'Local and General'. *Otago Witness Supplement*, 24 October 1889.

MacKinnon, Evelyn. 'The Junior Red Cross'. *Junior Red Cross Record*, August 1919.

Maidment, Brian and Aled Jones, 'Illustration'. In *Dictionary of Nineteenth-Century Journalism*, edited by Laurel Brake and Marysa Demoor, 305–6. London: Academia Press and the British Library, 2009.

Mallan, Kerry. 'Empathy: Narrative Empathy and Children's Literature'. In *(Re)Imagining the World: Children's Literature Response to Changing Times*, edited by Yan Wu, Kerry Mallan, and Roderick McGillis, 105–14. Berlin: Springer, 2013.

Margaret. 'The Little Missionary Collector'. *Wesleyan Juvenile Offering*, February 1850.

Maton, Karl. 'Habitus'. In *Pierre Bourdieu: Key Concepts*, edited by Michael James Grenfell, 48–64. Durham: Taylor & Francis, 2014.

Mauss, Marcel. *The Gift: The Form and Reason for Exchange in Archaic Societies*. Abingdon: Routledge, 2002.

Mayall, Berry and Virginia Morrow. *You Can Help Your Country: English Children's Work During the Second World War*. London: Institute of Education, 2011.

Mays, Kelly J. 'The Disease of Reading and Victorian Periodicals'. In *Literature in the Marketplace: Nineteenth-Century British Publishing and Reading Practices*, edited by John O. Jordan and Robert L. Patten, 165–94. Cambridge: Cambridge University Press, 1995.

McAllister, Annemarie. '*Onward*: How a Regional Temperance Magazine for Children Survived and Flourished in the Victorian Marketplace'. *Victorian Periodicals Review* 48, no. 1 (2015): 42–66.

— *Writing for Social Change in Temperance Periodicals: Conviction and Career*. New York: Routledge, 2023.

Bibliography   259

McFadyen, Ella. 'Competition Results'. *New South Wales Red Cross Record*, April 1916.

— 'Mother Goose to Date'. *New South Wales Red Cross Record*, May 1916.

Merish, Lori. 'The Poverty of Sympathy'. In *Philanthropic Discourse in Anglo-American Literature, 1850–1920*, edited by Frank Q. Christianson and Leslee Thorne-Murphy, 13–29. Bloomington: Indiana University Press, 2017.

Miller, Susan A. 'Assent as Agency in the Early Years of the Children of the American Revolution'. *Journal of the History of Children and Youth* 9, no. 1 (2016): 48–65.

Milman, Helen. 'To the Children'. *Our Waifs and Strays*, February 1892.

Milton, Frederick. 'Uncle Toby's Legacy: Children's Columns in the Provincial Newspaper Press, 1873–1914'. *International Journal of Regional and Local Studies* 5, no. 1 (2009): 104–20.

'More Successful Collectors'. *At Home and Abroad*, 1900.

Morrison, Hugh. '"Impressions Which Will Never Be Lost": Missionary Periodicals for Protestant Children in Late Nineteenth-Century Canada and New Zealand'. *Church History* 82, no. 3 (2013): 388–93.

— '"Little vessels" or "little soldiers": New Zealand Protestant Children, Foreign Missions, Religious Pedagogy and Empire, *c*.1880s–1930s'. *Paedagogica Historica* 47, no. 3 (2001): 303–21.

Morrison, Hugh and Mary Clare Martin. 'Introduction: Contours and Issues in Children's Religious History'. In *Creating Religious Childhoods in Anglo-World and British Colonial Contexts*, edited by Hugh Morrison and Mary Clare Martin, 1–20. London: Routledge, 2017.

Moruzi, Kristine. 'Charity, Affect, and Waif Novels'. In *Affect, Emotion, and Children's Literature: Representation and Socialisation in Texts for Children and Young Adults*, edited by Kristine Moruzi, Michelle J. Smith, and Elizabeth Bullen, 33–55. New York: Routledge, 2018.

— *Constructing Girlhood Through the Periodical Press, 1850–1914*. Aldershot: Ashgate, 2012.

— 'Serializing Scholarship: (Re)Producing Girlhood in *Atalanta*'. In *Seriality and Texts for Young People: The Compulsion to Repeat*, edited by Mavis Reimer, Nyala Ali, Deanna England, and Melanie Dennis Unrau, 166–89. Houndmills: Palgrave Macmillan, 2014.

Moruzi, Kristine, Beth Rogers, and Michelle J. Smith. 'General Introduction: Reading, Writing, and Creating Communities in Children's Periodicals'. In *The Edinburgh History of Children's*

Periodicals, edited by Kristine Moruzi, Beth Rogers, and Michelle J. Smith, 1–21. Edinburgh: Edinburgh University Press, 2024.

Murdoch, Lydia. *Imagined Orphans: Poor Families, Child Welfare, and Contested Citizenship in London*. New Brunswick: Rutgers University Press, 2006.

Mussell, James. 'Repetition: Or, "In Our Last"'. *Victorian Periodicals Review* 48, no. 3 (2015): 343–58.

'The New Adelaide Creche Opening Ceremony'. *Adelaide Observer*, 15 August 1896.

'The New Magazine for Our Young Helpers'. *Night and Day* 16, February 1892.

'The New Ship "John Williams"'. *Juvenile Missionary Magazine*, June 1844.

'News from the J. R. C. Mountain Home'. *Red Cross Record*, May 1924.

Nicholls, James. *The Politics of Alcohol: A History of the Drink Question in England*. Manchester: Manchester University Press, 2009.

Noren, Carol M. 'Origins of Wesleyan Holiness Theology in Nineteenth-Century Sweden'. *Methodist History* 33, no. 2 (1995): 112–22.

'Notes by Uncle Ned'. *At Home and Abroad*, 1903.

Nussbaum, Martha. *Cultivating Humanity: A Classical Defense of Reform in Liberal Education*. Cambridge: Harvard University Press, 1997.

Olsen, Stephanie. 'Children's Emotional Formations in Britain, Canada, Australia, and New Zealand Around the First World War'. *Cultural and Social History* 17, no. 5 (2020): 643–57.

Olsen, Sherry and Peter Holland. 'Conversation in Print Among Children and Adolescents in the South Island of New Zealand, 1886–1909'. *Journal of the History of Children and Youth* 12, no. 2 (Spring 2019): 219–40.

'Opinions of Girls on "The Press"'. *Ups and Downs*, February 1896.

Oppenheimer, Melanie. *The Power of Humanity: 100 Years of Australian Red Cross 1914–2014*. Sydney: HarperCollins, 2014.

— 'Realignment in the Aftermath of War: The League of Red Cross Societies, the Australian Red Cross and Its Junior Red Cross in the 1920s'. In *The Red Cross Movement: Myths, Practices and Turning Points*, edited by Neville Wylie, Melanie Oppenheimer, and James Crossland, 130–47. Manchester: Manchester University Press, 2020.

'Organisation of the League, and Its Work'. *Young Helpers' League Magazine*, January 1892–December 1894.

'Otago Witness Little Folks' Kindergarten Fund'. *Otago Witness*, 19 December 1895.

'Our Emigrants'. *Ups and Downs*, December 1898.
'Our First Junior Red Cross Home: The Story of "Shuna"', *Junior Red Cross Record*, March 1924.
'Our Girls'. *Ups and Downs*, January 1896.
'Our Juvenile Associations'. *At Home and Abroad*, April 1882.
'Our Juvenile Associations'. *At Home and Abroad*, February 1895.
'Our Juvenile Associations'. *At Home and Abroad*, 1901.
'Our Juvenile Associations'. *At Home and Abroad*, 1902.
'Our Juvenile Associations'. *At Home and Abroad*, 1904.
'Our Juvenile Associations: Important Notice to Secretaries'. *At Home and Abroad*, 1901.
'Our Juvenile Collectors'. *At Home and Abroad*, 1903.
'Our Juvenile Missionary Associations'. *Wesleyan Juvenile Offering*, December 1867.
'Our Little Folks'. *Otago Witness*, 16 July 1886.
'Our Little Folks'. *Otago Witness*, 23 July 1886.
'Our Little Folks'. *Otago Witness*, 7 January 1892.
'Our Little Folks'. *Otago Witness*, 17 March 1892.
'Our Little Folks'. *Otago Witness*, 12 May 1892.
'Our Little Folks'. *Otago Witness*, 30 June 1892.
'Our Old Friends' Directory'. *Ups and Downs*, October 1895.
Owen, Alfred B. 'Echoes of the Month'. *Ups and Downs*, January 1895.
— 'Echoes of the Month'. *Ups and Downs*, December 1895.
Owen, David. *English Philanthropy, 1660–1960*. Cambridge: Belknap Press, 1964.
Oxford English Dictionary. s.v. 'charity, n', September 2023. https://doi.org/10.1093/OED/3068262751
Oxford English Dictionary. s.v. 'philanthropy, n', July 2023. https://doi.org/10.1093/OED/4790171312
Oxford English Dictionary. s.v. 'transnational, adj', July 2023. https://doi.org/10.1093/OED/3337940338
Parker, Roy. *Uprooted: The Shipment of Poor Children to Canada, 1867–1917*. Chicago: Policy Press, 2010.
Parkes, Christopher. *Children's Literature and Capitalism: Fictions of Social Mobility in Britain, 1850–1914*. Houndmills: Palgrave Macmillan, 2012.
Parr, Joy. *Labouring Children: British Immigrant Apprentices to Canada, 1869–1924*. Toronto: University of Toronto Press, 1994.
Phillips, Kendall R. 'Rhetorical Maneuvers: Subjectivity, Power, and Resistance'. *Philosophy & Rhetoric* 39, no. 4 (2006): 310–32.

262   Philanthropy in Children's Periodicals, 1840–1930

Piesse, Jude. *British Settler Emigration in Print, 1832–1877*. Oxford: Oxford University Press, 2015.

Piper, R. E. 'Invalid Cookery'. *Junior Red Cross Record*, March 1921.

Plateau, Lucienne. 'From a Little French Girl'. *Junior Red Cross News*, September 1919.

Poole, Eva Travers Evered. 'Four Questions Fully Answered'. *Night and Day*, February 1892.

— 'What One Little Sunbeam Did!' *Young Helpers' League Magazine*, January 1892–December 1894.

Pooley, Siân. 'Children's Writing and the Popular Press in England, 1876–1914'. *History Workshop Journal* 80 (2015): 75–98.

Potter, Simon J. *News and the British World: The Emergence of an Imperial Press System, 1876–1922*. Oxford: Oxford University Press, 2003.

Prentis, Malcolm. *The Scots in Australia*. Sydney: UNSW Press, 2008.

Pritchard, John. *Methodists and Their Missionary Societies, 1900–1966*. London: Taylor & Francis Group, 2014.

Prochaska, Frank. 'Little Vessels: Children in the Nineteenth-Century English Missionary Movement'. *Journal of Imperial and Commonwealth History* 6, no. 2 (1978): 103–18.

— *Women and Philanthropy in Nineteenth-Century England*. Oxford: Clarendon Press, 1980.

Pykett, Lyn. 'Reading the Periodical Press: Text and Context'. *Victorian Periodicals Review* 22, no. 3 (1989): 100–8.

Ramsland, John. 'Grasby, William Catton [1859–1903]', *Australian Dictionary of National Biography*, Australian National University, https://adb.anu.edu.au/biography/grasby-william-colton-6459/text11059, 1983, accessed online 19 September 2023.

Reay, Diane. '"It's all becoming a habitus": Beyond the Habitual Use of Habitus in Educational Research'. *British Journal of Sociology of Education* 25, no. 4 (2004): 431–44.

Reed, Rev. Joseph. 'Famine Waifs'. *At Home and Abroad*, 1901.

'Reflections from a Board Room Mirror', *The Nursing Record and Hospital World*, 4 January 1896.

'Remembrance Card'. *Junior Red Cross Record*, April 1919.

Report of the British Red Cross Society for the Year 1924. London: np, 1924.

The Report of the Directors to the Fifty-First General Meeting of the Missionary Society. London: London Missionary Society, 1845.

'Report of the Select Committee of the House of Commons in Immigration and Colonization'. *The Globe*, 13 April 1875.

Bibliography 263

The Report of the Wesleyan Methodist Missionary Society. London: Wesleyan Missionary Society, 1842.

'Reproduction of the First Prize Poster in the Children's Prize Poster Competition', *Canadian Red Cross Junior* (January 1923): 14.

Richards, Eric. 'Varieties of Scottish Emigration in the Nineteenth Century', *Historical Studies* 21, no. 85 (1985): 473–94.

Rietzler, Katharina. 'From Peace Advocacy to International Relations Research: The Transformation of Transatlantic Philanthropic Networks, 1900–1930'. In *Shaping the Transnational Sphere: Experts, Networks and Issues from the 1840s to the 1930s*, edited by Davide Rodogno, Bernhard Struck, and Jakob Vogel, 173–93. New York: Berghahn Books, 2015.

Robertson, James W. 'Peace-Time Policy and Health Progress of the Red Cross in Canada'. *Canadian Medical Association Journal* 19, no. 1 (July 1928): 91–3.

Rodgers, Beth. 'Competing Girlhoods: Competition, Community, and Reader Contribution in *The Girls' Own Paper* and *The Girl's Realm*'. *Victorian Periodicals Review* 45, no. 3 (Fall 2012): 277–300.

Rose, Clare. 'Raggedness and Respectability in Barnardo's Archive', *Childhood in the Past: An International Journal*, 1, no. 1 (2009): 136–50.

Rose, Jacqueline. *The Case of Peter Pan; or the Impossibility of Children's Fiction*. London: Macmillan, 1984.

Royle, C. J. 'Foreword'. *Junior Red Cross Record*, March 1919.

Ruiz, José Gomez. 'How the Junior Red Cross Was Born'. *International Review of the Red Cross (1961–1997)* 4, no. 36 (1964): 146–50.

Salmon, Edward. *Juvenile Literature As It Is*. London: Henry J. Drane, 1888.

Sánchez-Eppler, Karen. 'Childhood'. In *Keywords for Children's Literature*, edited by Philip Nel and Lissa Paul, 35–41. New York: New York University Press, 2011.

Schrad, Mark Lawrence. 'The Transnational Temperance Community'. In *Transnational Communities: Shaping Global Economic Governance*, edited by Maria-Laure Djelic and Sigrid Quack, 255–81. Cambridge: Cambridge University Press, 2010.

Scott, George. 'A Child's Self-Denial for the Mission Cause'. *Wesleyan Juvenile Offering*, April 1844.

The Seventh Annual Report of the Oxfordshire Band of Hope and Temperance Union, 1881–82. Oxford: Oxfordshire Band of Hope and Temperance Union, 1882.

264   Philanthropy in Children's Periodicals, 1840–1930

Sheehan, Nancy M. 'Junior Red Cross in the Schools: An International Movement, a Voluntary Agency, and Curriculum Change'. *Curriculum Inquiry* 17, no 3. (1987): 247–66.

Sherman, James. 'Every One Can Do Something for Jesus Christ'. *Juvenile Missionary Magazine*, July 1844.

Shilling, Chris. *The Body in Culture, Technology and Society*. London: Sage Publications, 1995.

'A Single Woman: Miss Findley Charged With Killing a Boy'. *The Globe*, 14 November 1895.

Smith, Lindsay. 'The Shoe-Black to the Crossing Sweeper: Victorian Street Arabs and Photography'. *Textual Practice* 10, no. 1 (1996): 29–55.

Smith, Michelle J., Kristine Moruzi, 'The Child Reader: Children's Literary Culture in the Nineteenth Century'. In *Literary Cultures and Nineteenth-Century Childhoods*, edited by Kristine Moruzi and Michelle J. Smith, 53–67. Cham: Palgrave Macmillan, 2023.

— 'Transnational Children's Periodicals'. In *Handbook of Transnational Periodical Research*, edited by Marianne Van Remoortel and Fionnuala Dillane. Leiden: Brill, forthcoming.

Smith, Michelle J., Kristine Moruzi, and Clare Bradford. *From Colonial to Modern: Transnational Girlhood in Canadian, Australian, and New Zealand Children's Literature, 1840–1940*. Toronto: University of Toronto Press, 2018.

S. T. 'Address to the Juvenile Contributors Towards the New Missionary Ship'. *Juvenile Missionary Magazine*, October 1844.

'Story of the Girls' Donation Fund'. *Ups and Downs*, March 1896.

Studebaker, John W. 'A Letter of Greeting'. *Junior Red Cross News*, September 1919.

'"Sunbeam" In Memoriam Lifebuoy Fund'. *Adelaide Observer*, 3 February 1900.

'The Sunbeam Society Dinner to the Ragged School Children'. *Adelaide Observer*, 8 February 1896.

Sutherland, Neil. *Children in English-Canadian Society: Framing the Twentieth-Century Consensus*. Waterloo: Wilfred Laurier University Press, 2000.

Swain, Shurlee. 'Sweet Childhood Lost: Idealized Images of Childhood in the British Child Rescue Literature'. *Journal of the History of Childhood and Youth* 2, no. 2 (Spring 2009): 198–214.

Swain, Shurlee and Margot Hillel. *Child, Nation, Race and Empire: Child Rescue Discourse, England, Canada and Australia, 1850–1915*. Manchester: Manchester University Press, 2010.

'Telegraphic'. *Otago Witness*, 22 April 1887.

'Theodora'. 'Lady Rosamund'. *Young Helpers' League Magazine*, January 1901–December 1902.

Thomas, Lynn M. 'Historicizing Agency'. *Gender and History* 28, no. 2 (August 2016): 324–39.

Thorne-Murphy, Leslee. *Bazaar Literature: Charity, Advocacy, and Parody in Victorian Social Reform Fiction*. Oxford: Oxford University Press, 2022.

'The Three-Letter League'. *Young Helpers' League Magazine*, January 1901–December 1902.

'To Authors and Authoresses'. *Young Helpers' League Magazine*, January 1901–December 1902.

Tomanović, Smiljka. 'Family Habitus as the Cultural Content for Childhood'. *Childhood* 11, no. 3 (August 2004): 339–60.

'To Our Juvenile Collectors'. *Wesleyan Juvenile Offering*, November 1847.

'To Our Readers'. *Band of Hope Review and Children's Friend*, September 1852.

'To Our Young Readers'. *Wesleyan Juvenile Offering*, January 1844.

Triolo, Rosalie. *Our Schools and the War*. Melbourne: Australian Scholarly, 2012.

'The Two Pledges'. *Band of Hope Review and Sunday School's Friend*, October 1861.

'The Universal Language of Service'. *Junior Red Cross News*, January 1925.

Valdes, Annemarie. '"*I, being a member of the Junior Red Cross, gladly offered my services*": Transnational Practices of Citizenship by the International Junior Red Cross Youth'. *Transnational Social Review* 5, no. 3 (2015): 161–75.

Vallgårda, Karen, Kristine Alexander, and Stephanie Olsen. 'Emotions and the Global Politics of Childhood'. In *Childhood, Youth and Emotions in Modern History: National, Colonial and Global Perspectives*, edited by Stephanie Olsen, 12–34. Houndmills: Palgrave Macmillan, 2015.

Vipond, Frank. 'At the Editor's Desk'. *Ups and Downs*, January 1895.

— 'At the Editor's Desk'. *Ups and Downs*, September 1895.

— 'With Our Friends'. *Ups and Downs*, September 1895.

Wagner, Gillian. *Barnardo*. London: Eyre & Spottiswoode, 1979.

'Waiting for More'. *Ups and Downs*, March 1896.

'The Way to Health'. *Junior Red Cross Record*, October 1921.

W. C. 'Juvenile Sympathy'. *Wesleyan Juvenile Offering*, January 1844.

'We Don't Want Prizes!' *At Home and Abroad*, October 1903.

'What Is the Junior Red Cross?' *Red Cross Junior*, June 1922.

266 Philanthropy in Children's Periodicals, 1840–1930

'What Other Papers Say'. *The Globe*, 30 March 1895.

'What the Canadian Juniors Think of Our Portfolios'. *Junior Red Cross News*, November 1924.

'Where Are the Nine?' *Ups and Downs*, February 1896.

'Why You Should Take THE JUNIOR RED CROSS RECORD'. *Junior Red Cross Record*, January 1921.

Williams, Carlyle T. 'Flying Aboard the "Friendship"'. *Junior Red Cross News*, May 1920.

Williams, Gwylmor Prys and George Thompson Brake. *Drink in Great Britain, 1900–1979*. London: Edsall & Co., 1980.

Wilson, Woodrow. 'To the School Children of the United States'. *Junior Red Cross News*, September 1919.

'With Our Friends'. *Ups and Downs*, August 1895.

'With Our Friends'. *Ups and Downs*, December 1895.

'A Woman Friend'. *Ottawa Citizen*, 15 November 1895.

Zelizer, Viviana A. 'The Priceless Child Revisited'. In *Studies in Modern Childhood: Society, Agency, Culture*, edited by Jens Qvortrup, 184–200. Houndmills: Palgrave Macmillan, 2005.

Index

activism, 23, 166
Adelaide Observer, 17, 166, 167, 176, 181–93
adult, 3, 8, 9, 11, 12, 15, 25, 26, 29, 30–1, 35, 36, 41, 47, 59, 60–1, 63, 64, 79, 100, 104, 137, 187, 188, 201, 204, 228, 231, 240, 242, 243, 244
  publications, 1, 2, 8, 9, 10, 17, 100, 167, 217, 218, 244
adulthood, 6, 12, 203, 210–11, 222, 244
affect, 16, 25, 26, 67, 100, 101, 104, 108, 112, 185, 244
agency, 2, 13, 15–16, 59–92, 100, 111, 135, 239, 242
Anderson, Benedict, 24
animal protection, 1, 28, 240
At Home and Abroad, 15, 59, 65, 83–92
Aunt Judy's Magazine, 10, 14, 23, 27, 33–4, 37–40, 44, 47–52, 77, 87, 88, 89, 114, 176, 241
Australia, 10, 14, 17, 18, 69, 166–7, 168, 169, 174, 177, 181–93, 195n, 197n, 199n, 210, 216–25, 226, 227, 231, 235n, 236n

badges, 9, 36, 89, 102
Baker, Louisa, 194n
Band of Hope, 34, 36, 42, 43, 181, 182
Band of Hope Review, 2, 11, 14, 23, 28–30, 36, 43, 47, 54n, 240
Barnardo, Thomas, 22, 30, 33, 35, 99, 170–6, 183
Barnardo's, 8, 14, 16, 17, 22, 30–1, 44, 90, 99–124, 129n, 132–61, 162n, 163n, 166, 167, 170–6, 178, 243
  ideal boy, 144, 148, 160
  ideal girl, 147, 148, 149, 160

Belgian Relief Fund, 34, 167, 178, 179, 180
beneficence, 6, 103
benevolence, 4, 5, 6, 64, 124, 155, 240
Birt, Louisa, 133, 162n
Bottrill, David, 181, 197n
Bourdieu, Pierre, 18, 103, 201, 203–4, 207
  habitus, 18, 30, 35, 201–31
Boy's Own Paper, 7
Boys of England, 9
Boys' Brigade, 181, 197n
Boys' Field Club, 181, 197n
British Home Children, 132, 141, 160
Brothers and Sisters, 8
Brunner Relief Fund, 189

Canada, 16, 18, 132–4, 136–61, 168, 171, 201, 202, 204–16, 218, 220, 221, 224, 226, 230, 231
Canadian Red Cross Junior, 18, 202, 204–16, 217
certificates, 9, 36
charitable
  activity, 1, 15, 25, 60, 76,87, 100, 101, 118, 174, 178, 186, 224
  agency, 82–91
  agents, 15, 59, 61, 63, 79, 86, 240
  behaviour, 5, 25, 62, 63, 102, 104, 105, 107, 120, 159, 169, 201, 203, 209, 244
  brand, 9
  cause, 1, 2, 6, 7, 8, 10, 12, 13, 14, 15, 16, 17, 18, 22, 23, 24, 25, 27, 35, 37, 38, 40, 41, 44, 49, 51, 52, 53, 70, 61, 82, 87, 90, 92, 102, 134, 167, 168, 172, 173, 175, 176, 178, 189, 192, 193, 202, 203, 228, 240, 241, 242, 243, 244, 245

267

268 Philanthropy in Children's Periodicals, 1840–1930

charitable (*cont.*)
  content, 28, 241
  contribution, 33, 51, 208
  donation, 67, 174, 186
  donor, 2, 13, 16, 17, 22, 27, 40, 66, 75,
    100, 111, 132, 133, 135, 140, 154,
    160, 166, 190, 243
  ethic, 4
  giving, 1, 6, 7, 12, 14, 16, 17, 22, 23,
    24, 30, 34, 38, 44, 47, 49, 61, 66,
    72, 73, 82, 92, 105, 112, 113, 132,
    154–61, 209, 201, 239; *see also* giving
  habits, 10, 18, 103, 201–31, 239, 241
  ideal, 1, 2, 13, 15, 24, 91, 172, 174,
    180, 183, 185, 190, 193, 204, 239,
    241, 242, 243, 244
  institution, 2, 4, 64, 166, 181, 189, 191,
    193
  motivation, 16, 99–124
  obligation, 17, 167
  public, 6, 14–15, 16, 22–53, 61, 66, 88,
    103, 160, 177, 240, 241
  subjectivity, 16, 132–61
  success, 37, 46–53, 124, 139–45
  work, 1, 3, 9, 10, 13, 15, 16, 17, 19, 26,
    33, 41, 43, 46, 48, 49, 51, 53, 60, 64,
    65, 66, 67, 71, 77, 87, 101, 102, 103,
    107, 108, 109, 111, 118 120–4, 167,
    171, 173, 175, 176, 178, 179, 180,
    182, 184, 185, 186, 188, 189, 191,
    192, 202, 224, 239, 240, 241, 242
charity
  bazaar, 4, 10, 118, 120, 123, 171, 175,
    183, 184, 187, 188, 189, 191, 192,
    198n, 220, 240
  definition of, 4, 6, 18, 26, 202
  international, 17, 167, 176, 189, 243
  reports, 8, 13, 14, 23, 37, 44, 46, 47, 48,
    49, 51, 52, 53, 64, 65, 71, 73, 75, 77,
    79, 80, 83, 84, 86, 100, 117–18, 124,
    129n, 133, 135, 159, 169, 170–1,
    177, 180, 181, 185, 186, 195n, 211,
    212, 213, 214, 219–20, 224, 239,
    244
  transnational, 17, 166–93
child
  as donor, 2, 16, 17, 22, 27, 40, 52, 64,
    66, 67, 75, 100, 111, 132–3, 134,
    135, 140, 148, 154, 160–1, 166, 190,
    243
  as object of charity, 1, 2, 239–40
  definition of, 206
  emigration, 132, 136, 139, 140, 150

Indigenous, 12, 68, 215
  readers, 4, 9, 17, 19, 22, 23, 25, 34, 37,
    38, 41, 52, 63, 64, 65, 66, 67, 68, 71,
    72, 73, 76, 82, 83, 88, 89, 90, 91, 92,
    99, 100, 103, 104, 105, 111, 122,
    132, 133, 154, 166, 167, 175, 185,
    190, 201, 208, 209, 239
childhood
  Australian, 17, 167
  definition of, 6, 12, 25, 26
  dependency, 12
  ideology, 17, 18, 71, 202
  innocence, 3, 9, 25, 31, 100, 101, 242
  vulnerability, 3, 9, 24, 101
children
  impoverished, 4, 132, 142, 155, 174
  neglected, 3, 4, 100, 101, 124, 133, 137
children's
  columns, 1, 2, 6, 7, 10, 11, 13, 17, 18,
    27, 88, 122, 141, 166–93, 201, 217,
    240, 241
  magazine, 8, 14, 23, 27, 36, 40, 46, 52,
    61, 64, 67, 69, 75, 82, 92, 103, 170,
    193, 213, 214, 221, 225, 230
  voice, 26
Children's Union, 30, 33
Christian, 4, 7, 31, 62, 68, 76, 89, 101,
    111, 122, 141, 145, 240
Christian Endeavour, 181, 182, 198n
Christmas Dinner Fund, 185, 187
circulation, 30, 168, 169, 174, 183, 185,
    186, 230, 233, 242
citizenship, 18, 204, 205, 206, 210, 212,
    213, 214, 216, 228
class, 2, 3, 4, 6, 7, 12, 16, 17, 31, 33, 64,
    72, 90, 100, 101, 103, 105, 108, 111,
    112, 113, 120, 124, 132, 136, 139,
    141, 203, 242, 243
collective action, 18, 41, 72, 80, 202
community, 9, 23, 24, 33, 36, 41, 42, 66,
    68, 88, 130n, 133, 139, 141, 147,
    149, 150–4, 174, 178, 180, 193, 214,
    215, 224, 226, 230
competition, 7, 46, 88, 90–1, 122, 130n,
    157, 182, 184, 207–8, 216–17, 218,
    244
contributions
  child authored, 18, 201
correspondence, 7, 11, 13, 17, 26, 27, 33,
    37–8, 48, 63, 71, 88, 92, 130n127,
    133, 141, 150, 160, 167, 170, 174,
    177, 178, 178, 180, 191, 193, 214,
    215, 230, 231, 239, 243, 244

Index   269

Dependents' Day, 220, 236
Distressed Farmers' fund, 190
Dorcas Society, 183, 198n

earthquake, 213, 224
editorial persona, 11, 83, 170
emigration, 16, 132–61, 184, 199n, 240
emotion, 16, 24, 26, 67, 75, 82, 100–2, 104–13, 118, 122, 123–4, 148, 156, 206, 210
emotional formation, 105, 109

famine, 9, 87, 167, 190–2
Fenwick, William, 194n
fiction, 2, 6, 8, 11, 14, 22, 27, 36, 37, 46,47, 63, 65, 76, 105, 110, 111, 112, 121, 217, 229, 239
First World War, 6, 7, 18, 34, 46, 167, 178, 201, 202, 204, 205, 210, 225–6, 241
foreign mission, 23, 59, 90
fundraising, 4, 6, 7, 9, 10, 15, 23, 37, 41, 44, 46, 49, 52, 65, 70, 72–92, 99, 100, 135, 156, 167, 169, 171, 175, 178, 181, 182, 185, 187, 188, 191, 201, 202, 204, 209, 212, 213, 224, 231, 240, 241, 244, 245
    activities, 14, 61, 62, 64, 189
    campaign, 3, 16, 42, 52

Gatty, Margaret, 33, 34, 51, 176
gender, 2, 12, 203, 216
gift theory, 5
Girl's Friendly Society, 10
Girl's Own Paper, 10
giving
    behaviour, 5, 66
    reciprocal, 3, 67
    religious, 65, 72
    see also charitable giving
Good Words for the Young, 9
Grasby, Catton, 197n
Guild of Kindness, 183, 184, 198n

happiness, 2, 69, 100, 107, 108, 109, 111, 120, 121, 124, 223
health, 3, 14, 18, 24, 33, 35, 46, 115, 117, 118, 201–31, 236n, 241
home mission, 1, 30
hospitals, 4, 10, 14, 23, 24, 33, 34, 38, 40, 47–8, 51, 52, 99, 105, 106, 108, 109, 115, 117, 155, 156, 176, 181, 182,

183, 184, 185, 189, 217, 218, 223, 239, 240, 242

illustration, 2, 14, 27, 37, 40, 48, 82, 102, 112, 113–21, 124, 230, 235n, 239
informational article, 14, 27, 37, 205, 230, 239
'In Memorium Lifebuoy Fund', 190, 200n
intimate public, 14, 23, 24–7

Jack's Day, 220, 236n
Japanese Relief Fund, 214, 234n
Junior Red Cross, 7, 8, 18, 34–5, 44, 46, 103, 201–31, 241, 243
Junior Red Cross News, 18, 202, 225–31
Junior Red Cross Record for New South Wales, 18, 20, 202, 216–25, 234n, 235n
Juvenile Missionary Magazine, 7, 28, 37, 41, 48, 49, 62

Leader, 192, 196n
literacy, 8, 16, 62–3, 132
London Missionary Society, 28, 37, 41, 48, 61, 62, 72

McFadyen, Ella, 217, 235n
McKinnon, Evelyn, 222
Macpherson, Annie, 133, 162n30
magazine
    charity, 8–9, 10, 14, 20, 27, 28, 37, 40, 43, 103, 104, 154, 203, 240
    children's see children's
    commercial, 14, 27, 40, 51
    missionary, 14, 27, 40, 51
    religious, 15, 34, 61, 62
Milman, Helen, 30, 33
Ministering Children's League, 181, 182, 198n
missionary activities, 4, 23, 49, 64, 65, 69, 72, 92, 241
moral development, 16, 104
moral values, 7

narrative strategy, 65–71, 105–12
New South Wales Red Cross Record, 216
newspaper, 1, 2, 10, 17, 18, 27, 30, 88, 122, 141, 166–7, 168, 173, 174, 180, 184, 186, 196, 201, 217
Night and Day, 8, 30, 162n, 171, 195n
non-fiction, 2; see also informational article

270   Philanthropy in Children's Periodicals, 1840–1930

Otago Witness, 17, 166–7, 170–80, 181, 185, 194n, 194n, 241
Our Waifs and Strays, 8
Owen, Alfred B., 139, 140, 147, 150, 154

participation, 8, 11, 13, 15, 16, 17, 22, 25, 26, 36, 38, 60, 61, 80, 110, 118, 167, 189, 193, 203, 230, 231
peace, 18, 29, 179, 202, 205, 226, 228–9, 231, 244
philanthropy
  definition of, 4
  discourse, 17, 166
  intercultural transfer, 167, 169
  see also charity
photography, 14, 83–7, 102, 113, 144, 147, 148, 157, 208, 210, 213, 221, 230, 239, 244
poetry, 8, 11, 27, 170, 217
poverty, 5, 24, 34, 63, 100, 101, 111–12, 113, 136, 181, 186, 208, 212, 243
print culture, 2, 4, 6, 7, 10, 11, 14, 17, 18, 21n, 62, 122, 168, 169, 241
puzzles, 11, 170, 184

race, 2, 12
Ragged School, 110, 167, 185–7, 189
readership, 6, 8–9, 23, 24, 28, 29, 64, 68, 122, 140, 154, 186, 193, 218, 241, 244
  ageing, 9, 35, 53, 244
  dual, 29
reading, 7, 16, 24, 29, 37, 62, 66, 68, 75, 101, 102–5, 122, 144, 192, 218
Red Cross, 4, 8, 46, 202
religion, 5, 15, 24, 33, 41, 59, 61–2, 103
rhetorical manoeuvres, 17, 132–5, 140, 147, 160, 243
Rose, Jacqueline, 239
Rye, Maria, 133, 136, 162n

sacrifice, 2–3, 11, 65, 70, 71, 76, 79, 92, 123, 173, 179, 180, 187, 188, 190, 193, 217, 220, 240
Salmon, Edward, 7
scrapbook, 214
secular, 4, 7, 46

seriality, 36–7, 40, 48, 51, 65, 168, 244
service, 7, 18, 46, 86, 88, 120, 141, 150, 201–31, 241
social responsibility, 6, 103
social welfare, 3, 11, 111
soldiers, 4, 34, 190, 192, 200, 202, 216, 217, 218, 220, 221, 223, 225, 226, 236n
South Africa, 190
subject position, 17, 31, 132–3, 134, 135, 148, 161
subscription list, 14, 37, 44, 49–52, 63, 77, 102
Sunbeam Society, 17, 167, 176, 181–93
Sunday School, 23, 29, 41–2, 44, 62, 63, 77, 149, 171, 241, 242
sympathy, 35, 68, 99, 103, 104, 105, 114, 171, 176, 177, 179, 188, 193, 210, 214, 216, 227

teetotalism, 16, 47
temperance, 4, 14, 16, 23–4, 28–30, 35–6, 41, 42–4, 47, 62, 112, 169, 182, 240, 242, 243
transatlantic, 166

United States, 18, 166, 177, 201, 225–31
Ups and Downs, 16, 17, 132–61

visual strategy, 16, 83–7, 113–21

Weekly Herald, 183–4
Wesleyan Juvenile Offering, 7, 8, 14, 15, 37, 41, 59–92, 100
Wesleyan Missionary Society, 15, 41, 43, 52, 59–92
  'John Wesley' missionary ship, 69, 70, 82–3
  Juvenile Associations, 52, 63, 73–5, 83, 86, 87–8, 92
Whitford, Samual, 33
Wilson, Woodrow, 225–6

Young Helpers' League, 22, 31, 35, 44, 99–124, 162n, 175–6, 179
Young Helpers' League Magazine, 8, 14, 16, 22, 30–3, 44–5, 99–124, 162n, 240